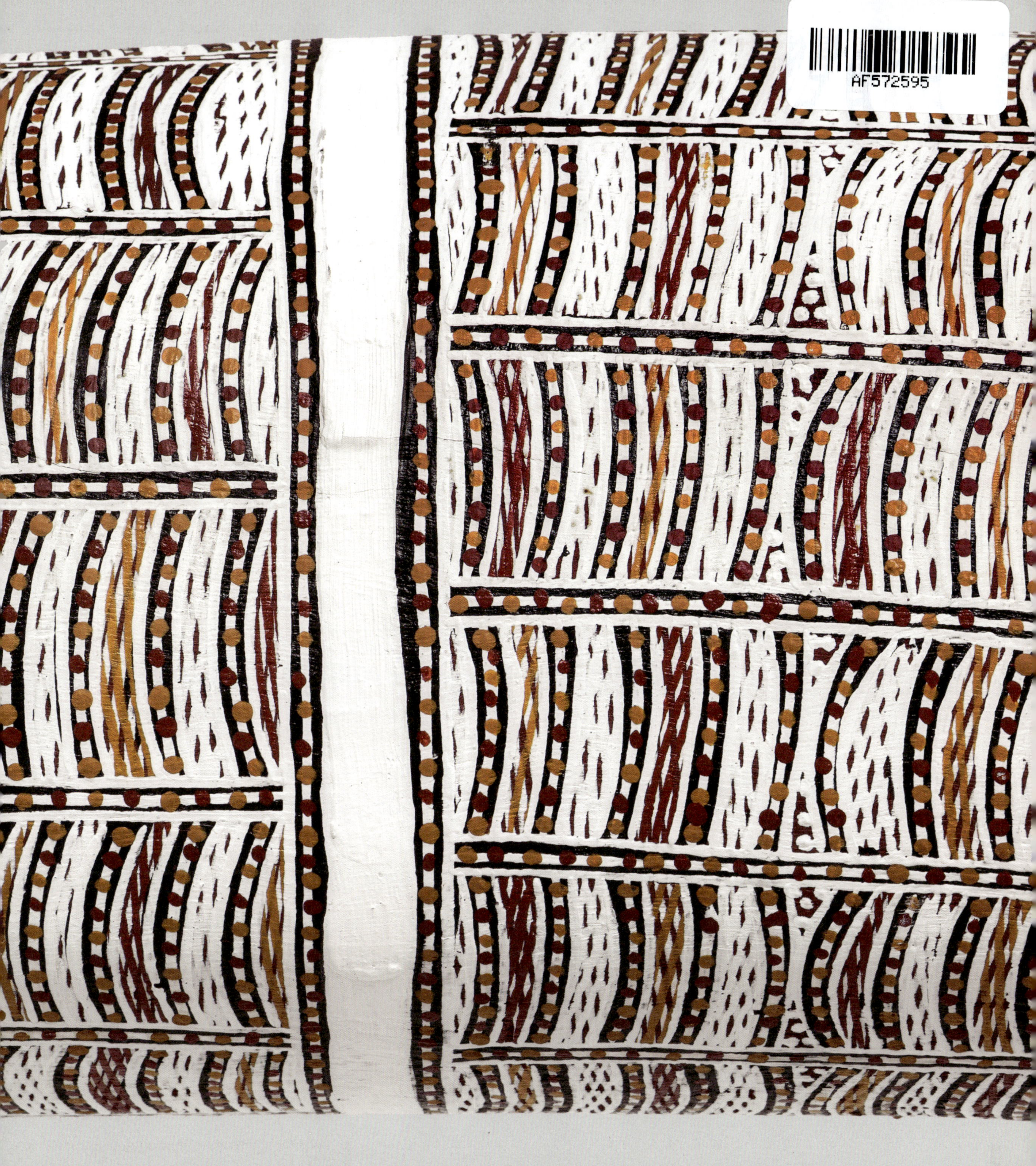

The Inside World

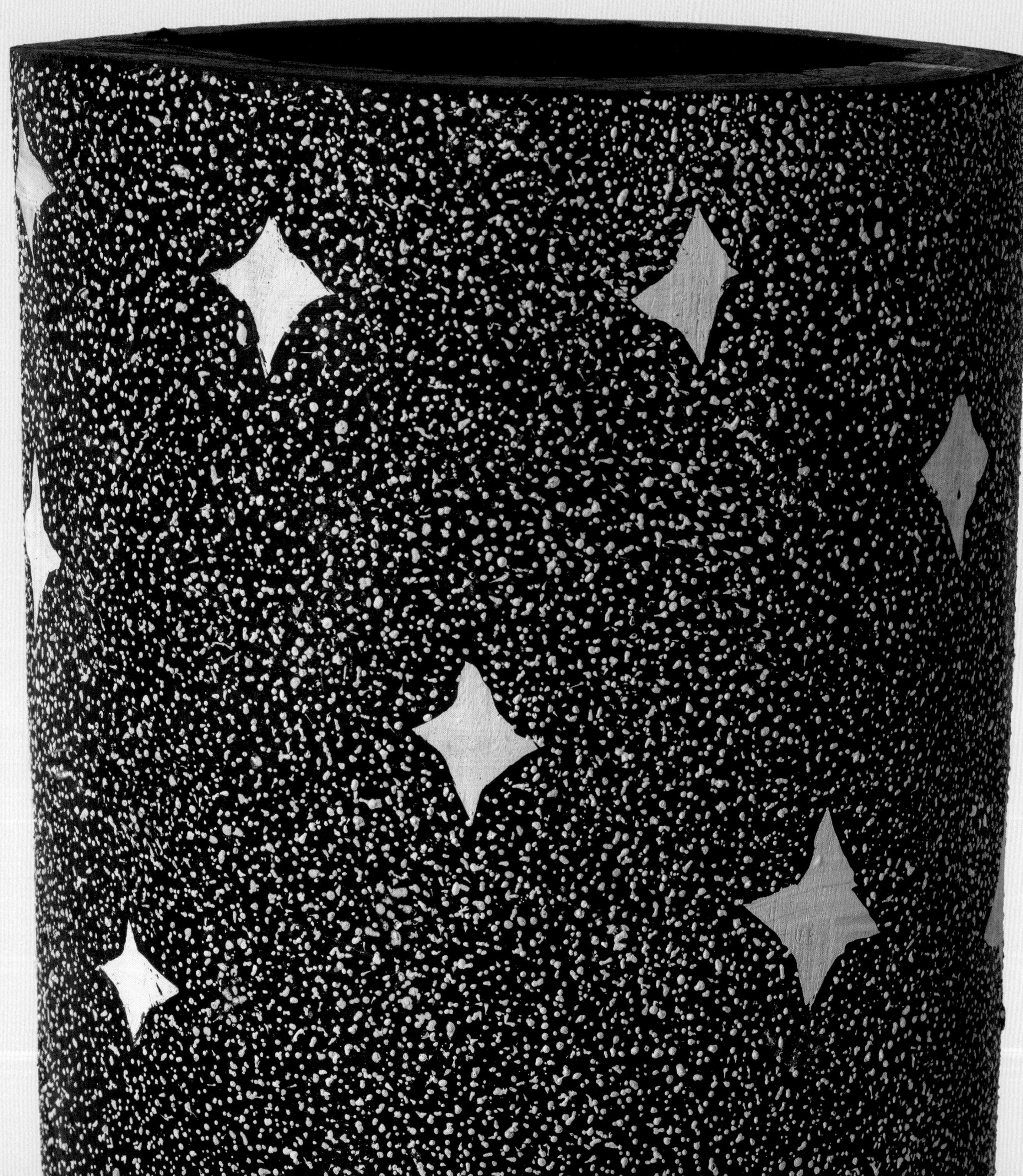

The Inside World
Contemporary Aboriginal Australian Memorial Poles

From the Debra and Dennis Scholl Collection

Edited by

Henry F. Skerritt

With contributions by

Murray Garde
Louise Hamby
Howard Morphy
Kimberley Moulton
Diana Nawi
Wukun Wanambi
David Wickens

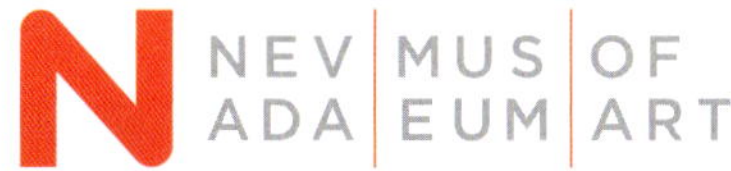

DelMonico Books • Prestel
Munich London New York

This publication accompanies the exhibition *The Inside World: Contemporary Aboriginal Australian Memorial Poles* from the Debra and Dennis Scholl Collection

Nevada Museum of Art, Reno, NV
February 9, 2019–June 23, 2019

Charles H. Wright Museum of African American History, Detroit, MI
July 18, 2019–December 29, 2019

Fralin Museum of Art, University of Virginia, Charlottesville, VA
January 24, 2020–June 28, 2020

Patricia and Phillip Frost Art Museum, Florida International University, Miami, FL
July 2020–December 2020

Published in 2019 by DelMonico Books, an imprint of Prestel Publishing
Prestel, a member of Verlagsgruppe Random House GmbH

Prestel Verlag
Neumarkter Strasse 28
81673 Munich
Germany
Tel.: +49 89 4136 0

Prestel Publishing Ltd
14–17 Wells Street
London W1T 3PD
Te.: +44 20 7323 5004

Prestel Publishing
900 Broadway, Suite 603
New York, NY 10003
Tel.: +1 212 995 2720
E-mail: sales@prestel-usa.com

www.prestel.com

ISBN 978-3-7913-5816-1

Design: Rita Jules, Miko McGinty Inc.
Production: Claire Bidwell, Miko McGinty Inc.
Printed in Italy by Trifolio S.r.L, Verona

Library of Congress
Cataloging-in-Publication Data

Names: Skerritt, Henry F., 1979– editor. | Nevada Museum of Art.
Title: The inside world : contemporary Aboriginal Australian memorial poles from the Debra and Dennis Scholl collection / edited by Henry F. Skerritt; with contributions by Murray Garde, Louise Hamby, Howard Morphy, Kimberley Moulton, Diana Nawi, Wukun Wanambi, David Wickens.
Other titles: Inside world (Nevada Museum of Art)
Description: Munich ; New York : DelMonico Books Prestel, 2019. | "This publication accompanies the exhibition The Inside World: Contemporary Aboriginal Australian Memorial Poles, Nevada Museum of Art, Reno, NV." | Includes bibliographical references.
Identifiers: LCCN 2018041454 | ISBN 9783791358161 (hardback)
Subjects: LCSH: Larrakitj—Exhibitions. | Scholl, Dennis—Art collections—Exhibitions. | Scholl, Debra (Debra Sue)—Art collections—Exhibitions. | Sculpture—Private collections—United States—Exhibitions. | BISAC: ART / Australian & Oceanian. | ART / Collections, Catalogs, Exhibitions / Group Shows. | ART / History / Contemporary (1945–).
Classification: LCC NB1101 .I57 2018 | DDC 730.75—dc23
LC record available at https://lccn.loc.gov/2018041454

A CIP catalogue record for this book is available from the British Library

Front cover: Gunybi Ganambarr, *Milŋurr Ŋaymil* (detail), 2016 (see p. 116)
Back Cover: Gabriel Maralngurra, *Lorrkkon* (detail) 2016 (see p. 54)
Endpapers: Guwaykuway Wan̲ambi, *Yanawal* (detail), 2016 (see p. 147)
Frontispiece: Naminapu Maymuru-White, *Milŋiyawuy (Milky Way)* (detail), 2016 (see p. 125)
Page 7: Manini Gumana, *Garraparra* (detail), 2016 (see p. 117)
Page 9: Nicky Djawutjawuku, *Milminydjarrk at Garriyak (Sacred Waterholes)* (detail) 2016 (see p. 96)
Pages 40–41: Marrnyula Munuŋgurr, *Djapu L̲arrakitj* (detail), 2016 (see p. 128)

Throughout this book, authors have chosen to use the Yolŋu Matha orthography. This is most evident in the use of macrons to indicate retroflexed sounds and the venar nasal or "tailed n" [Ŋ/ŋ]. Retroflexed sounds are pronounced while the tip of the tongue curls back to the roof of the mouth. The venar nasal "Ŋ:ŋ" denotes the sound *ng* as in the English word sing.

Members of Indigenous communities are respectfully advised that a number of people mentioned in writing or depicted in photographs in the following pages have passed away.

Contents

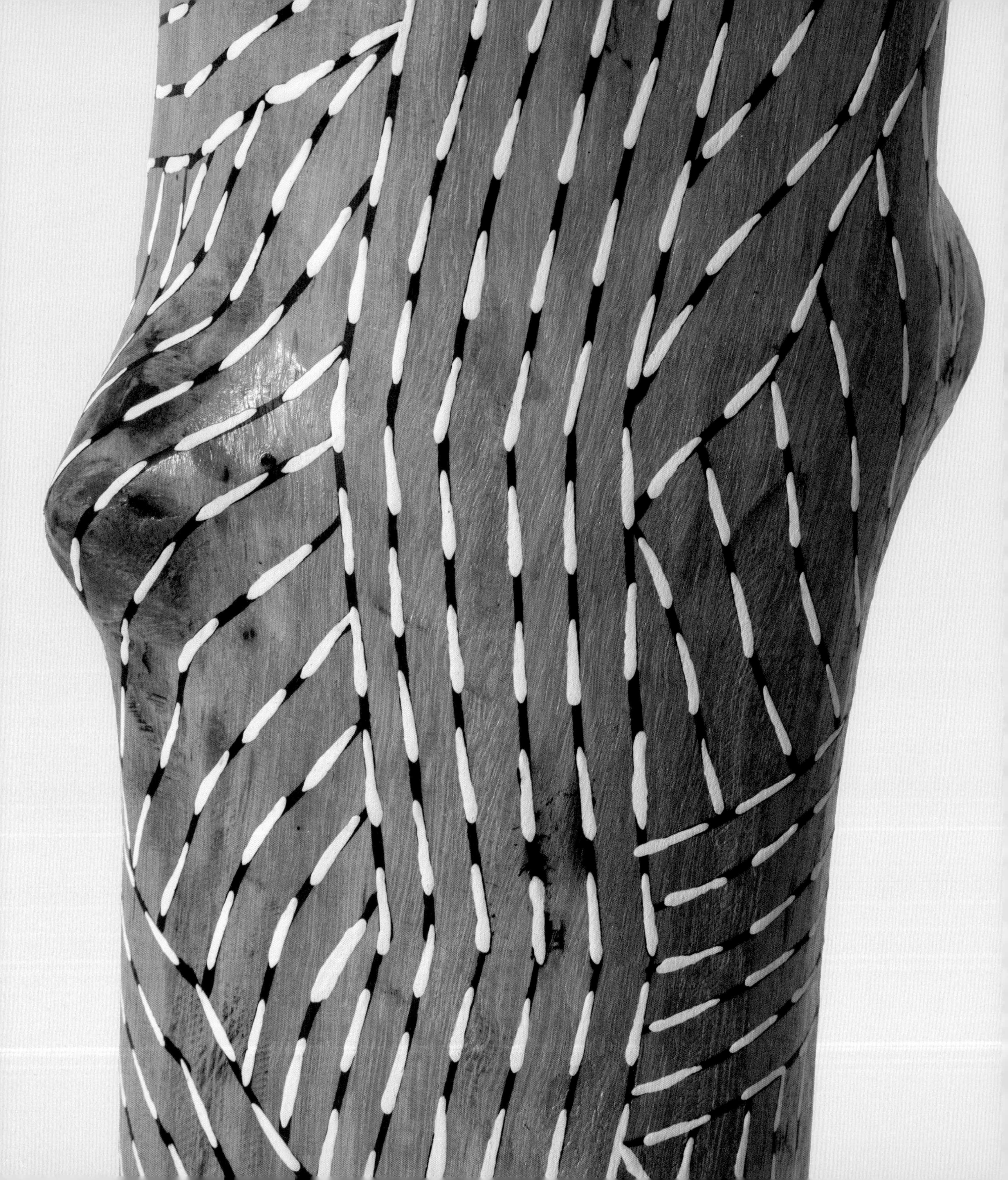

Director's Preface

David B. Walker
Executive Director | CEO, Nevada Museum of Art

When we began working with collectors Debra and Dennis Scholl in 2012, we had no idea that we would organize and tour three exhibitions of contemporary Aboriginal Australian art from their holdings. Nor that in 2017 we would announce that they were gifting a significant portion of those works to the Nevada Museum of Art. The Scholls have made it their practice to focus on a particular area—say, conceptual art or contemporary drawing—and assemble a large and deep survey of those works representing the state of the field. And then they would give most of it away to like-minded museums, in order to make room for new areas of interest. It is an enlightened and elegant way to collect that satisfies their curiosity, quest for new knowledge, and joy of collecting, and also benefits society at large.

In the case of Aboriginal art, the Scholls' fifth distinct collection, they began acquiring works more than a decade ago, and within a few years had amassed one of the most significant private collections in the United States. Their emphasis was on contemporary Aboriginal works that were fine examples of abstract art, and in fact the title of their first exhibition toured by the Museum in 2015 was *No Boundaries: Aboriginal Contemporary Abstract Painting*. The exhibition traced the evolution of the painting careers of nine senior Aboriginal men, and was followed in 2017 by *Marking the Infinite: Contemporary Women Artists from Aboriginal Australia*.

After several years of buying Aboriginal paintings through galleries, the Scholls moved into working directly with local Aboriginal art centers to commission new works that were often of a far-larger scale than the artists had tackled before. And, in part, they were driving the international market for Aboriginal painting within the context of contemporary art. That was certainly the case when they commissioned approximately one hundred memorial poles from the Northern Territory of Australia. The poles, based on the hollow-log coffins used in burial ceremonies, are painted tree trunks that present not only the power of contemporary Aboriginal painting but also reflect the traditions underlying the paintings.

Museum collections of Aboriginal Australian art in the United States have mostly arisen from the generosity of private collectors, but the Nevada Museum of Art had begun working with Aboriginal artists in remote desert communities in 2011 through research projects in association with our Center for Art + Environment. By 2017 the Center had brought more than a hundred paintings from field projects to the Museum; but, when the Scholls announced that they were donating almost an equal number of works by the most important Aboriginal artists in Australia, we realized that we were well on the way toward assembling one of the largest public collections of Aboriginal art in the United States—and that we would have the largest collection of memorial poles in the Americas.

Our own interest in these works grew out of the idea that Nevada and Australia share many cultural and geographic similarities: vast expanses of open land, rich natural resources, diverse Indigenous peoples, colonialism, and the ongoing conflicts that inevitably arise when these factors coexist. Aboriginal art has its deepest roots in the transmission of essential knowledge from generation to generation through stories, song, dance, and body decorations for more than forty thousand years. And Aboriginal contemporary art is relevant to all of our collections and educational endeavors, whether those are focused on art and the environment, how humans alter the landscape and work within it, and even how we code data and knowledge. It is a continuing privilege to work with our good friends Debra and Dennis Scholl whose philanthropy demonstrates that humans still pass down gifts to serve future generations.

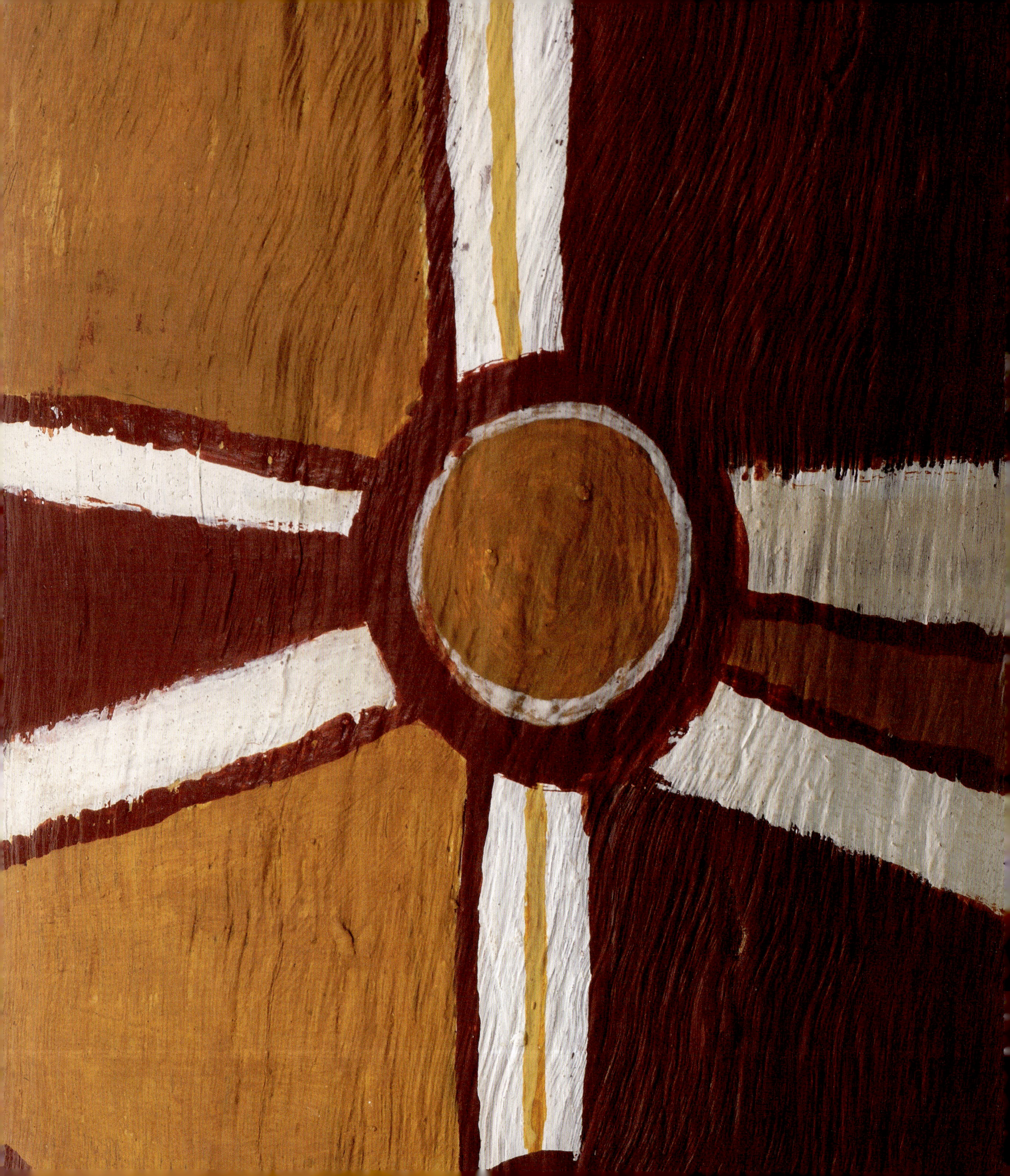

Preface

Dennis Scholl

This third and final exhibition is the culmination of a dozen years resulting in sixteen museum exhibitions of Aboriginal Australian art. It has been one of the finest adventures of my life.

After an exhibition of men's contemporary art titled *No Boundaries* and an exhibition of women artists, *Marking the Infinite*, I found that there was one set of objects that stood out, beyond the paintings we had been collecting. These were the memorial poles. The essays in this catalogue describe their original funereal purpose far better than I can. They came to me as art objects, first and foremost, not ceremonial objects. And I found them dazzling.

Watching the "pole whisperers" go into the forest in Arnhem Land, tap on a series of termite-eaten dead trees and instruct assistants which one to chop down, as it was not too thick or too thin, was a lesson in material selection. Then the careful peeling and soaking to remove the bark, which can be used for a canvas of its own. And finally the preparation of the log by rubbing it to harden and smooth the surface. The preparation of the ochres—clays taken from the river—in white, black, red, and brown. Only then would the log be laid down on the ground and the artist begin work.

I spent many an hour, particularly in Yirrkala, on the porch, watching the methodical work of Nyapanyapa Yunipiŋu and Noŋgirrŋa Marawili in particular, mixing the ochre on a small stone with just a drop of water. Sometimes when supplies were short, they would arrive with a twig, reach up to their own head, pull out a few long hairs, wrap them around the twig, and drag them through the thick ochre paint. Instant bush paintbrush! Laying down their designs on the logs, working methodically without haste, singing some days; they treated my presence as a silly nuisance, ignoring me on one hand and gossiping about me in their native tongue, Yolŋu Matha.

And, oh my, the results of those daily sessions. Hollow logs turned into astounding three dimensional works of art that dominate any room they are in, with designs handed down through generations. And lately as these incredible art objects began to gain in popularity, a freer hand began to emerge in their designs reminding me of the comment by the great painter Paddy Bedford, "I painted my Father's dreams, I painted my Mother's dreams, now I just paint." The hundred poles in this show provide a burst of creativity that takes you on a hundred journeys.

All of these poles come from a remote part of northeast Australia called Arnhem Land, where few urban Australians have been. In fact, the comment I received the most during this project when I told Australians where I had been traveling was, "I can't believe you have been there. I am Australian and I don't know anyone who has been there." Arnhem Land is a magical place, tropical and generally unspoiled, dotted with communities that have names like Milingimbi, Kunbarllanjnja, Maningrida, and Yirrkala. In each of them, artists are the revered leaders in the community: a level of respect I wish we could import back to the United States for our artists. The results reflect the seriousness with which the artists undertook the project. Knowing that these works were destined for four major museum shows in the US gave the artists a seriousness of intent for which we are forever grateful.

Twelve years ago we set out with the immodest goal of changing the western world's view of where these Aboriginal Australian artists belong in the canon. I am not sure we have succeeded, but I know my life has been changed forever.

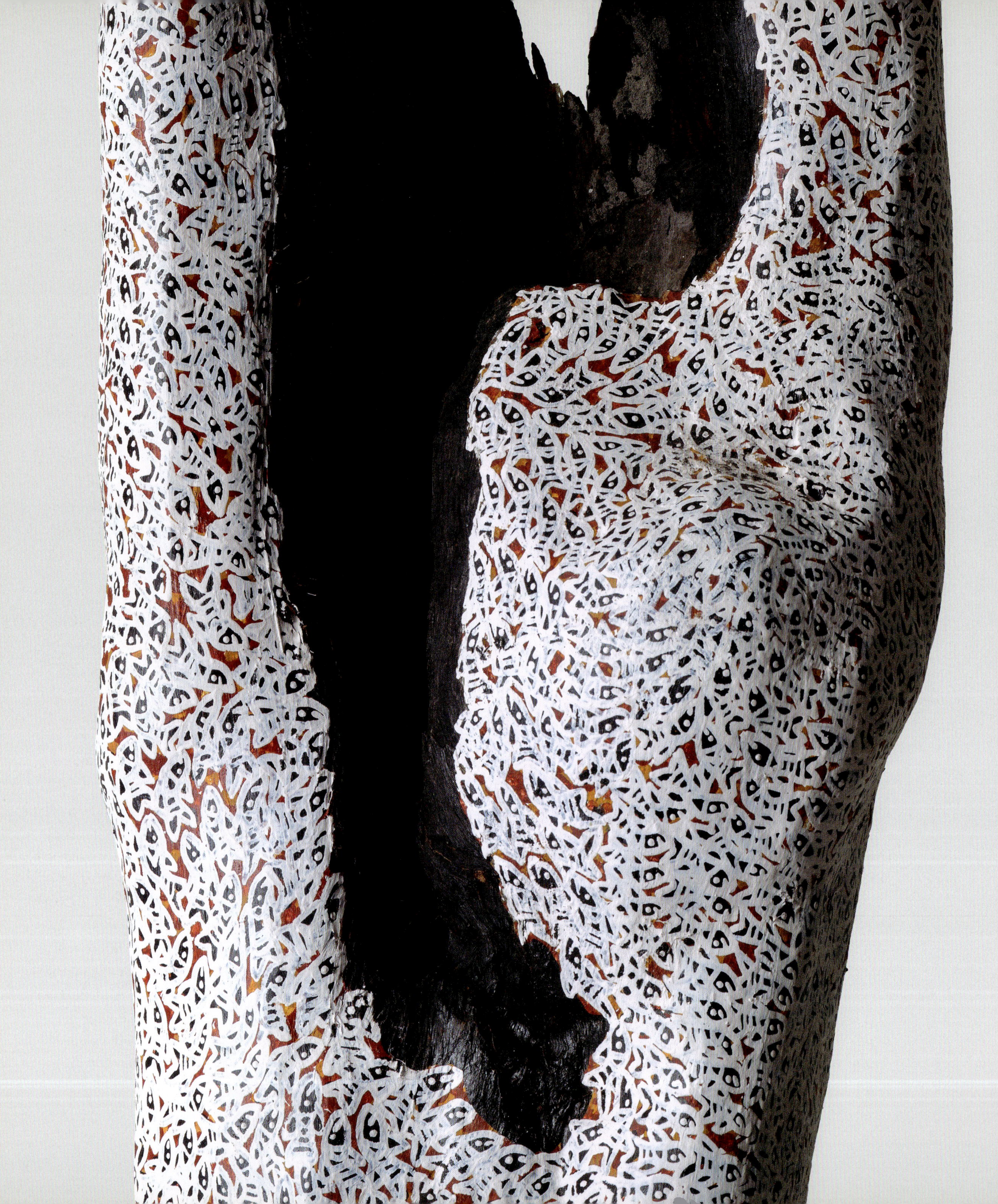

The Inside World

Henry F. Skerritt

Located in Australia's tropical north, Arnhem Land is another world: a place of spectacular natural beauty and irrepressible life. Occupying 37,000 square miles, it is home to some of the world's oldest continuing cultural traditions, with archaeological evidence confirming human habitation back over fifty thousand years. To the west, the rocky escarpments and sweeping flood-plains have long sustained the Bininj: the people of the stone country. While to the east, the white-sand beaches and sparkling bays are the sacred homelands of the Yolŋu. Between these poles live speakers of over a dozen different languages, each with their own distinctive cultural and artistic traditions. These differences are reflected in the diversity of works in this exhibition.

The Inside World presents ninety-nine memorial poles by forty-nine artists from four remote Aboriginal communities. It is not the first exhibition of Aboriginal memorial poles. Indeed, since *The Aboriginal Memorial* (Sydney Biennale, 1988; p. 37), memorial poles have been a regular feature in contemporary art exhibitions in Australia.[1] These exhibitions have, however, tended to focus on the work of a single community. *The Inside World* is the first exhibition to attempt to map the production of contemporary memorial poles across Arnhem Land—drawing on works produced through the art centers Injalak Arts (Kunbarrllanjnja), Maningrida Arts and Culture (Maningrida), Milingimbi Art and Culture (Milingimbi) and Buku-Larrŋgay Mulka (Yirrkala). Many of the works were commissioned specifically for this exhibition, and in several instances, as David Wickens notes in his essay, these commissions have resulted in the revival of the practice of producing memorial poles. In other instances—most notably the artists of Buku-Larrŋgay Mulka—the exhibition captures a profound moment of artistic development, as artists such as Wukun Wa<u>n</u>ambi (b. 1962), Gunybi Ganambarr (b. 1973) and Nyapanyapa Yunupiŋu (b. ca. 1945) push the boundaries of the form into new and unexpected trajectories.

Traditionally, memorial poles like those in *The Inside World* would have been used as ossuaries: the final resting place for the bones of the dead. The poles would be made from the trunk of a carefully selected *Eucalyptus tetradonta* (stringybark tree) that had been naturally hollowed out by termites. The most perfectly cylindrical trunk would be selected and its bark stripped so that it could be painted with powerful clan designs that would identify and protect the spirit of the deceased. Today, many artists have chosen to incorporate natural imperfections in their work, heightening the sense of connection between the human and natural worlds.

In western Arnhem Land, these objects are generally called *lorrkkon;* in central Arnhem Land, *ḏupun* is the more common term; while in northeastern Arnhem Land, they are usually called *larrakitj* (with underlined l). As Louise Hamby documents in her essay in this volume, there are a myriad other clan-specific names for memorial poles, reflecting the linguistic and cultural diversity of Arnhem Land. We have respected this diversity here, allowing for variations in spelling and terminology that indicate local differences.[2] Similarly, in English, these objects have gone by a range of descriptors, most commonly "hollow-log coffins" or "burial poles." We have opted for the term "memorial poles" to register their movement beyond the confines of the mortuary process, as well as to capture their broader symbolic and aesthetic roles in both Aboriginal society and the contemporary art world.

Wukun Wa<u>n</u>ambi, *Bamurruŋu* (detail), 2016 (see p. 134)

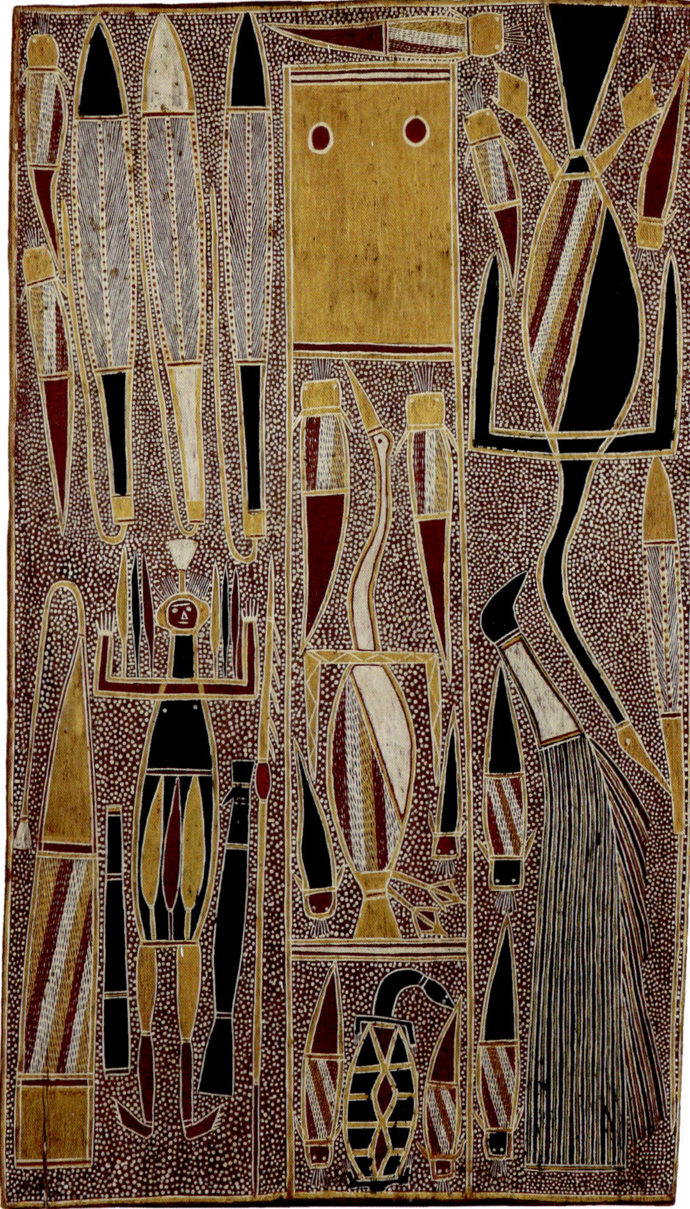

Fig. 1. John Buŋuwuy (Australian/Gupapuyŋu, c. 1922–1982), *Gupapuyŋu Mortuary Ceremony*, before 1966. Earth pigments on bark, 41½ x 24½ in. (105.4 x 62.2 cm). Kluge-Ruhe Aboriginal Art Collection of the University of Virginia. Edward L. Ruhe Collection. Gift of John W. Kluge, 1997

The symbolic nature of these objects is not something new, as Murray Garde notes in his essay in this book, these poles are never hollow: they are filled with memories of those loved and lost, reminding us of our connection to those who came before us. Indeed, in Aboriginal cosmology, the entire world exists on a highly metaphorical plane, as everything in the universe is considered mimetic of ancestral actions. Aboriginal ceremony renews and affirms these ancestral connections. Like all ritual, it is high in metaphor, allegory and symbolism. Generally speaking, memorial poles would be produced to mark the end of the mortuary process. In the early parts of the funeral rites, the body of the deceased would be placed on a raised platform. Once the flesh had decayed, their bones would be collected and worn round the neck of close family members in a woven dilly-bag. Once the grieving process was complete, these bones would be placed in a hollow-log coffin as part of an elaborate ceremony (such as the *Lorrkkon* ceremony recounted in Garde's essay). Not everyone would be granted this honor: often it was restricted to high-ranking or ritually powerful members of a clan.

Interment in a memorial pole marked the final point in a long and complex mortuary process designed to guide the spirit of the deceased on its final journey. It signified the moment when spirits were considered to have finally returned to their ancestral homes—when they had left all vestiges of the mundane "outside" world and become one with the "inside" realm of the ancestral world. This is matched in the symbolism of the hollow-log coffin. The trunk of the tree is stripped of its skin, till only its "inside" body remains. The bones of the deceased are then placed into this new body, which is painted with the clan designs that signify the "inside" identity of the deceased. As Morphy notes, at this point the bones have ceased to be the bones of the person and have, to use a Yolngu metaphor, become part of "the bones [*ngaraka*] of the clan."[3]

Embodying this complex symbolism of life, death, and eternity, the hollow-log coffin was ripe for artistic investigation. And if collectors and institutions were slow to grasp this potential, Aboriginal artists have explored it for some time. In particular, the depiction of hollow-log coffins has provided fertile ground for bark painters trying to represent the interconnected nature of Aboriginal cosmology. Take for instance *Gupapuyŋu Mortuary Ceremony* by John Buŋuwuy (ca. 1922–1982) (Fig. 1). At the center of the work Buŋuwuy depicts a large *djal̲umbu* (the Gupapuyŋu term for memorial poles), along with other ritual objects from the mortuary ceremony. Buŋuwuy does not distinguish the foreground of the *djal̲umbu* from the background of the painting, uniting them with a field of fine white dots. This serves to flatten the picture plane—but also creates a powerful metaphor for the *djal̲umbu* as a site at which the ancestral and physical realms meld. On the *djalumbu* he depicts a white diving duck (*burala*), while in the top left corner he depicts three ceremonial objects also known as *burala*.[4] To the right, a black diving duck balances the composition. The effect is a highly fluid and poetic merging and mirroring of the ancestral, ceremonial, and natural worlds.

INSIDE OUT

There are some things that unite the peoples of Arnhem Land. One is their belief that everything in existence has an "inside" and an "outside meaning." Morphy notes: "Inside things are ancestrally powerful and sacred, while outside things are mundane; inside things are restricted whereas outside things are unrestricted."[5] Despite this apparent binary, the division between "inside" and "outside" operates as a continuum that structures the entire universe. In his essay in this volume, Wukun Wanambi describes the complexity of this continuum, and the ways in which it shapes Yolŋu teaching and learning. In the cross-cultural context of the art world, memorial poles become a tool for explaining the interrelation between the "inside" spiritual world and the "outside" world of the mundane. This is a frequent refrain of Wanambi's, as he has noted elsewhere:

> The outside surface of things hides what is inside. I want to share what is hidden. In Yolngu, understanding the life of the spirit is a circle. The *larrakitj* is a circle. We are looking for our identity and we search around and around until we find our destiny and we go straight to that circle and join it and become a part of family. We used *larrakitj* as a coffin but now instead of digging it in the ground we want to show it as art. We believe that the spirit travels through the water and returns to its source and then is born anew. The body dissolves and the bones return to the land as the *larrakitj* decays. I have wanted to share this understanding with non-Indigenous people for a long time. To show them what is inside. Inside the *larrakitj*. Inside our destiny. Inside our hearts.[6]

With the arrival of missionaries in Arnhem Land in the 1920s and 30s, the use of hollow-log coffins slowly diminished. In some cases, missionaries discouraged traditional practices, while in others it was just a matter of modern convenience, as the artist Joe Guymala (b. 1969) notes, "*balanda* brought more easy coffin box one with key." This is not to say that traditional practices died out, but rather, that they were refashioned. In many regions today, the painting of coffin lids remains an important part of the funeral process. In the late 1970s and 80s, there was a resurgence in the production of memorial poles for the developing Aboriginal art market. While not being used as funerary objects, the production of these poles was most clearly framed in terms of Aboriginal cultural resistance to the tide of westernization. Moving into the category of fine art, memorial poles retained all of their power as objects that embodied life, death, and memory. As Morphy notes in his essay in this catalogue, these have long been the major subjects of art because they transcend existence, connecting the living and the dead. But in the political context of Indigenous rights, they also represent a wholly *different* take on these universal experiences. It is in this sense that the memorial pole becomes both a powerful pedagogical tool for Aboriginal artists to explain their culture to outsiders, while drawing to the fore the profound differences in our comprehension of human existence. This is the essence of great contemporary art: to communicate across worldviews without losing any of its distinctiveness, in order that it reveals both our differences and our shared humanity.[7]

ENCOUNTERING MEMORIAL POLES IN THE PRESENT

At the time of his death, the great Ganalbiŋu artist Johnny Bulunbulun (1946–2010) was working on an imposing memorial pole. He had painted the underlying forms: a menagerie of fish and lizards that danced around more abstract shapes signifying sacred sites within his ancestral homelands in the Arafura Swamp. All that remained was to "finish" the piece with the shimmering bands of cross-hatched infill (or *rarrk*) that distinguished the great master's oeuvre. With Bulunbulun's passing, however, the piece lay silent: an unfinished requiem cut short before it could be sung. In accordance with Aboriginal protocols, the pole was hidden from view in a back-room of the Maningrida Arts and Culture center where Bulunbulun had worked.

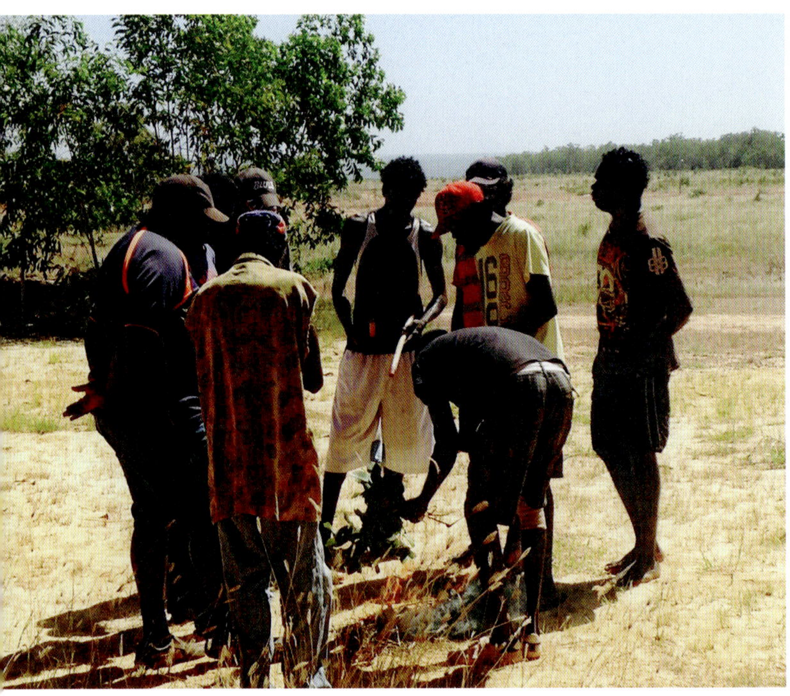

Fig. 2. Men preparing for a smoking ceremony at Maningrida, May 2015. Photograph by Henry Skerritt

In 2015, following a lengthy process of grieving, Bulunbulun's widow Laurie Marburduk (b. 1951) decided to complete her husband's final statement. Marburduk had a steady and practiced hand: she had assisted her husband many times before on the laborious task of infilling *rarrk*. This time, she sat alone. One can only imagine the thoughts that passed through Marburduk's head as she performed this final act of devotion, completing the clan designs of her late husband on this form (the hollow-log coffin) that for millennia had been used to guide the spirits of the deceased back to their ancestral homelands.

Traditionally, in Aboriginal Australian societies, objects associated with the dead were destroyed. The fine art economy—like other elements introduced following the British invasion of Australia in 1788—has necessitated some modification to such traditions. Rather than destroying Bulunbulun's majestic final artwork, a smoking ceremony was planned to "cleanse" the pole and ensure than any lingering spirits were sent on their way. So, on a hot day in May 2015, I was invited to witness a group of ten men perform this solemn ritual in the sandy clearing in front of the art center (Fig. 2). I stood back with a group of women, children, and other *balanda* (non-Aboriginal people) as the men moved rhythmically around the pole with smoldering eucalyptus branches; the sweet, sharp smell of burning leaves hanging in the humid air. As they circled, the men sang the lilting hymns of the Ganalbiŋu, a gentle murmur rising to a pulsing climax. Marburduk wiped tears from her eyes.

When the brief ceremony was complete, the men promptly assembled around Bulunbulun's pole to have their photographs taken—participating in that most contemporary form of memory preservation (Fig. 3). As a non-participant observer, I was quickly roped in to help, with several cell phones thrust into my hands. I noted with amusement later in the day that some of these photos turned up on the social media accounts of the younger men. For non-Aboriginal commentators, this mix of ancient cultural practices and modern technology is often characterized as disjunctive. Indeed, it has become something of a cliché to speak of Indigenous peoples as living "across two worlds." And yet, for most Indigenous Australians that I have spoken to, there is little tension between tradition and modernity. Indigenous Australians do not view their cultures as being out of step with the present, but rather, they see continuity and change as being in dynamic relation. Nowhere is this more clearly evidenced than in the contemporary Aboriginal art movement. As Howard Morphy has noted for the Yolŋu, the artistic system exists in a state of creative tension: "art mediates between the ideology of immutable forms and order originating in the ancestral past, and the reality of sociocultural change and political process."[8]

Contemporary Indigenous Australian conceptions of time, tradition, and memorialization have their roots in some of the oldest continuous philosophical traditions on the planet. In recent years, these ideas have found increasing global traction as EuroAmerican artists and academics have sought ways beyond the limiting paradigms of modernity. Following the collapse of modernism as the dominant artistic discourse in the West (and what Peter Osborne calls the "pyrrhic victory" of dematerialized and conceptual art practices), much EuroAmerican contemporary art and theory has begun to adopt parallel concerns to those that Indigenous artists have long championed.[9] Where the classic narratives of modern art have tended to eschew tradition—as epitomized in Ezra Pound's famous dictum, "make it new"—contemporary artists have reveled in the complex relationships between past, present, and future. This is evidenced as much in those artists attempting to reinvigorate the modernist tradition (such as Gerhard Richter [b. 1932] or Mark Bradford [b. 1961]), as it is in those whose explorations tap more explicitly into the processes of collective and individual mourning (take for example Doris Salcedo [b. 1958] or Rabih Mroué [b. 1967]). In this context, it is perhaps unsurprising that Aboriginal memorial poles from remote northern Australia have emerged as one of the most intriguing forms of contemporary Australian art.

MEMORIALIZING THE ART WORLD

In his contribution to this volume, Morphy explores the somewhat paradoxical history of memorial poles as contemporary art. On the one hand, their scale and weight were often a deterrent to collectors of Aboriginal art, who preferred the portability of paintings on bark or canvas. Moreover, their form, with its clear reference to pre-colonial mortuary rites, was often cast in negative terms as "ethnographic," "tribal," or "primitive," creating a considerable barrier to their appreciation within the category of "fine art." On the other hand, these physically imposing and symbolically loaded objects were well suited to the cavernous halls of modern art museums. As Morphy notes, one of the first significant institutional acquisitions of Aboriginal art was the Art Gallery of New South Wales's 1958 commission of seventeen Pukumani grave posts from senior artists of the Tiwi Islands. Aboriginal art had long been exhibited in natural history museums, but this marked a significant entry into the contemporary art world.

Four decades later, memorial poles featured in arguably the most decisive intervention by Aboriginal artists into contemporary art: *The Aboriginal Memorial*, 1987–88, exhibited at the 1988 Sydney Biennale. Conceived by curator Djon Mundine and the artists of Ramingining in response to the events surrounding the bicentennial of British colonization, *The Aboriginal Memorial* consisted of two hundred memorial poles—one for each year of British occupation. Describing the installation in the Biennale catalogue, Mundine noted: "Each Hollow Log is ceremonially a

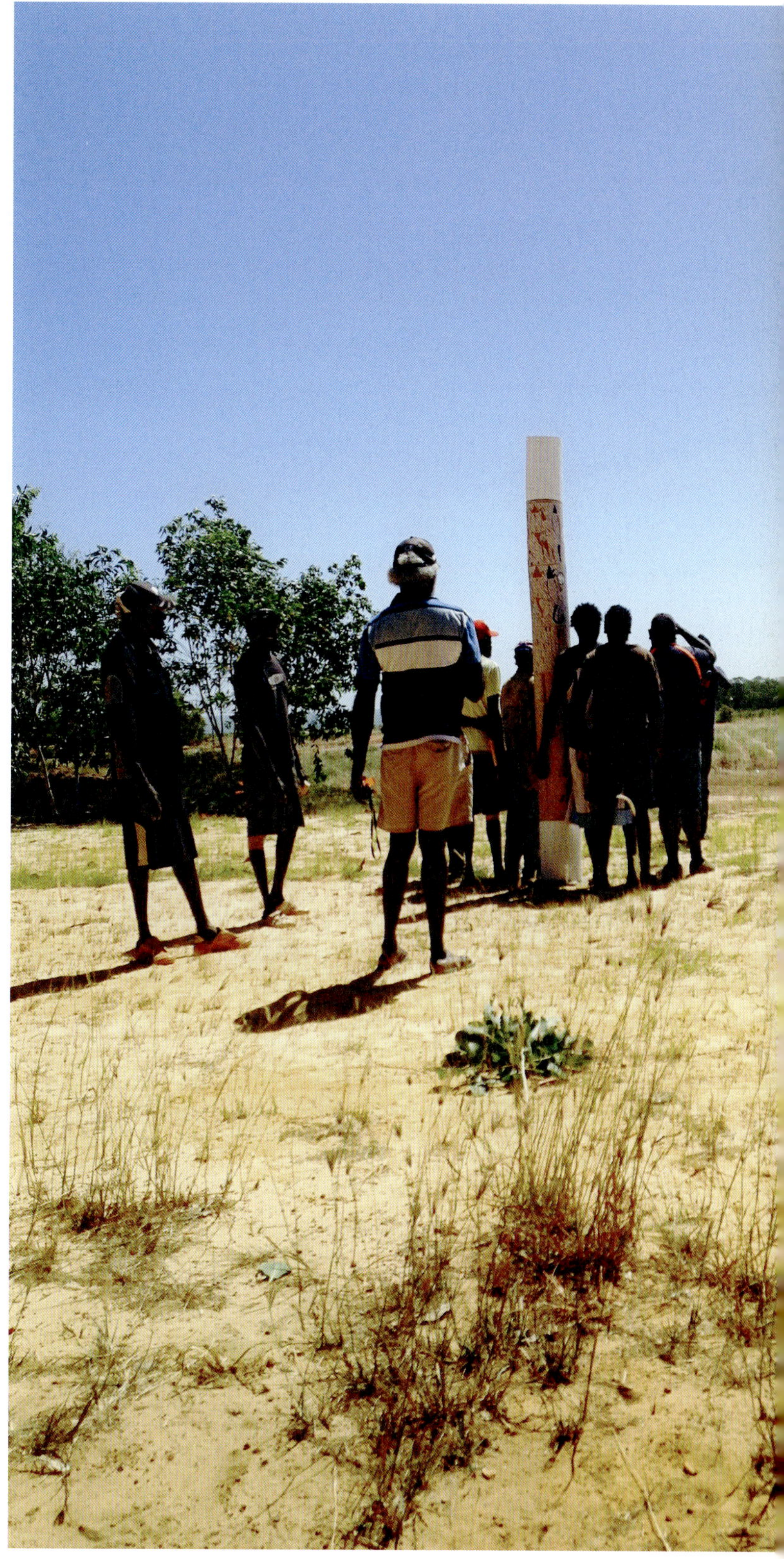

Fig. 3. Men having their photographs taken with Johnny Bulunbulun's final memorial pole. Maningrida, May 2015. Photograph by Henry Skerritt

Bone Coffin, so in essence the forest is really like a large cemetery of dead Aboriginals, a War Cemetery, a War Memorial to all those Aboriginals who died defending their country."[10] Unlike Aboriginal paintings, which were often characterized by their uncanny similarities to modernist abstraction, in the context of the Biennale, *The Aboriginal Memorial* resonated as a work of installation art. As Kimberley Moulton eloquently argues in her essay in this book, a large part of this resonance came from the profundity of the political challenge that *The Aboriginal Memorial* posed to mainstream Australian notions of colonial sovereignty. The art historian Terry Smith draws a similar conclusion in his analysis of *The Memorial*:

> A key point is that such interventions not only strongly assert the presence of those peoples who will not fit into an imposed, colonial fabricated nationality but also radically subvert western modernity's model of nationality as such. Aboriginal peoples, in this context, are basically saying: *We refuse your model of the nation state, for we have quite other practices of sociality; the only way you can deal with us is to reenact your early attempts at obliteration, which we know you cannot do.* This keeps nationality open, like a promise and a running sore.[11]

For Smith, at the heart of *The Aboriginal Memorial's* claim to be important contemporary art was its strategic balance of cultural incommensurability with the possibility of cross-cultural dialogue. Despite its seemingly impenetrable cultural difference, Smith concludes, "its aesthetic richness, its open sharing of sacred imagery, and its suggestion of persistence of life after death makes it an extraordinary yet entirely accessible template for reconciliation."[12] In his more recent art historical investigations, Nigel Lendon has shown that the very conception of *The Aboriginal Memorial* was a highly collaborative act—a work of "relational art" whose agency was dispersed between its "conceptual producer" Djon Mundine, the artists of Ramingining, and the institutions that have exhibited *The Memorial.*[13] This is not to deny *The Memorial*'s pivotal role in the history of contemporary art, but rather, to confirm it as an embodiment of the types of transactional practice that define both contemporary art and contemporary life. As every essay in this volume attests, what makes Aboriginal memorial poles such compelling contemporary art is the insistence with which they work across distinctions such as art and ethnography; tradition and modernity; locality and globalism; cultural difference and our shared humanity. As Diana Nawi notes, Aboriginal memorial poles transcend and confound these binaries around which conventional histories of contemporary art have been written.

LIVING MEMORIES

> One of the most surprising cultural and political phenomena of recent years has been the emergence of memory as a key concern in western societies, a turning toward the past that stands in stark contrast to the privileging of the future so characteristic of earlier decades of twentieth-century modernity.[14]
>
> Andreas Huyssen

Memory has emerged as a crucial concern of contemporary artists. This has been particularly noticeable in (although not limited to), the work of artists from previously marginalized and oppressed cultural backgrounds. Often this memory discourse has centered around historical trauma and the uncovering of previously concealed histories (such as Paddy Bedford's [1922–2007] depictions of previously unrecorded massacres of Aboriginal people, or Paul Rucker's [b. 1968] obsessive documenting of the Ku Klux Klan). In other instances, it has been at the behest of keeping cultural practices strong—as in the ceramics of Janet Fieldhouse (b. 1971) (Fig. 4) which reimagine traditional weaving practices of the Torres Strait Islands into fragile elegies in porcelain. For other Indigenous Australian artists, memory has served to reaffirm connections to their ancestral country in exile, such as the luminous abstractions of artists like Weaver Jack (1928–2010) or Nyilpirr Spider Snell (1925–2016). Indeed, the ceremonial songlines of Indigenous Australia are themselves a highly sophisticated mnemonic device for navigation and survival.

The pervasive interest in memory amongst contemporary artists is clearly indicative of shifting attitudes towards

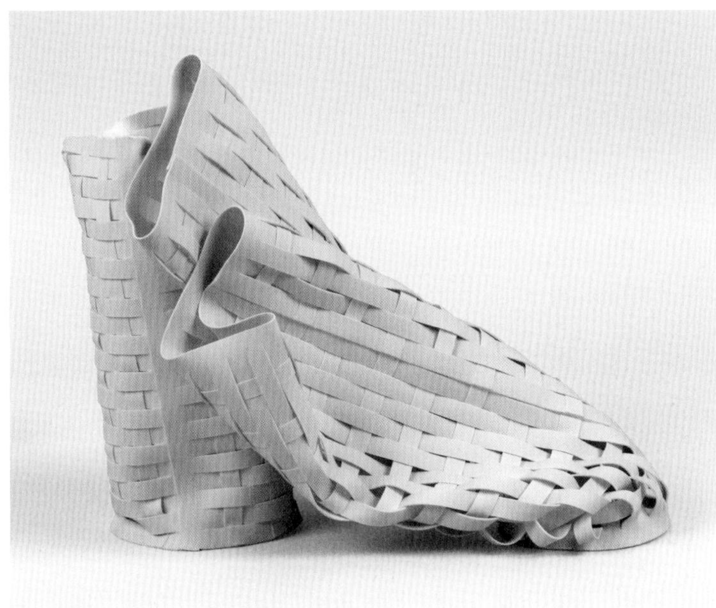

Fig. 4. Janet Fieldhouse (Australian/Meriam Mir, born 1971), *Memory Series 2*, 2014. Porcelain, 7⅞ x 10¼ x 6 in. (20 x 26 x 15 cm). Kluge-Ruhe Aboriginal Art Collection of the University of Virginia. Gift of the artist, 2017

temporality brought about by the changed conditions of globalization. As Huyssen notes, the acceleration of global movement and communication has radically transformed our experience of time, making us acutely aware of the "discrepant temporalities" of the contemporary.[15] Whereas modernity tended to be framed in terms of linear progress, contemporaneity is characterized by a coming together of different, but equally "present" times: a recognition of the myriad ways of inhabiting the present.[16] This is the very definition of "contemporary" which means to share one's time with others. In this "temporal turn," contemporary artists have increasingly turned to memory for its ability to marshal both the individual and the collective.[17] Unlike history—which is often characterized as official, institutional or national—memories are deeply personal. And yet, while memories structure our being (what are we but our memories?), they also shape our shared understandings of the past, present, and future (our *collective* memory).

My sense is that the memory embedded in the memorial poles in this exhibition operates on a slightly different level. For the artists of Arnhem Land, *ḻarrakitj, ḏupun* and *lorrkkon* embody living memories: the sign of a past that remains embedded in the present. In this sense, the wielding of memory becomes an act of *authority*. It is perhaps unsurprising that memory and trauma are so often bedfellows. Hal Foster has argued that trauma, much like memory, has absolute authority. "One cannot challenge the trauma of another: one can only believe it, even identify with it, or not. *In trauma discourse, then, the subject is evacuated and elevated at once.*"[18] Jill Bennett reasons that, in this regard, "trauma-related art is best understood as *transactive* rather than *communicative*. It often touches us, but it does not necessarily communicate the 'secret' of personal experience."[19] In doing so, it avoids what Jennifer Biddle has described as the "violence of identification," in which understanding the Other is filtered through the logic of resemblance.[20] In memorial poles we see the transaction of memory as lived experience—as part of a worldview that has both surface ("outside") meanings and hidden ("inside") meanings. We see the Other as a shimmering surface, whose depth we know, but which lies always out of view. As Waṉambi notes: "*Balanda* can see the surface side of the designs—like looking at the surface of the water—but underneath is the bigger part that only we know." In doing so, memorial poles offer the aesthetic contours of the Aboriginal worldview—the awareness of a "whole structure" that Waṉambi describes—while maintaining the restrictedness of this inside world.[21]

Today, the *ḻarrakitj*, *ḏupun*, and *lorrkkon* that travel the world as art stand as the embodiment of the rich, living cultures of Arnhem Land. They are not ritual objects in themselves, but metaphors for the crossing of cultures: spirit vessels designed to hint at the existence of an elusive "inside" world. As artworks, each one expresses this in a unique way: while many of the poles refer to clan designs, most use these designs as the launchpad for highly individuated expessions. The result is not a picture of dying cultures, but a celebration of life. In an interconnected world, in which the fear of difference is being increasingly marshalled by the supporters of xenophobic nativism, these works offer a remarkable olive branch: a model for considering the potential for dialogue within a world of diversity. Walking in this forest of bones, we find ourself reborn. Faced with this joyous elucidation of a culture so distant and different to our own, the world is made more alive.

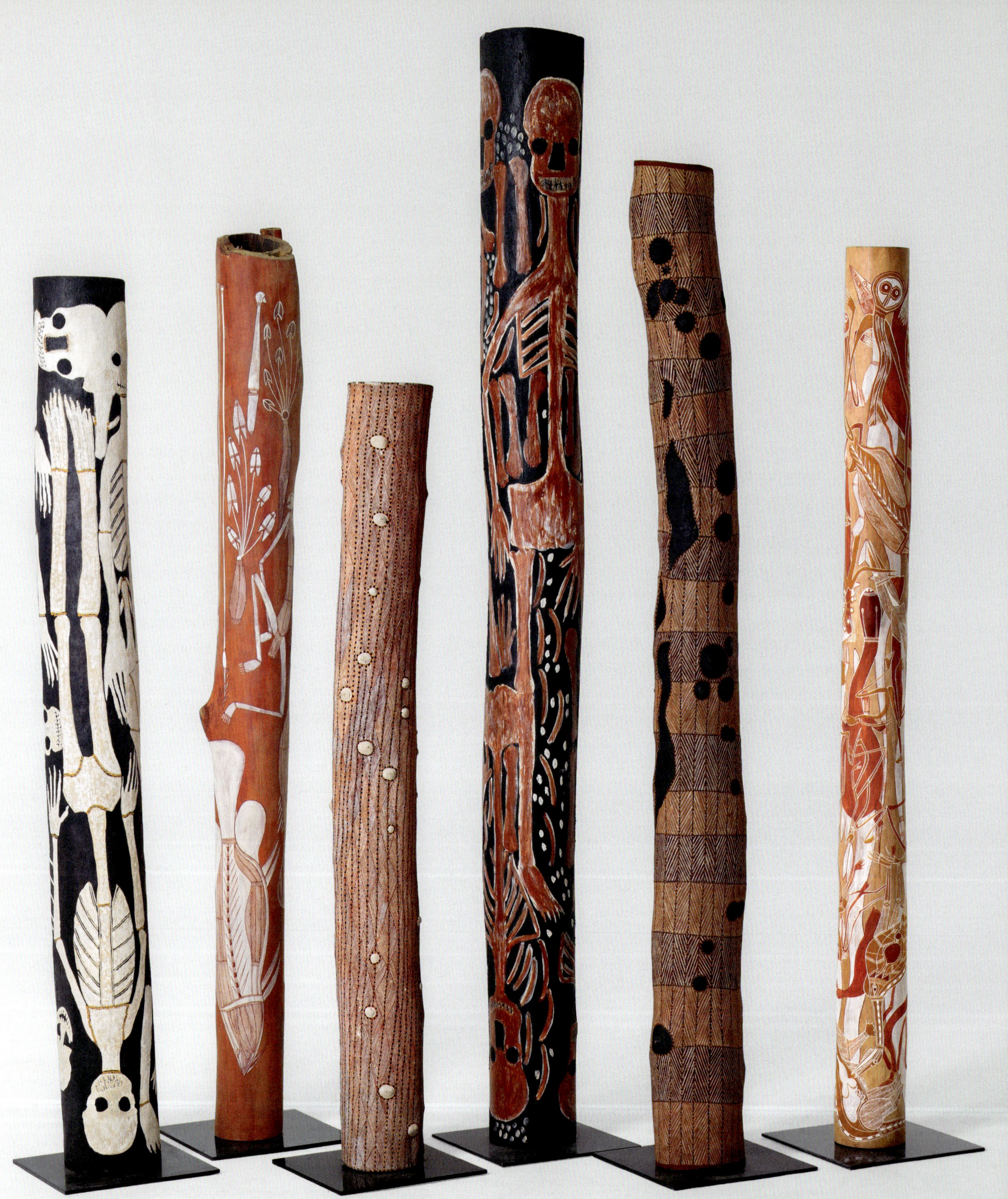

L̠arrakitj: Death and Memory

Howard Morphy

Perhaps for all human societies, death provides one of the main contexts for art. In death a person's past is present, and memories and emotions come together in communal expressions of sadness and hope. Music and poetry can be the means to evoke the spirit world by connecting people to places beyond the now, transcending the everyday. Paintings, sculptures, photographs, and texts provide means of representing the dead, giving them a continuing presence in the world of the living. Architectural spaces—buildings and ceremonial grounds—provide arenas for ritual performance and commemorative events that celebrate the lives of those who have died and bring the living together to look to the future. Many artworks endure for centuries after death; they become heritage, bringing memories of past lives to future generations. Pyramids, sarcophagi, memorial sculptures, poetry, sagas continue to be meaningful long after their creation, perhaps even achieving the enduring presence hoped for at the time of their making.

Indigenous mortuary rituals and burial practices vary greatly across Australia. Burial practices differ according to regional beliefs and customs as well as being influenced by environmental factors. In many parts of tropical north Australia hollow logs were used as coffins for interring the bones of the deceased. In Arnhem Land the final stage of the mortuary ritual was the placing of the bones of the dead in a hollow log coffin. *L̠arrakitj* is one of the Yolŋu terms for these coffins. *L̠arrakitj* were made from the trunks of stringybark trees that had been naturally hollowed out by termites. The trees were cut down and stripped of their bark leaving a surface that could be painted.

In the past mortuary rituals took place over an extended period of time. Following a death, the body was either buried in the ground or exposed on a wood and bark platform. Months later the bones were removed and placed in a bark container (*dan'parr*). Close relatives kept this bark coffin for several years before final interment in the *l̠arrakitj*.[1] In the escarpment country of western Arnhem Land these coffins were often placed in crevices and platforms in caves or rock shelters that formed natural ossuaries. In eastern Arnhem Land there were special cemetery areas where bones were brought to be placed in their *l̠arrakitj*. But often the ceremony would be held in the deceased person's clan country and the coffin remained in the ground as a memorial to them. The poles were left standing in place; sometimes they remained there for many years a reminder of the person buried within them. Finally, as they were weathered by wind and rain, or burnt in bush fires, all physical trace of them disappeared.

Changing burial practices have meant that bones are no longer placed in log coffins. The forms of mortuary rituals have

Opposite, left to right:
Joe Guymala, *Lorrkkon Story*, 2016. Earth pigments on wood, 84¼ in. (214 cm)
Gabriel Maralngurra, *Mimih Spirit Hunting*, 2017. Earth pigments on wood, 89 in. (226 cm)
Joey Nganjmirra, *Burrar (Water Goanna) Lorrkkon*, 2016. Earth pigments on wood, 74⅛ in. (188 cm)
Joe Guymala, *Lorrkkon Story*, 2016. Earth pigments on wood, 106⅓ in. (270 cm)
Joey Nganjmirra, *Burrar (Water Goanna) Lorrkkon*, 2017. Earth pigments on wood, 93¾ in. (238 cm)
Gabriel Maralngurra, *Lorrkkon*, 2016. Earth pigments on wood, 86⅝ in. (220 cm)

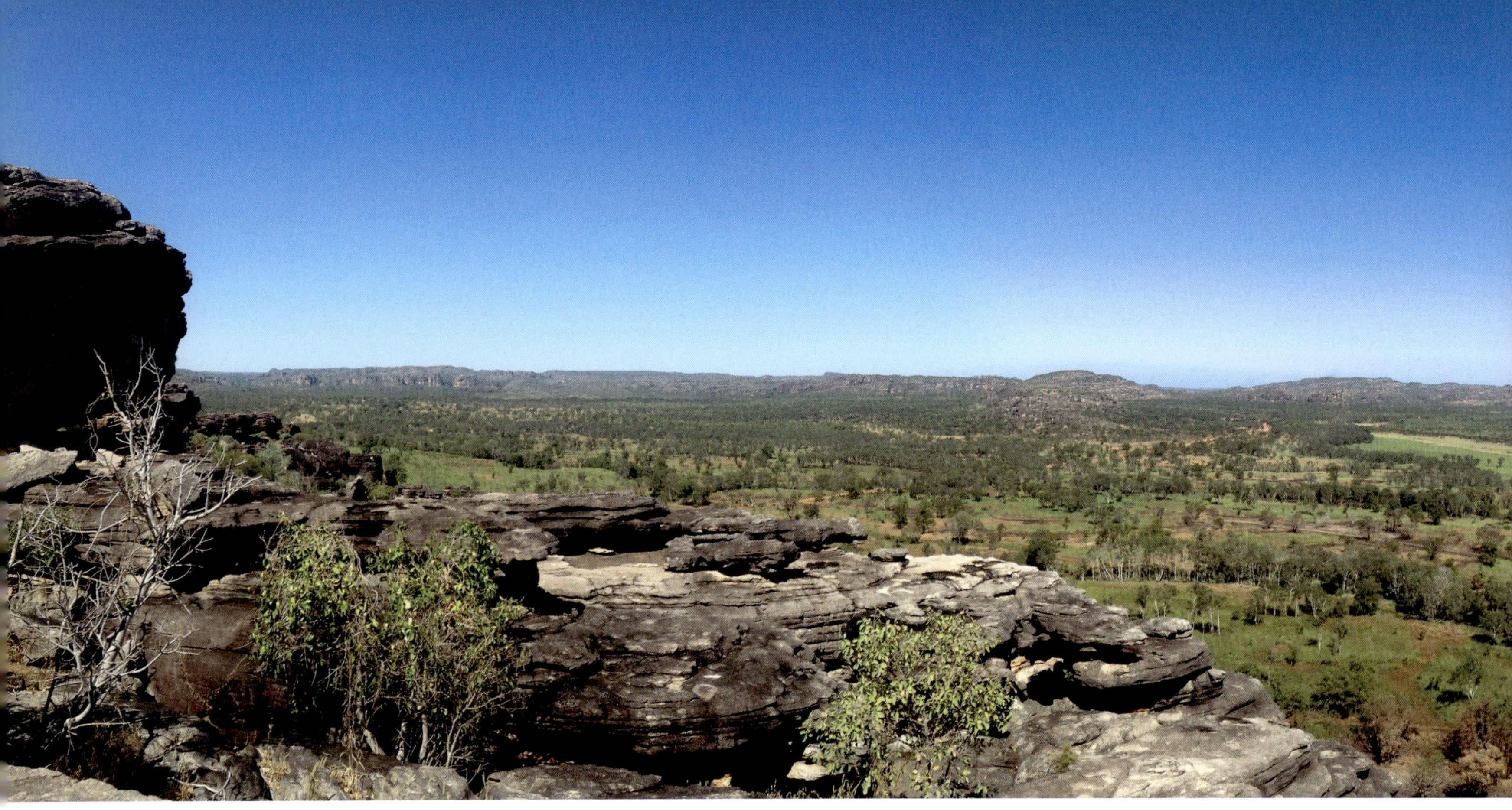

Fig. 1. View of Kunbarrllanjnja from Injalak Hill. Photograph by Henry Skerritt

adapted to changes that have followed from European colonization. However, religious beliefs and practices exist in continuity with the past, and the songs, paintings, and dances that are central to people's spiritual identity continue to be performed in new contexts.[2] As artifact, the hollow-log coffin is not only part of memories of the past but a continuing theme of life in the present. The rituals that were once part of final burial in a hollow log are now performed in other contexts and the hollow coffins have a renewed life as works of art. Painted hollow logs are still made for other kinds of ceremonies and as memorials for the dead in public contexts.

THE SOUL'S JOURNEY

In Arnhem Land people are closely connected to the beings of the Ancestral World, *Waŋarr* in the Yolŋu languages. The world was created by *Waŋarr* beings associated with the countries of different social groups. These ancestors left their mark on the landscape and their spirit is ever-present. Yathikpa in the country of the Maḏarrpa clan is associated with fire and the ancestral crocodile, Bäru. Bäru was originally human in shape. He had an argument with his wife who set fire to the bark hut in which he was sleeping. Engulfed in flames, the sheets of bark burning into his back, he began to change into the shape of a crocodile. He dived into the waters of Blue Mud Bay to quench the flames. The flames can still be seen in the waving red fields of sea grass in the waters of the bay, and Bäru's powerful presence can be felt in the turbulence of the waters on a stormy day. The ancestral events are represented in designs and in the form of sacred objects, as well as being the subjects of songs and dances (see for instance Djambawa Marawili's [b. 1953] *Dhakandjali*, 2015, p. 118). *Waŋarr* beings established the laws by which people live, the systems of marriage and authority that are the "footprints"—*djalkiri*—that people follow today.

People are born into country and gain their spiritual identity from the *Waŋarr* beings associated with the sacred places and waterholes in their clan estates. They are named after the ancestral beings and throughout their lives their spiritual identity is reinforced through participation in ceremonies. On death a person's soul returns to the *Waŋarr* domain; it is re-incorporated in the sacred waters of the clan.[3] Spirits can also be seen in the

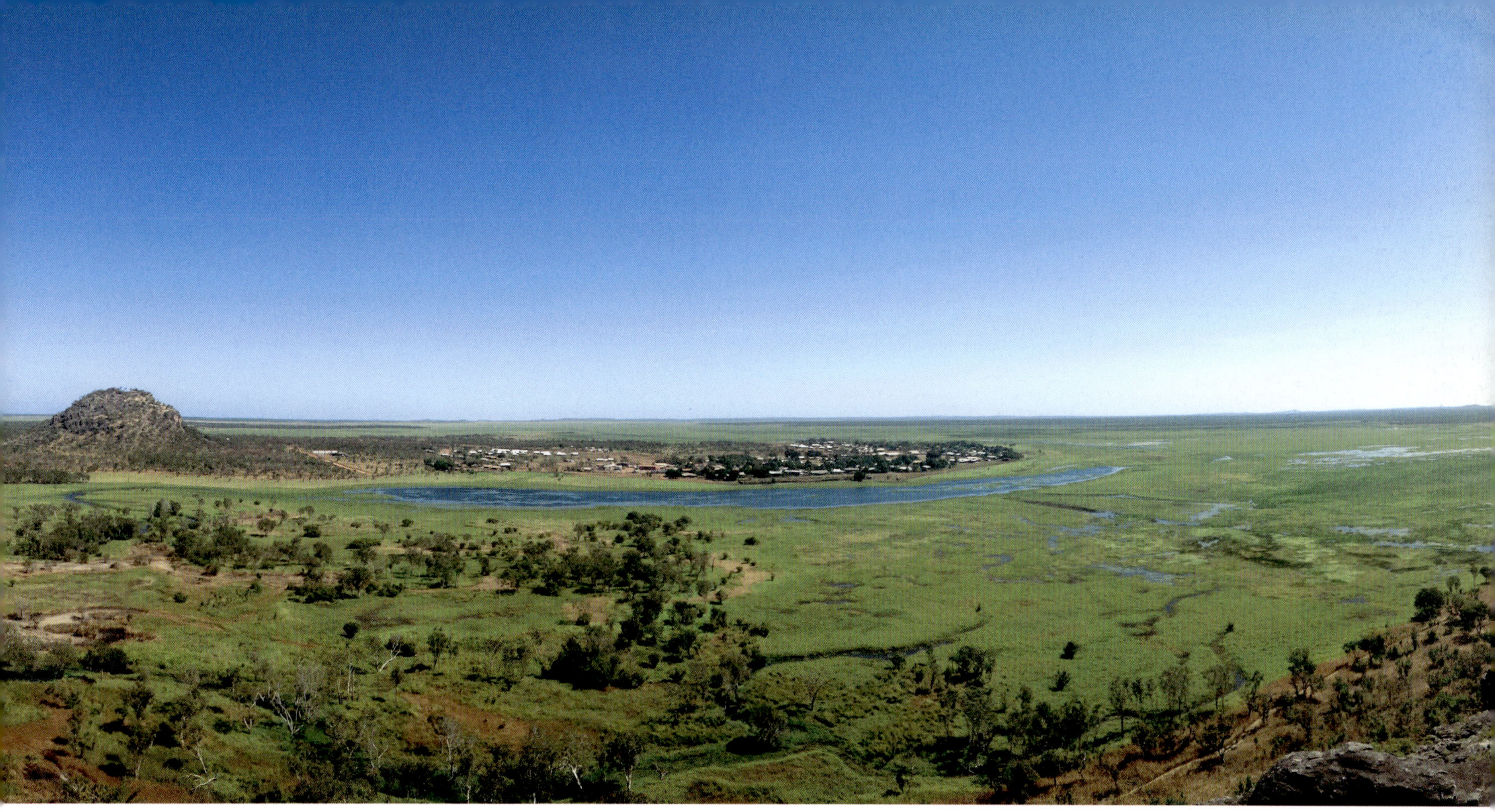

night sky in the form of stars. Yolŋu mortuary rituals fulfil several important functions in returning the person's soul to the spiritual domain, in repairing the emotions felt on their death and in bringing people together in the celebration of their life. Mortuary rituals are extensive and take place over several months following the death. The ceremonies are structured on the basis of the journey of the soul from the place of death to its final resting place in its own clan territory. The journey is envisaged as taking place over a period of time and its progress is assisted by the ceremonies that are performed at different stages of the mourning process. In the past that involved the three stages described above: primary burial, keeping the bones in a bark container and finally interment in the hollow-log coffin. By the time that the bones were placed in the hollow log the soul had already returned to the spiritual domain. The ceremony was the culmination of a journey whereby the soul leaves the body, is reincorporated within the *Waŋarr* domain, and becomes a source of spiritual sustenance for the living.

Today the main emphasis is on primary burial. The ceremonies last longer than in the past and are often followed later by others that enable the person's soul to continue on its journey, such as the cleansing of the person's house, the burial of their possessions or a circumcision ceremony which links the initiate to the soul of the person who has died. Bones are no longer placed in *l̲arrakitj* but remain buried in the ground. However painted poles, *djuwany*, are still made for the Djuŋguwan ceremony. *Djuwany* posts represent female ancestral beings and are distinguished by a fringe of bark around the top (see for instance, Dhurrumuwuy Marika's [b. 1981] *Rulyapa*, 2016, p. 119).

BECOMING ART

European colonization affected Aboriginal people in different ways across Arnhem Land. Western Arnhem Land was close to the developing township of Darwin, and that proximity had devastating consequences for the regional population. Eastern Arnhem Land was protected by distance from the initial impact. Mission stations were established in the 1920s and 30s by the Methodist Church, from Warruwi (Goulburn Island) in the west to Milingimbi in the east. The Yolŋu population was able to maintain its strength and considerable autonomy. People in

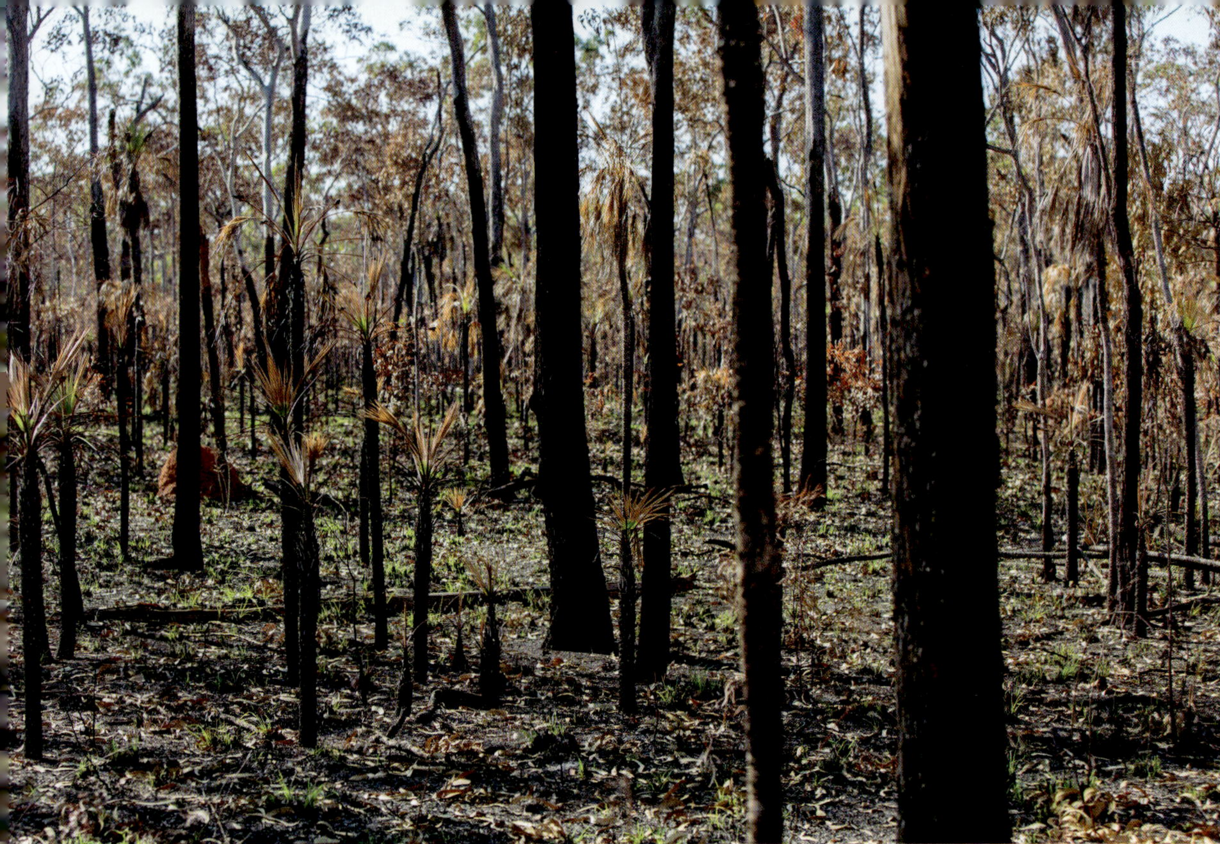
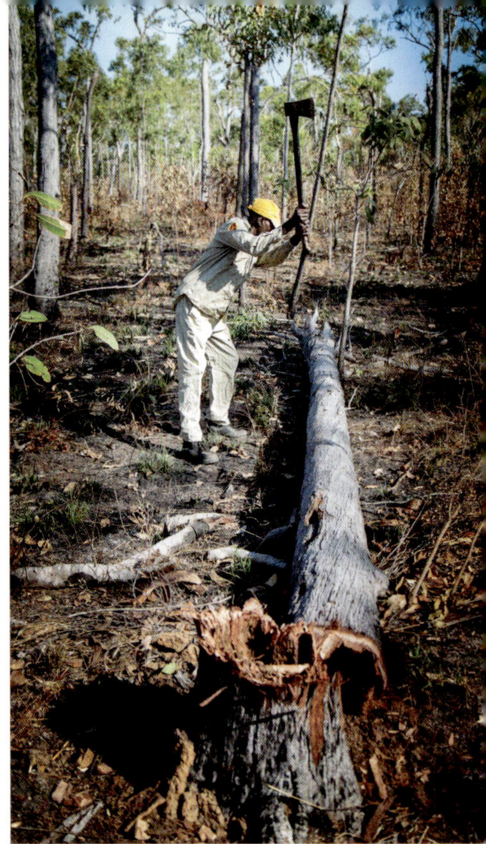

Arnhem Land had for many centuries traded with visitors from South Sulawesi and they continued the tradition with Europeans when possible. The Methodist Church used trade in artifacts both as a means of introducing their congregations in South Australia to Aboriginal culture and also as a source of income to encourage people to stay at the mission.

Hollow-log coffin ceremonies were performed across Arnhem Land and were among the more public rituals that involved the whole community, including the resident missionaries. These customs were sometimes the subject of documentary films.[4] Hollow logs used in mortuary rituals were not themselves objects of exchange, but much of the paraphernalia used in the ceremonies was traded. Bark paintings reproducing designs on hollow-log coffins were made for sale and a few were filled with kangaroo bones as examples for museum collections.

Yolŋu people engaged with the art and artifact market both for commerce and also as a means to persuade outsiders of the value of their culture and the richness of their way of life. Over time the sale of art became entangled with the struggle for recognition of their rights and the acknowledgement of difficult histories. Hollow-log coffins were rarely made for sale until the end of the twentieth century—their weight and scale made them difficult and costly to transport.

External recognition of art in Arnhem Land centred on bark paintings. In western Arnhem Land the first major collections of bark paintings were made in 1912 at Kunbarllanjnja (Oenpelli) by Baldwin Spencer. In eastern Arnhem Land bark paintings began to be marketed by the Methodist Overseas Mission in the years immediately prior to the Second World War. The style of paintings varied greatly across the region. In western Arnhem bark paintings were in dialogue with the rock art of the escarpment. The majority of paintings comprised beautifully detailed figurative representations of animals of the region, often showing their internal organs; others referenced the spirit beings that inhabited the bush; and some employed the geometric designs associated with the Mardayin regional initiation ceremony.[5] In eastern Arnhem Land the whole range of art produced in ceremonial and secular contexts became the subject of bark paintings.

A key moment for the recognition of Aboriginal art as fine art was its inclusion in the Art Gallery of New South Wales in 1959. Tony Tuckson, then deputy director of the Gallery, and Stuart Scougall, an orthopedic surgeon with a passionate interest in Aboriginal art, made major collections—Pukumani poles from the Tiwi Islands and bark paintings from Yirrkala. The works were exhibited in the forecourt of the gallery and, although the subject of initial controversy, they became the

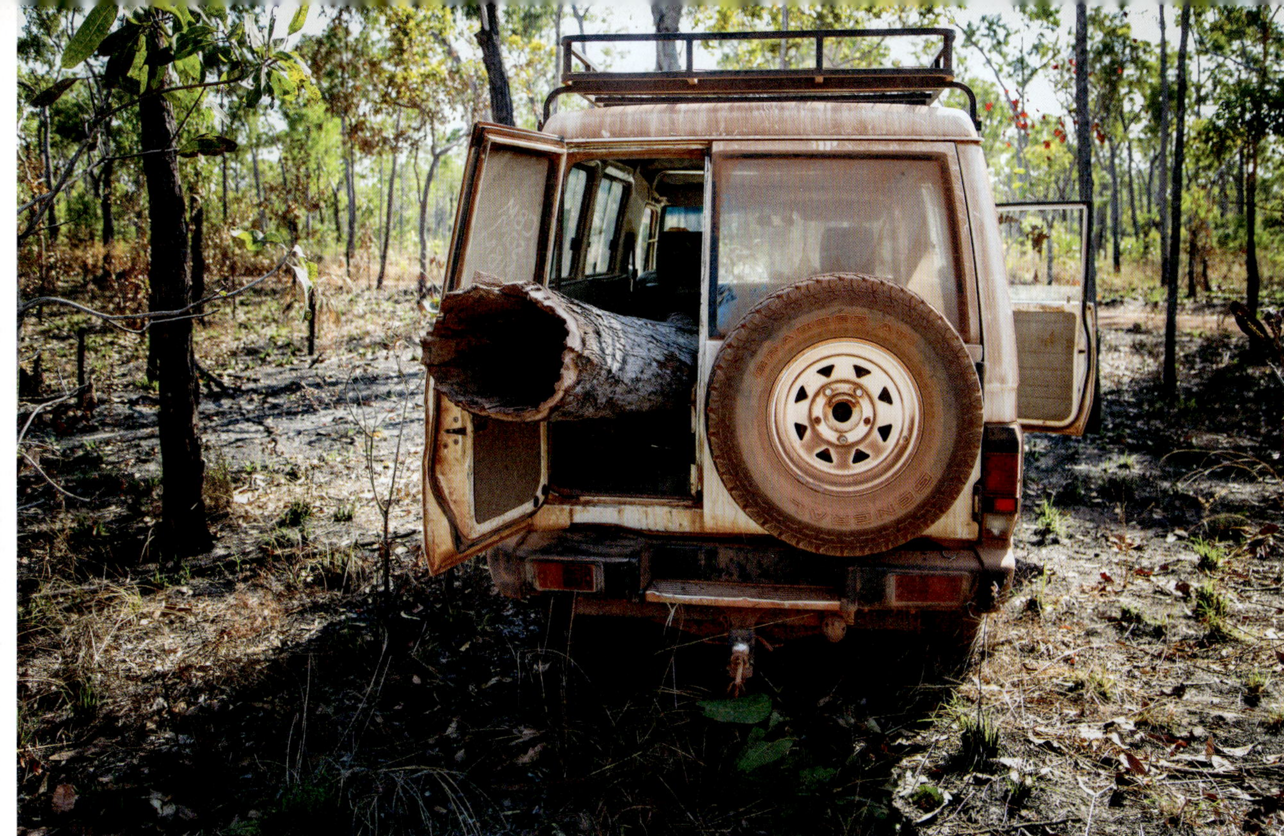

Figs. 2–4. Napuwarri Marawili harvesting *l̲arrakitj*. Courtesy of Creative Cowboy Films

building blocks for the expansion of collections of Aboriginal art in museums across Australia.[6]

The scale of bark paintings varied in size from miniature "canvases" to works of up to two meters in height. Subjects ranged from narrative illustrations of mythic episodes to geometric designs that covered the entire surface of the bark, based on the form of sacred clan designs. The final stage of the painting was the infilling of the designs with dotted patterns and hatching applied with a thin brush made of strands of human hair. Aesthetics combined with meaning to create a surface shimmer that expressed the power and nature of the ancestral beings. Variation in the design's form signaled different ancestral identities. The art continued to be produced in internal as well as external contexts and a dynamic relationship existed between the different contexts of the art as it moved into national and global collections and venues. By the 1980s Aboriginal art had gained widespread recognition within Australia and was beginning to be appreciated overseas.

Painted hollow logs continued to be a rare medium for art. However, in 1988 the situation was to change. Aboriginal artists from the community of Ramingining in central Arnhem Land, on the boundary between eastern and western styles of representation, worked with the curator Djon Mundine on an art project for the anniversary of the arrival of the First Fleet in Sydney—the effective beginning of the British colonization of Australia.[7] Rather than celebrating that event the artists developed the idea of making two hundred hollow-log coffins to demonstrate the survival of Indigenous artistic traditions and to commemorate the deaths and dispossession of Aboriginal people that had occurred in the intervening two hundred years. *The Aboriginal Memorial*, as it became known, was eventually acquired by the National Gallery of Australia and is permanently installed in its own space at the entrance to the building (see p. 37). *The Aboriginal Memorial* showed both the potential of *l̲arrakitj* as a medium of expression and the powerful impact of displaying them as sculptural forms in installations. The memorial was a contemporary curatorial idea that integrated well with an Indigenous past—creating ossuaries without bones.

THE TRAJECTORY OF *L̲ARRAKITJ* AS SCULPTURAL FORMS

L̲arrakitj reveal diversity both in their forms and in the paintings that cover their surfaces; there have always been variations on the basis of region, ceremony, and clan. Some poles were simply tall cylindrical forms of different width and height, but all, with their bark peeled off, providing a smooth surface for painting. Other poles had one or more carved ridges or incised channels to demarcate separate spaces on the surface. Some poles had circles cut through them and many were carved at the top with geometric projections, or in some cases figurative forms. The variations reflected the clan or moiety of the deceased and the ancestral origin of the particular *larrakitj*—the carved top might represent the tail of a whale, the jaw of a barracuda, or the serrated "nose" of a sawfish. Once prepared, the poles were painted with designs depending on factors such as region, the affiliation and status of the dead person and the location of the ceremony. The paintings could be predominantly figurative in form, relating to themes of the ceremony, or they could include geometric clan designs that signaled the final destination of the soul in its clan country.

Following the installation of *The Aboriginal Memorial* in the National Gallery of Australia hollow logs became a major medium for art making. The forms of the pole initially followed those used in the past for mortuary rituals, creating an ideal surface for painted designs. While Arnhem Land artists continue in dialogue with the past, recursively drawing on themes and compositional elements from their own transmitted art history, there has always been a dynamic element to their practice. The forms of the painted designs changed and moved across the different media of art from bark paintings, to hollow log coffins, to figurative carvings and prints. Variations of the same paintings occur in different media in different contexts. However innovations began to occur in the forms of the *larrakitj* themselves as the tradition continued to develop. Yolŋu artists have always been attuned to the properties of the surface form of the natural "canvas," fitting the designs to the shape of the human body, the contours of a sheet of bark, or the structure of a woven bag. Turning aside from straight logs with smooth surfaces, Yolŋu artists began to explore the potential of irregularities in nature's forms—splits in the trunk, projecting bosses—imperfections that offered potential for the expression of new aesthetic ideas.

Many of the paintings on *larrakitj* are based on the form of clan designs that mark the presence of ancestral forces in places and track the journey of *Waŋarr* beings across land, along watercourses and in the waters off shore. Djambawa Marawili's paintings of the fire carried by Bäru into the sea off Yathikpa show the movements of currents and tidal flows as they bend to the contours of the shore and respond to changing conditions (p. 118). Irregularities in the shape of the logs he selects work in harmony with the dynamism of the sea. Wukun Wan̲ambi's *larrakitj* are set in the Marrakulu country of Gurka'wuy (p. 135). He paints the inrushing tide that sprays up onto the rocky outcrops in the centre of the bay. He uses nodules in the body of the trunk to mark the islands and the places where the spirits of the ancestral mullet *buku-duŋgulmirri* are marked by an abundance of fish. The fish themselves are the basic elements in an almost abstract pattern that charts the flow of the waters in the bay.

Yolŋu artists conceive of sets of poles as sculptural installations that work as a whole. They are very conscious of the logs as the product of natural processes, which, standing together, provide a perspective on the forest—a glimpse of where they once grew. Wukun Wan̲ambi explicitly uses the natural irregularities of tree trunks to evoke the process of pole making as well as the life cycle of the forest itself. Splits in the tree trunks, natural holes in the side, places where branches broke off, edges charred by forest fires—all provide potential to bring the forest to life. They also give an insight into how the poles as hollow-log coffins were seen: a glimpse of the hidden world of the inside.

Painted designs on the poles often make reference to Yolŋu mortuary rituals. Galuma Maymuru's (1951–2018) paintings show colonies of sand crabs on the beach at low tide (p. 124). The crabs emerge from holes in the beach to scavenge for food, eating the remains of dead fish then retreating back beneath the sand. Her paintings refer to the process of death and decay and the renewal of life each day as the tide washes memories away and life begins again. The paintings on Naminapu Maymuru-White's (b. 1952) poles reference Milŋiyawuy, the Milky Way (p. 125). Milŋiyawuy, a river of stars across the night sky, is a manifestation of the spirits of the dead of the Yirritja moiety. The striped designs of the L̲iyagawumirr poles from Milingimbi are associated with the journeys of the Djan'kawu Sisters who traveled from east to west through the wetlands, giving birth to clans of the Dhuwa moiety (pp. 100–103). All such designs have a multiplicity of meanings keyed in by the songs that the Djan'kawu sang, and that are still sung today. They sang about the animals that they saw on their journeys and the events that took place. One of the meanings evoked by the striped design is the flash of the kingfish as it dived through the filtered light in a forest pool.

The poles from western Arnhem Land reflect a similar complex art history in which the contemporary works emerge from a dialogical and recursive relationship with the past. Artists from Maningrida and Kunbarllanjnja are closely related and take part together in regional ceremonies, but their painted poles reflect different contemporary trajectories in the art from the region. Sets of poles from Maningrida are predominantly "abstract" in form. The designs reference the geometric forms of body paintings and sacred objects from the Mardayin ceremony, transformed as layers on the landscape created by the ancestral beings, each painting is associated with a particular site of ancestral power. The paintings by John Mawurndjul (b. 1952), Ivan Namirrkki (b. 1961) and others have an intense focus on surface form, with beautifully executed cross-hatching creating a sense of luminescence (pp. 79–83).

Poles from Kunbarllanjnja show great diversity. Joey Nganjmirra's (b. 1980) poles reflect the Mardayin style (pp. 56–9), whereas others reference the complex figurative traditions of the region. Gabriel Maralngurra's (b. 1968) works combine styles from different eras of rock art, providing a perspective on the art history of the region that stretches back many thousands of years—a history of connection that is still very much part of the present (pp. 54–5). The super-positioning of images on the surface, overlapping but somehow distinct, captures the feel of rock art transferred to the contoured surface of the wood. In Joe Guymala's works, powerful skeletal forms confront the viewer with the reality of death and our shared destiny (pp. 52–3). These poles from Kunbarllanjnja transport the viewer into the passages and rocky overhangs and evoke the hollow-log coffins from the past that rest in crevices and on natural platforms inside the caves. The poles move the viewer from the rich vibrant animal life of the escarpment and adjacent wetlands to the interior of rock walls, from outside to inside the hollow-log coffins, creating a sense of a sacred space shared across Arnhem Land as a whole.

CONCLUSION

The journey of *ḻarrakitj* from Arnhem Land to homes and museums across Australia and beyond shows art's capacity to create a sacred place where people from various backgrounds and with different histories can share emotional understandings. The engagement is always in more than one direction and is inevitably experimental. It takes time. Hollow-log coffins were once primarily made as bone containers. But works of art never have a single purpose—they function in terms of what they are as much as what they do. They carry with them a particular sense of history, a perspective on the world, a body of technical knowledge and an aesthetic sensibility—past practices and bodies of knowledge that can have new meanings in the present. *Ḻarrakitj*, as an art form that develops in time and space, can allow the viewer to enter the forests of Arnhem Land, move from one language group to another, see styles change. The engaged viewer can reflect on the movement of tide on the beach, see the layerings of paintings on the walls of rock shelters and sense the richness of the environment in which the artists live. The hollow-log coffins can act as memorial poles, bringing history into the present, because they have a richness of meaning in the context of Aboriginal society that the artists are able to share with others. *Ḻarrakitj* bring with them the artists' own sense of history, but also engage in a process of persuasion—helping others to understand how the makers of *ḻarrakitj* see the world.

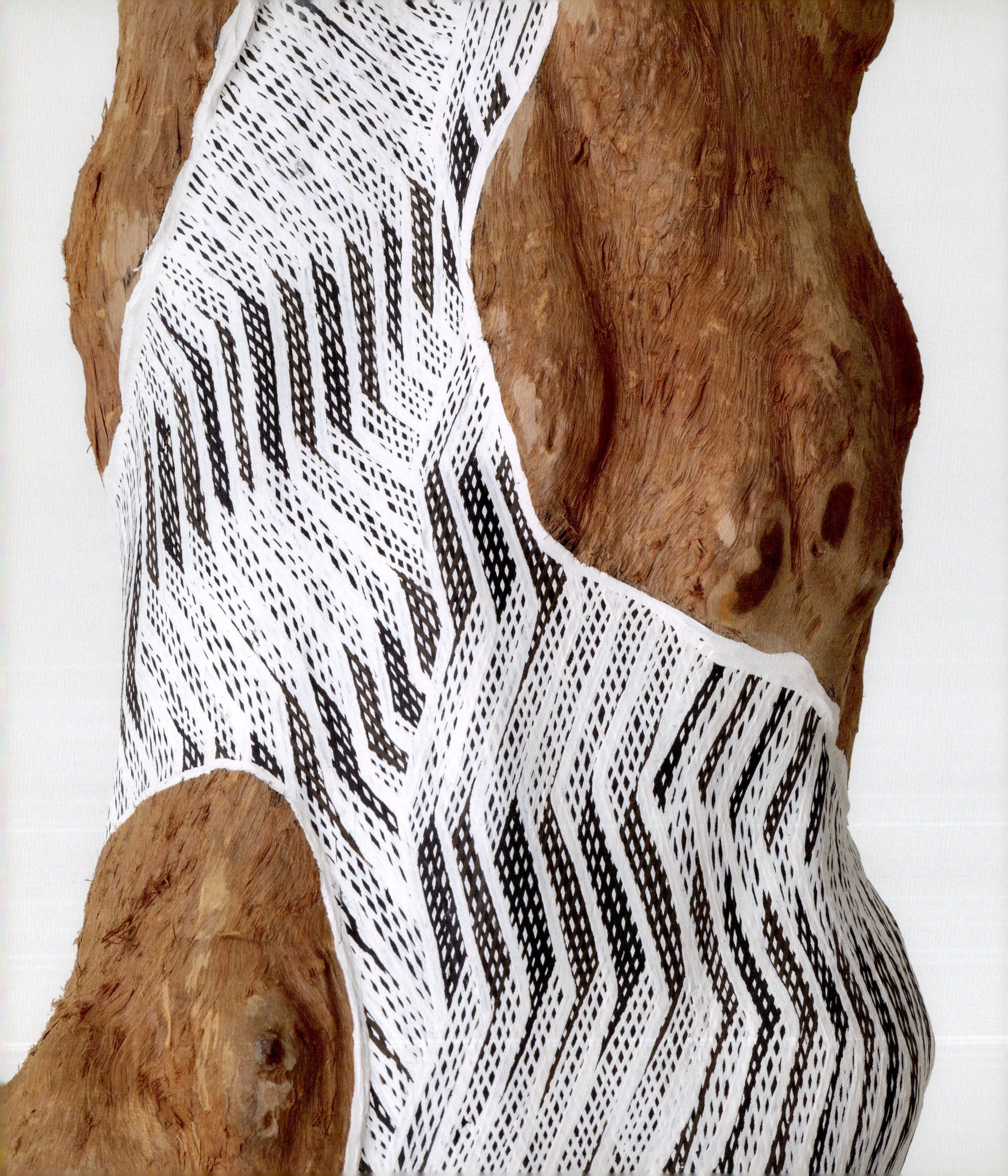

A Longer Contemporary

Diana Nawi

How might real and perceived dichotomies find their marriage and dialogue within a form of artmaking? How might we read the distinction between painting and sculpture, between abstraction and representation? Aboriginal Australian memorial poles suggest this unification, a seemingly effortless pivot between, or perhaps against, the central structures and languages that are used to classify, consume, and display works of art within the western canon. They allow us to reconsider the binaries that art history so often compels us to express, at once transcending and confounding them.

Memorial poles circulate in a global contemporary context—they are made by contemporary artists—but they resist the dominance of western categorizations of contemporary art and the modern museum. They are decorative objects that have no ostensible purpose; they are paintings that occupy space; they are sculptures that rely on a language of painting, be it derived from works on the body, board, bark, or canvas. They offer a particular challenge to the conventions that comfortably define a modernist break with history, an avant garde dependent on rupture with the past. Memorial poles are a traditional form and a contemporary one, self-consciously engaging with a long history and continuously innovating, both formally and conceptually. They do not suggest contemporary art as an outgrowth or a fracture, but rather imply the radical potential of the possibility of continuity.

Introducing his seminal text on northeast Arnhem Land art, Howard Morphy makes explicit the problematics of considering the work under an either/or paradigm of Aboriginal or European and western rubrics. While he acknowledges that Aboriginal art, considered under one categorization or the other, may have different meanings, and importantly, different receptions, he articulates the fact that these two realms are inextricably linked through proximity, lived experience, and history.[1] His analysis revolves around the hybrid nature of the works' origin, and it is also critical to understand how this hybridity operates in the reception of these works. Context is often the central means through which we understand contemporary art. When we analyze the objects of contemporary art we do so under particular paradigms of history and culture, but as these works enter the shared and often indeterminate space of global institutional and market reception, there is a presumption of some level of shared methodologies, stakes, and vocabularies.

In the case of Aboriginal artworks, their circulation in both Aboriginal and non-Aboriginal contexts forces the reconsideration of them under new criteria and histories. Aboriginal artworks emerge from specific places and cultural backgrounds (contexts that are themselves notably hybrid), but are largely created for outside audiences. As they move between these contexts, the way they are understood necessarily changes. In moving onto a global stage, the meaning of these works is not strictly bound to that of its original context, nor does it entirely lose this specificity (for instance, being characterized by purely western formal or aesthetic qualities). Instead, Aboriginal artworks force a unique set of questions that museums, collectors, historians, and markets must seek to address.

The contemporary memorial poles in this exhibition emerge from historical traditions of burial. This history animates them, and seemingly remains their defining feature in the realm of

Gunybi Ganambarr, *Garraparra and Gunyuru* (detail), 2016 (see p. 117)

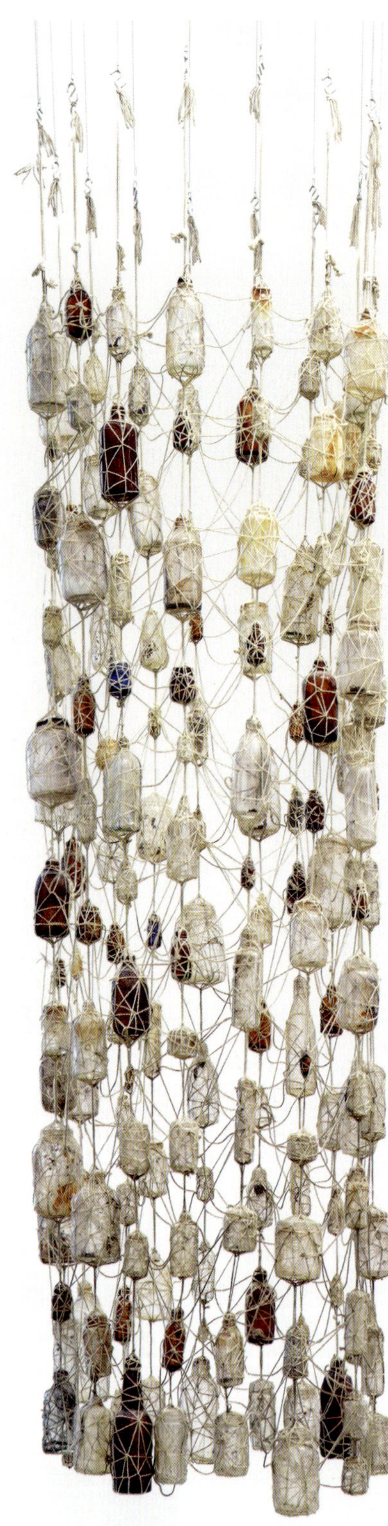

Fig. 1. Nari Ward (American, born 1963), *Vertical Hold*, 1996, yarn and found bottles, 107 x 30 in. (diameter) (271.8 x 76.2 cm). Installation view, Pérez Art Museum Miami, *Nari Ward: Sun Splashed*, November 19, 2015–February 28, 2016. Museum of Modern Art, New York; Gift of the Hudgins Family in memory of J. I. Nelson and Sarita Nelson-Nunnelee

mainstream contemporary art, even as the artists and objects themselves have moved beyond this paradigm. Two-dimensional Aboriginal painting practices have found a foothold in the art world, its exhibition spaces, and its market places, but the memorial poles present an intriguing conundrum for a system that wishes to absorb them into conventions of an art history broken down by medium, geography, and temporality, rather than function. In their fundamental structure—the hollowed-out tree—these works insistently reiterate their difference from tropes of western contemporary art; they assert their relationship to particular histories and the specificities of unique cultural practices, as well as to the prioritization of the act of remembering, practicing, and enlivening one's own culture.

The idea of remembrance is built into the form of memorial poles through their literal function as burial objects. Now divorced from this act, the poles remain tied to a notion of collective remembrance, of continuing to work within and evolve cultural vocabularies and traditions. Like much contemporary art, these objects have a communicative function—an outgrowth of their conceptual underpinnings that allows them to operate not only as phenomenological encounters, but as discursive pivots around which we might think and converse. Aboriginal memorial poles communicate on multiple levels, their form inherently suggests echoes of history and culture, but their singular qualities—the unique palette, marks, and imagery of each work, and the way in which these features articulate personal remembrances and expressions, operate, like much of contemporary art, as a form of visual language. Individually, each work has its own formal and expressive logics, some suggest narrative via figuration and others implicate mapping and topographic patterns, still others bear a relationship to time and the rhythms of abstracted mark-making. While the logs themselves are formed by natural processes, the works are invariably handmade. They are organic objects and by virtue of each artist's work they are tied to the human hand, implying selfhood and the assertion of presence within the larger and natural world—individual and collective memory embedded in a form that contains the implication of environmental cycles and geological time.[2]

The adaptive nature of this way of working—of self-expression within a trajectory of shared cultural forms—finds parallels in much of global artmaking today. This is evident in a vast range of works; for instance the self-conscious adaptation of the form of the Afro-Caribbean bottle tree as we see in projects by Wangenchi Mutu (b. 1972), Gary Simmons (b. 1964), and Nari Ward (b. 1963) (Fig. 1), among others; artists like Jeffrey Gibson (b. 1972) (Fig. 2) and Brian Jungen (b. 1970) (Fig. 3), who adapt and mash-up Indigenous forms with new materials, ideas, and objects; and any range of artists who are interested in the intersection of modernist, craft, and folkloric forms. Additionally this way of working offers a rejoinder to western modernism's compulsion for the new, creating a differently paced temporality implied by the long history of the form itself (reinforced by the organic nature of the tree and the inherent relationship to death and memory) that suggests long time rather than the punctuation of invention. Growing out of historical and traditional forms, these forms remain visually and conceptually intertwined with centuries-old cultural practices, while being resolutely authored and new. They offer a challenge to the possibility of reception within an anthropological and art-historical framework.

These structures privilege a notion of authenticity tied to ideas of cultural purity and a belief that historical distance confers critical gravitas on an object—a conundrum faced by countless non-western cultures when explored under the rubric of western knowledge systems. Memorial poles are made by living artists, influenced by the forces of global modernity but primarily drawing on vocabularies established within the confines of Aboriginal visual culture and from personal expressions; they reflect the moment and space in which they were created and absorb evolving meaning as they circulate in the larger world. We might consider this to be the true mark of contemporaneity—a kind of cultural and temporal hybridity, or, at the very least, cross-cultural acknowledgment that gives primacy to the challenging space of encounter, contradiction, and response.[3]

Morphy writes specifically about the Yolŋu, who live in northern Australia, [they] "live in a world that includes both

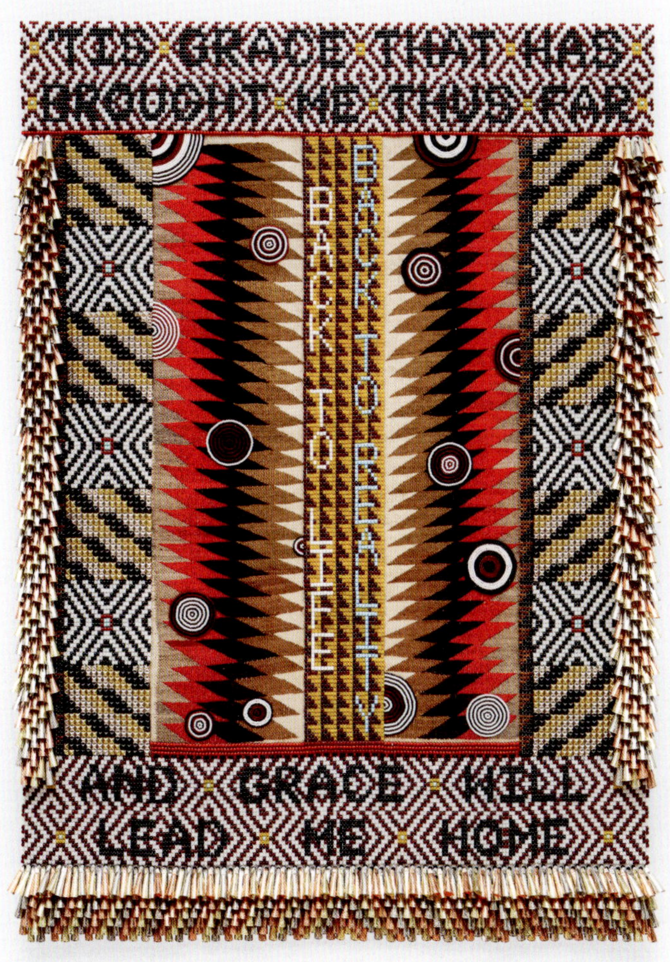

Fig. 2. Jeffrey Gibson (American/Choctaw-Cherokee, born 1972), *Amazing Grace*, 2017. Glass beads, artificial sinew, trading-post weaving, steel studs, copper and tin jingles, acrylic felt, canvas, and wood. 76 x 54 in. (193 x 137.2 cm)

European and Aboriginal institutions, systems of knowledge, and languages; they are influenced by both . . . The process is a two-way one . . ."[4] His description of this sort of bilateral cross-cultural influence can also be conceived of more broadly, as applying to the hybrid and mutual world most of us exist and produce culture within. Contemporaneity can then perhaps be understood as a rejection of binary modes of thinking that rely on systems of classification; the work is of the now and connected to the past, it is entirely specific to its context and exists within fluid and global channels of reception—a way of

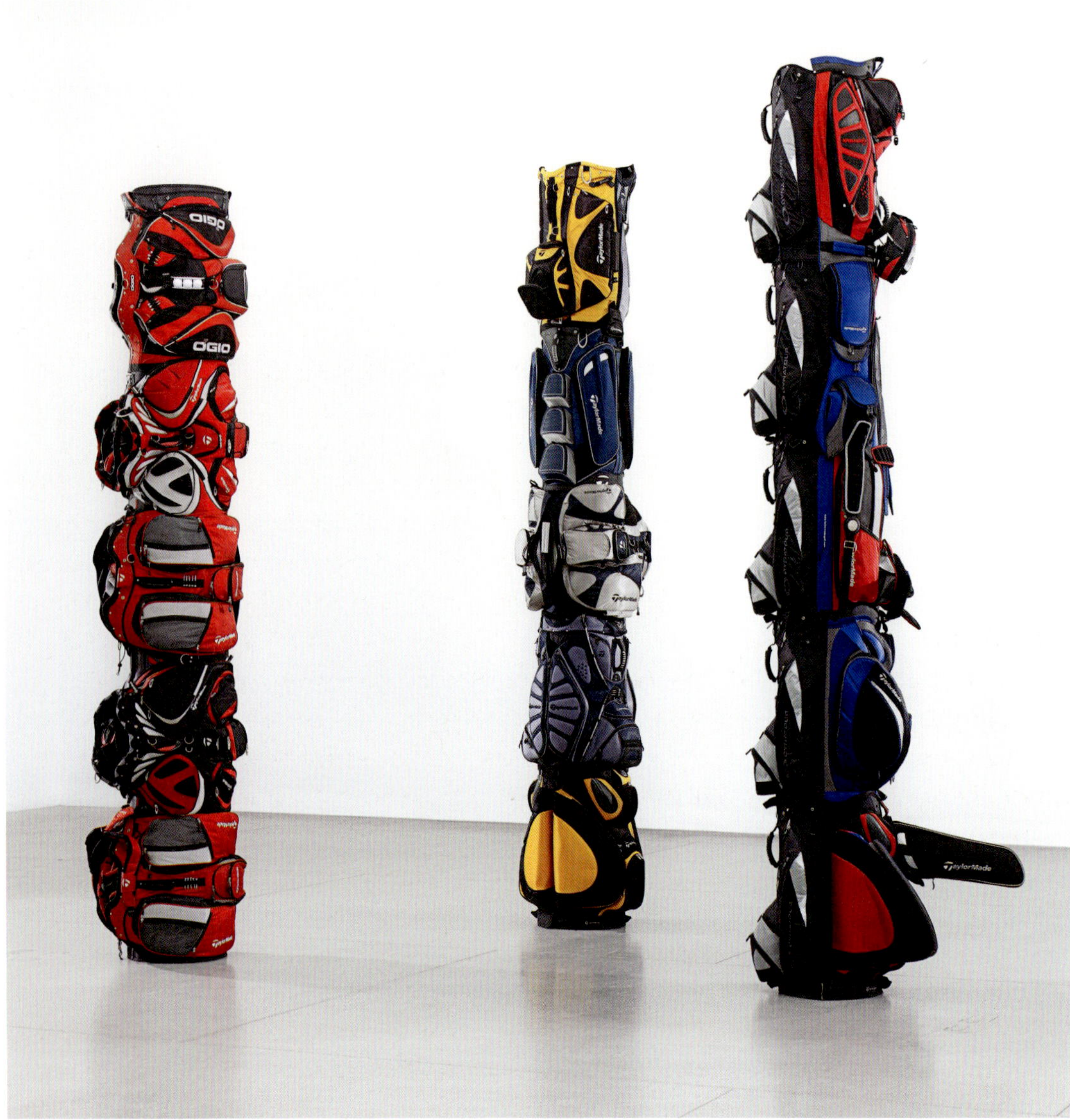

Fig. 3. Brian Jungen (Canadian/Dane-Zaa, born 1970). Left to right: *1980*, 2007. Polyester, metal, painted wood on paper sonotube, 139 x 38 x 27 1/16 in. (353 x 96.5 x 68.8 cm). Art Gallery of Ontario. Purchased with the assistance of The David Yuile and Mary Elizabeth Hodgson Fund, 2007. *1970*, 2007. Polyester, metal, painted wood on paper sonotube, 151 1/16 x 29 x 30 in. (383.7 x 73.6 x 76.2 cm). Art Gallery of Ontario. Promised Gift of Rosamond Ivey. *1960*, 2007. Polyester, metal, painted wood on paper sonotube, 156 x 48 1/16 x 36 in. (396.2 x 122 x 91.4 cm). Art Gallery of Ontario. Promised Gift of Michael and Sonja Koerner

being that reflects the status of cultural practice throughout the world. Cultural production is not rendered less authentic by necessary, responsive, and ongoing shifts in form, meaning, circulation, and market; in fact, relevant and vibrant cultural production is marked by adaptation within ever-shifting contexts.

The collection of Debra and Dennis Scholl, from which this exhibition is drawn, with its varied areas of depth—photography, conceptual art, drawing, Aboriginal painting, and now memorial poles—is a living example of how we might picture and think through these questions of changing contexts. These varied trajectories literally sit side-by-side within their collection, distinct but in conversation. They suggest the critical ways through which we might understand the autonomy and specificity of objects, and the trajectories from which they emerge, as well as the shared and adaptive qualities we might begin to understand when we see them together. The works produced in Kunbarllanjnja at the Injalak Arts center are notable for their deft interplay of figuration and abstraction, and for their innovative handling of the form of the logs themselves; the work emerging from this center is acutely aware of the formal possibilities of the memorial poles and the ways in which they might be extended and complicated. Joe Guymala's works, in particular, seem to provide a self-conscious riff on the traditional history of the poles as burial vessels. When the poles were used in this way, they were decorated in specific modes; however, their re-popularization as non-functional art objects has opened up myriad modes of visual expression used to adorn the surfaces of the hollowed-out logs. Guymala's *lorrkkon* are covered in images of skeletons that interlock and are disassembled to form a kind of playfully morose surface of skulls, ribcages, femurs, and other bones (p. 52).

Likewise, the work of Nawurapu Wunuŋmurra (1952–2018), from Yirrkala in northeastern Arnhem Land, and in particular *Muŋurru*, 2016 (p. 141), offers detailed patterned decoration in brown and white, broken by a band of black filled in with white bones arranged like puzzle pieces—as if we were seeing a cross section into the log itself. These invocations of the deceased and the human body decomposing conjure the history of this form and imply that these artists maintain a connection to such a tradition, while updating it and reframing its visual expression. Gabriel Maralngurra also suggests tradition within his painting, creating almost narrative representations of animals and human figures. While the repetitive line work (known as *rarrk*) that characterizes much Aboriginal painting from Arnhem Land is evidenced, Maralngurra has used it to animate dynamic figures and activity. His elongated and expressive figures seem almost to move across the surface of the trees (pp. 54–5).

Memorial poles occupy a space between sculpture and painting in an intriguing way—a mode that allows us to think about adaptation and confounding as not only conceptual structures, but as giving rise to formal devices. The poles themselves are "found" objects; the forms they present to the artists who work on them are predetermined, and the artist's hand is evidenced in the painting he or she does on the surface—combining the two and three-dimensionality of the mediums into singular artworks. In this way the works reside between mediums, the logics of painting at play against the forms of sculpture and architecture. A number of artists make use of this in their works, allowing the uneven three-dimensionality of the logs to determine or at least intercede within their painterly strategies. *Burrar Lorrkkon*, 2016, by Joey Nganjmirra serves as a prime example (p. 56). Nganjmirra animates the surface of the log using an entirely abstracted vocabulary: a repetitive and finely rendered band of striped and criss-crossing browns, ochres, and reds that wraps the pole. His highly patterned earth-tone painting is broken up by black patches that follow the naturally occurring knots and protrusions of the tree (see p. 59). At a distance they appear like dots of varying scale, but up close, they are revealed as decorative accouterments to the tree's organic, uneven surface. Nganjmirra responds to the innate qualities of the wood in different ways in his different poles, but in each case he demonstrates a playful and innovative approach to the structured abstraction he establishes for himself, treating the imperfections of the log's surface as cues for painterly gestures.

While there are shared visual proclivities evidenced across the wide-ranging collection of works in *The Inside World*, namely an impulse towards all-over patterning and a *horror vacui* approach to treating the surface of the poles, there are distinctive vocabularies that emerge within regions and in the hands of individual artists. Like their two-dimensional counterparts on bark, canvas or board, the memorial pole imagery and patterning evokes mapping, storytelling, systems, and the cosmos, while expressing the openness and originality of formalism captured in the best of contemporary abstract painting.

If the question is fundamentally whether memorial poles are contemporary art, the answer is of course yes. As autonomous art objects they resound with dynamic visuality and tactility; as subjects of inquiry and ideas, they suggest new possibilities for how we might undo the limiting binaries and categorizations of art history and the exhibitions, markets, and discourse that emerge from these rubrics. It is the more nuanced questions that follow that are perhaps more critical: How does one exhibit them? What are the contexts for them? What is the language around them? What are their logics? Who are their peers? How do they communicate? What do they communicate? These questions offer a path toward a re-examination and intellectual retrofitting, and even possibly an expansion, of the categorizations and boundaries of our field. It is these questions to which we must attend and, to which this collecting endeavor, this exhibition and this catalogue offer a salient and meaningful step forward.

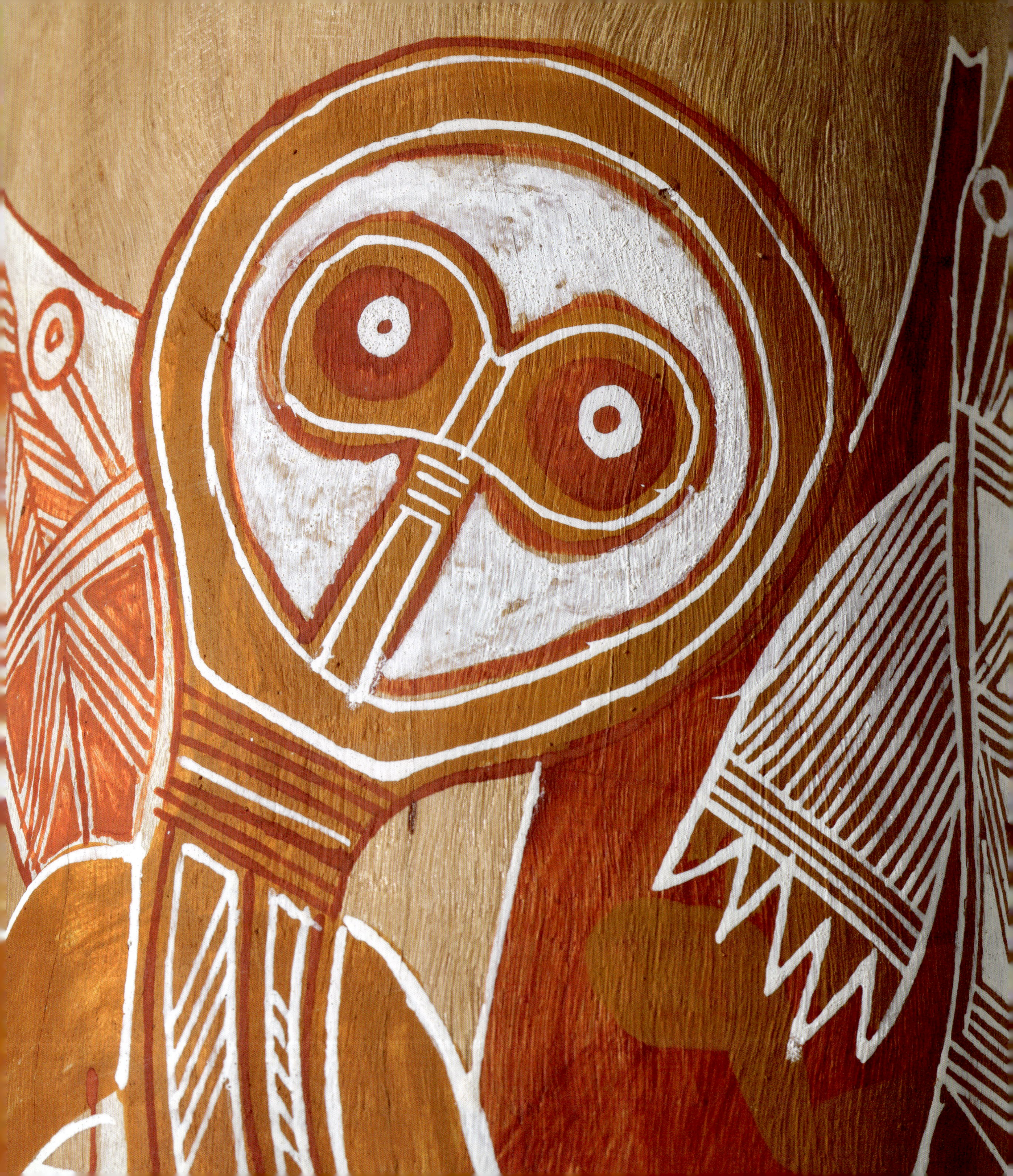

Sharing Culture to Maintain a Future

Kimberley Moulton

My history is alive today. My history keeps on building up. My identity is stronger. It is not dying. The more I share, the stronger I get. The more power I get. That's why, when we put a l̲arrakitj *as a piece in a museum, it has got the power.*[1]

Wukun Wan̲ambi

L̲arrakitj, d̲upun and *lorrkkon* are vessels that hold time and place. They are objects of remembering and of the present. Portals that transcend time, once used to hold people and safely guide them into the next life, today they share stories and histories of the First Peoples of Arnhem Land. They are not fixed within a temporality: tangibly and intangibly they sit in the *everywhen*[2]—a cyclical First Peoples' philosophy that encompasses both Ancestral creation and living cultural connections, long ago, now and for generations to come, all at the same time. This is also true of the art practice of the First Peoples of Australia, rooted in their connections to country from time immemorial and continuing to thrive, from the most northern to the southern part of the continent.

Painting and etching country, Ancestors and knowledge, what we now call "art," has been a central part of culture that physically asserts the Sovereignty of First Peoples—*always was, always will be Aboriginal land.* This mantra extends to our cultural objects in museums like the Smithsonian or the British Museum and to our contemporary works within galleries—*always was, always will be Aboriginal belongings.*

What does Sovereignty mean today within Australia and more broadly across the globe for Indigenous Peoples? We continue to fight for our lands and waterways, the right to hunt and fish, and protect our cultural heritage from pipelines and mining companies as our Ancestors have done from our times of UnSettlement. We continue to face land grabs, high rates of imprisonment, and dramatic health disparities with our non-Indigenous neighbors. Continuing to have limited opportunity for representation in government across the globe, our voices are carried through our artwork and are just as relevant as any western doctrine or constitution. Professor Tony Birch writes:

> In a society stuck within a colonial mindset constructed on the denial of its own true existence, let alone the autonomy and authority of Indigenous nations across Australia, Sovereignty is a word and concept beyond understanding. Conversely, within Aboriginal and Torres Strait Islander communities, Sovereignty is a reflection of a reality that people, custom and Country are inextricably linked, regardless of the impositions of colonisation.[3]

The art of the Yolŋu people since the British invasion has been a critical aspect of the trajectory of political action. The use of cultural knowledge across the country has raised the profile of the struggle for land and sea rights, for the human rights of the Yolŋu people. This has had a ripple effect across the country, art as a tool of resistance, art as evidence and art to ensure cultural continuity have all been significantly influenced by the Yolŋu and their practices from bark painting to the *l̲arrakitj* and *d̲upun*. The works are not just aesthetic. Curator, artist, and activist Djon Mundine, OAM, states, "Aboriginal bark paintings

Gabriel Maralngurra, *Lorrkkon* (detail), 2016 (see p. 55)

are more than just ochres on bark: they represent a social history; an encyclopedia of the environment; a place; a site; a season; a being; a song; a dance; a ritual; an ancestral story and a personal history."[4]

The *larrakitj* pole had its beginnings as part of the Yolŋu mortuary practice going back to *Waŋarr*, the time before the first morning.[5] It was a way in which people who passed might go back into the earth through the hollow log of the *larrakitj* that guided their spirit to its resting place through the ceremonies of the living. These practices of guidance through death, the cycle that begins and ends with the land, are central to the making and customary use of the *larrakitj*. They once stood as part of the ritual and ceremony of death, they were posts of cultural strength and an assertion of Sovereignty. Now they have been transformed into contemporary works that embody past traditions but also signal a new way of Yolŋu culture.

The English language I have cannot describe the crucial role these items play in both Yolŋu life and also that of the country we now know as Australia. What you must know is that they are important and are not merely painted logs, the *larrakitj* carry the energies of the land that once gave the log life, the energy and intent of the artist that painted them and they stand as conduits between the stars and the earth. It is a privilege to be in their presence and to share in the stories of the contemporary works that have expanded the *larrakitj* to where they sit in museums and galleries across the world today.

There are many meeting points for the viewer in connecting to these works, understanding the stories, the artists and their country and clan, losing themselves in the colours and textures and feeling the cultural power. As Chinese-Australian artist Lindy Lee notes, "the depth and breadth of Indigenous art—the personal, expansive relationship it has to 'country'—can only be experienced. It is in no way an intellectual thing, it is visceral and cellular."[6]

First Peoples' art, practice and methodology stretches above and beyond the western canon. It can be the literal, the conceptual and the imaginary that form within a work. It is often but not always restricted to the land and belonging that are essential meeting points in the work of many Sovereign peoples.

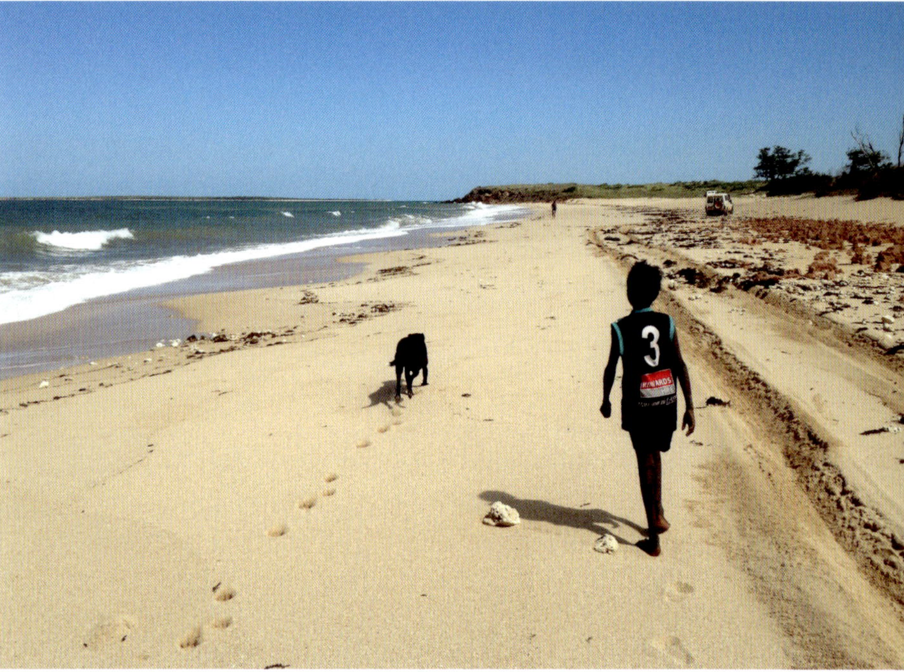

Fig. 1. Near Baratjula, Northern Territory, Australia. Photograph by Henry Skerritt

There is an inherent connection to country, and alongside this are family and community. The *larrakitj* tell the story of Yolŋu country—the fresh waters and salt waters and the animals, the Ancestral beings that created it and continue to live there.

The art that is created by First Peoples across Australia upholds the responsibility to future generations. Our art forms, patterns, and designs are passed down from elder to child, learned through connecting to Ancestral belongings (otherwise known as artifacts) in museums and archives, and channeled through our genetic memories. This may manifest itself through the cycling of iconographies that are markers of identity for a particular clan or individual, but it may also be expressed in a need to tell our stories and assert our Sovereignty through the tools we have today. First Peoples' art can be anything from *larrakitj* to film or photography, one practice or style does not have "authenticity" over the other. Gundijtmara and Wemba Wemba artist and curator Paola Balla states, "Sovereignty itself is an inalienable, innate and intimate right; its expression can be found buried within artistic works, gently emerging from inherited practices, or boldly spelled out in new artistic forms adorned with confident lines, camouflage, electric lights and bling."[7]

The power of art and creative activisms by First Peoples questions the Australian reluctance and the colonial blindfold that continue to prevail in acknowledging and facing the past. Using art for political action within western hegemonic spaces like government and other institutions means it not only physically intervenes within space but is an act of resistance and Sovereign being. First Peoples' art within these spaces also creates a presence within a discourse that decides, often without us, upon issues concerning our lands and futures. It is an act of ongoing cultural authority, which can in turn lead to healing.

The presence of diverse political First Peoples' art encourages consideration about where one is standing (consider now the First Peoples of where you are at this moment) and to think about the truth of history and the scars that are yet to heal. The Yolŋu people have strategically resisted the massacre of their peoples, the mining of their land and the displacement of their culture since Australian invasion. Their actions, in which art has been a consistent anchor, have not only proclaimed that they are Sovereign peoples of their homelands with cultural ways of being and doing, but they have also held Australian government and missionaries accountable for their destructive policies and legislations that affect First Peoples across the country.

MATERIALITY OF SOVEREIGNTY

Between 1962 and 1963 two significant art works were made by Yolŋu clan leaders representing the Dhuwa and Yirritja moieties. The two panels show the connections of the contemporary Yolŋu to the Ancestral beings and were painted with the intention that they would hang in the Methodist mission church. They are panels of incredible depth and knowledge, and technical genius that would compete with any master painting in cathedrals around the world. Their execution was a bold act of defiance and a statement that Yolŋu Sovereignty, law, and the Ancestral beings that made them continue to be the higher order, not the church. According to Mundine,

> The Church Panels were produced to assert the authority of the Yolŋu power structures and to show that there was no inherent incompatibility between Christian and Yolŋu belief. They were also made to reveal the designs which underpin the Yolŋu claim to land and sea. This was done while mining companies were already negotiating with the Government and the Church to disposses the Yolŋu of their country.[8]

In a brutal irony, as these panels were being made the government at the time was developing the mining of bauxite out of Yolŋu country near Yirrkala mission without any consultation.

These Dhuwa and Yirritja panels remained in the church through to the 1970s before being removed by a new minister who considered them to be an abomination. Will Stubbs, manager of the Buku-Larrŋgay Mulka art center, describes the force behind the works:

> The patterns themselves are powerful. Within Yolŋu law, to be in the presence of these designs is to be subject to, if you like, radioactive power.... The subterranean power emanating from Yolŋu law within and through Yolŋu art is one of the reasons why Yolŋu artists are happy for their work to go "out there." This is because whoever is in the presence of this power is being altered at a molecular level.[9]

The Yirrkala Church Panels were part of the beginning of the Yolŋu people's understanding of the power of art as a form of political protest and how, by utilising their customary designs and knowledge, some of which had never been shared outside of the sacred space of their community before, they could challenge the oppressive systems.

ART AS EVIDENCE

Shortly after the Dhuwa and Yirritja Church Panels were made in 1963 the Yolŋu people were fighting off miners and the unsolicited destruction of their homelands. In response and protest two Bark Petitions were created and sent to the Australian parliament (Figs. 2, 3). The barks represented the two moieties and were written in both Yolŋu and English, with cultural designs painted round their borders. The Bark Petitions stated that there was no consent for mining of their sacred land, the land on which they had been born and had hunted and gathered their food since time immemorial. The Yolŋu also

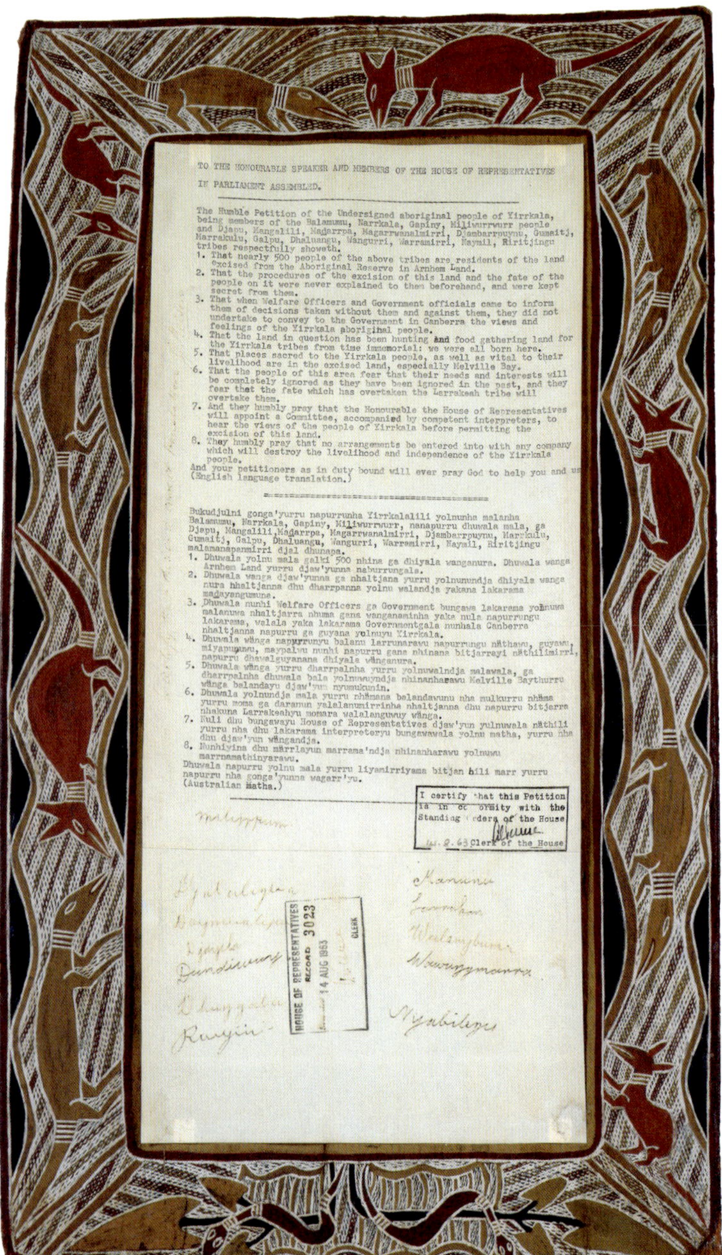

TO THE HONOURABLE SPEAKER AND MEMBERS OF THE HOUSE OF REPRESENTATIVES IN PARLIAMENT ASSEMBLED.

The Humble Petition of the Undersigned aboriginal people of Yirrkala, being members of the Balamumu, Narrkala, Gapiny, Miliwurrwurr people and Djapu, Mangalili, Madarrpa, Magarrwanalmirri, Djambarrpuynu, Gumaitj, Marrakulu, Galpu, Dhaluangu, Wangurri, Warramirri, Naymil, Riritjingu tribes respectfully showeth.

1. That nearly 500 people of the above tribes are residents of the land excised from the Aboriginal Reserve in Arnhem Land.
2. That the procedures of the excision of this land and the fate of the people on it were never explained to them beforehand, and were kept secret from them.
3. That when Welfare Officers and Government officials came to inform them of decisions taken without them and against them, they did not undertake to convey to the Government in Canberra the views and feelings of the Yirrkala aboriginal people.
4. That the land in question has been hunting and food gathering land for the Yirrkala tribes from time immemorial: we were all born here.
5. That places sacred to the Yirrkala people, as well as vital to their livelihood are in the excised land, especially Melville Bay.
6. That the people of this area fear that their needs and interests will be completely ignored as they have been ignored in the past, and they fear that the fate which has overtaken the Larrakeah tribe will overtake them.
7. And they humbly pray that the Honourable the House of Representatives will appoint a Committee, accompanied by competent interpreters, to hear the views of the people of Yirrkala before permitting the excision of this land.
8. They humbly pray that no arrangements be entered into with any company which will destroy the livelihood and independence of the Yirrkala people.

And your petitioners as in duty bound will ever pray God to help you and us.
(English language translation.)

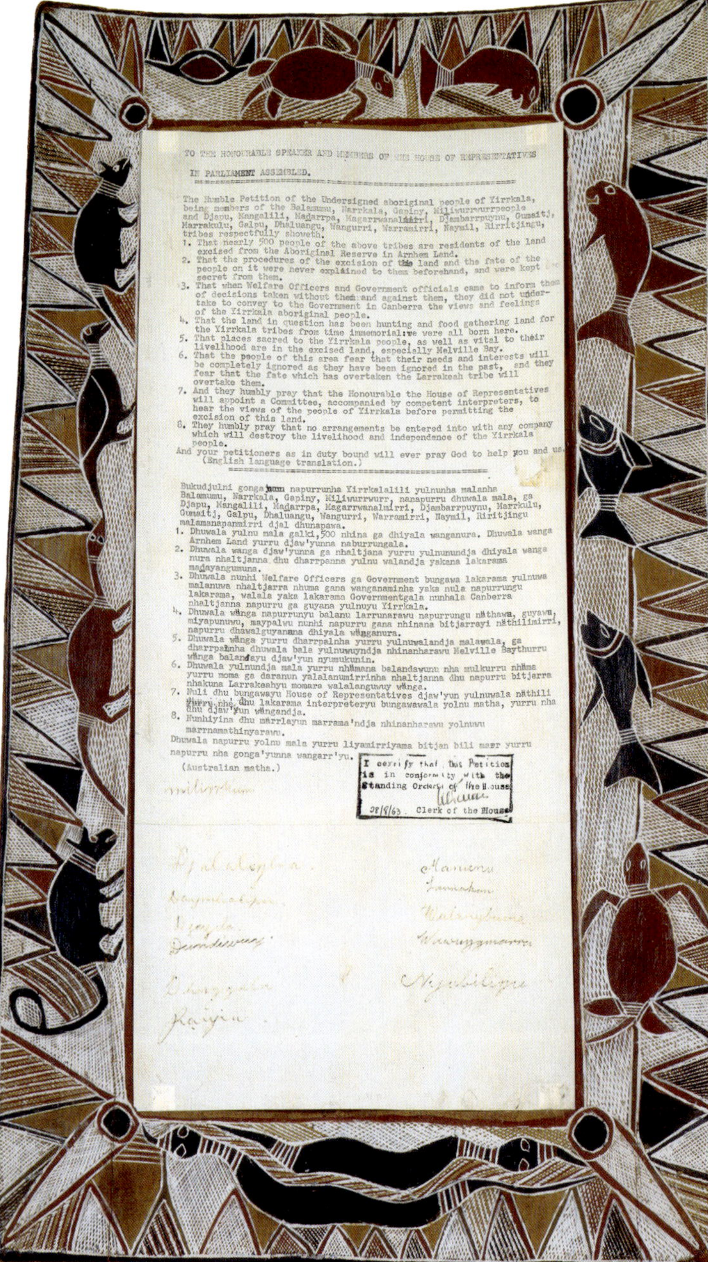

Figs. 2, 3. Various artists, *The Yirrkala Bark Petitions*, 1963. Earth pigments on bark and type-written paper, 23¼ x 13⅜ in. (59.1 x 34 cm). Presented to the Australian House of Representatives on 14 August 1963 and 28 August 1963. Parliament House, Canberra

requested a committee be appointed to hear the views of the people of Yirrkala with interpreters before allowing any mining to take place. The Petitions are groundbreaking works; they are the first traditional documents to have been recognised by the Commonwealth Parliament leading to the recognition of First Peoples in Australian law. The Petitions were, however, unsuccessful and the excision of the land from the Yolŋu continued. Although unsuccessful at the time these works had immense influence on the 1967 referendum that amended the constitution to include First Peoples, the acknowledgment of Aboriginal land rights in 1976 and to the Mabo land rights case of 1992 when the fallacy of *terra nullius* was overturned by the High Court of Australia.

THE PHYSICAL SOVEREIGN—WE ARE STILL HERE

Artistic intervention within the landscape maintains a significant role in the physicality of Sovereignty—making the invisible visible. There is a vast absence of any memorials or markers of

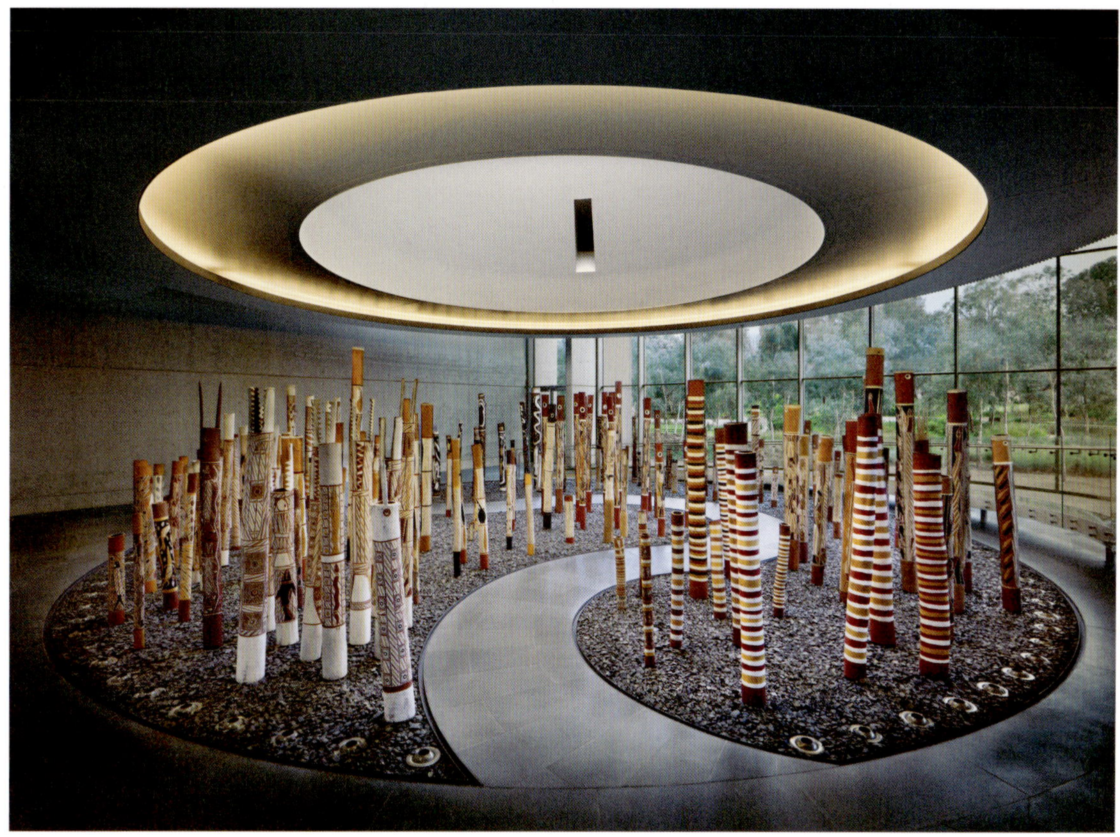

Fig. 4. Ramingining artists, *The Aboriginal Memorial*, 1987–88. Earth pigments on wood. National Gallery of Australia, Canberra. Purchased with the assistance of funds from the National Gallery admission charges and commissioned in 1987

significant Aboriginal sites in Australia. There is very little to acknowledge the frontier wars and the massacres on the "lucky country." However, one of the most important works of art made in Australia is *The Aboriginal Memorial* created in 1987–88 (Fig. 4). This installation of *larrakitj* shifted the way in which poles were situated within contemporary art—the first large-scale memorial of its kind.

Djon Mundine developed the monumental project of two hundred memorial poles as a response to the 1988 Bicentennial celebrations happening around the country and particularly in Sydney. The project emerged from Ramingining in the west of Yolŋu country and poles were painted by forty-three artists from central Arnhem Land. Although *larratikj* had started to be made and sold commercially in the early 1980s Mundine's project expanded on what the poles could be—conceptually and spatially—and how they could be used to assert Sovereignty and cultural power, just as the Church Panels and Bark Petitions had.

This memorial work was not only to challenge the notion that everyone in Australia was celebrating the anniversary of invasion but it also commemorated those First Peoples who had fallen on the frontier, a lament for loss, but also a statement of survival. The work was acquired by the National Gallery of Australia and now stands as the first work you see upon entry. The two hundred poles are positioned to reflect their geographical relationships, representing land, the people, and the art that gives life.

The art of the Yolŋu peoples and the *larrakitj* have played an integral role in First Peoples' rights and acknowledgment of Sovereignty both within government systems and in contemporary art spaces. The generous sharing of culture, knowledge, and deep time through these extraordinary works raises a consciousness of connection and understanding that First Peoples' lands and heritage are sacred. As a guest, wherever you are in this world, you must walk gently. The *larrakitj* from today, tomorrow, and yesterday express power and presence. We can learn from these pillars of strength from the inside world of the Yolŋu: they remind us to respect, and always to remember.

Our designs show that someone is entitled to a land, whether it is from the river, the bay or the sea. The pattern is in my soul and in my mind. I know the country and I know those patterns.

— Djambawa Marawili, AM

Comprising 37,000 square miles, Arnhem Land is the name given to the eastern half of the large peninsula that makes up the northernmost part of Australia's Northern Territory. The topography varies from the rocky escarpments in the stone country of western Arnhem Land, to the wetlands of the Arafura swamp in central Arnhem Land, to the glistening white sand beaches and sheltered bays of the Gove Peninsula. Arnhem Land is home to over 12,000 Indigenous Australians from around fifteen different language groups, including the Kunwinjku, Kuninjku, Dalabon, Rembarrŋa and Yolŋu. It is bordered by the Arafura Sea to the north, the East Alligator River and Kakadu National Park to the west, the Roper River to the south, and the Gulf of Carpentaria in the east. The climate is tropical monsoon, with a wet and dry season. Archaeological evidence shows that Indigenous Australians have been present in Arnhem Land for over 50,000 years.

The region was named for the Dutch ship *Arnhem*, captained by the explorer Willem van Colster, which visited the area in 1623. Fron the mid-eighteenth century on, Arnhem Land was regularly visited by sailors from Makassar (now Indonesia), who harvested trepang (sea-cucumbers) and traded with the Indigenous communities. From 1916 to the 1970s, missions and settlements were established through the region, and in 1931 it was declared an Aboriginal reserve. With the rise of the land rights movement in the 1970s, many of the Indigenous people of Arnhem Land returned to live on small outstations located on their traditional lands. Arnhem Land is home to some of the oldest rock-art sites on the planet, testament to thousands of years of continuous cultural tradition.

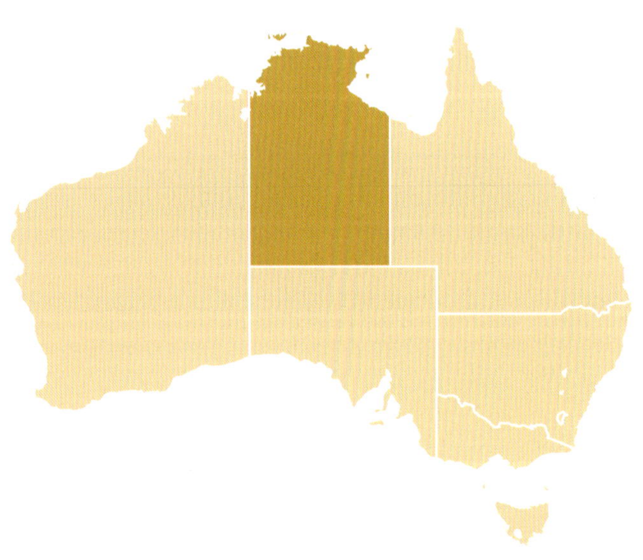

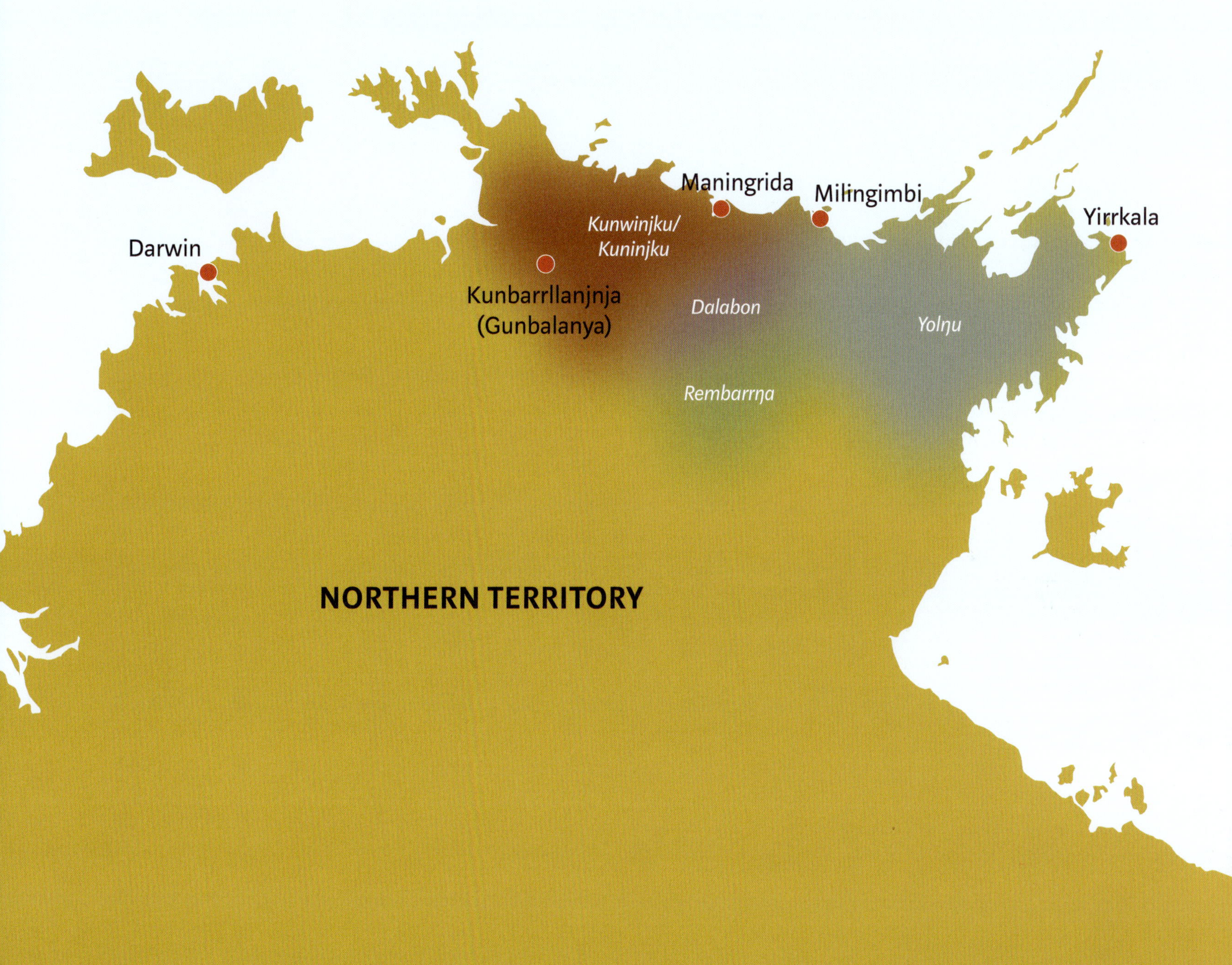
ARAFURA SEA
Darwin
Maningrida
Milingimbi
Yirrkala
Kunwinjku/
Kuninjku
Kunbarrllanjnja
(Gunbalanya)
Dalabon
Yolŋu
Rembarrŋa
NORTHERN TERRITORY

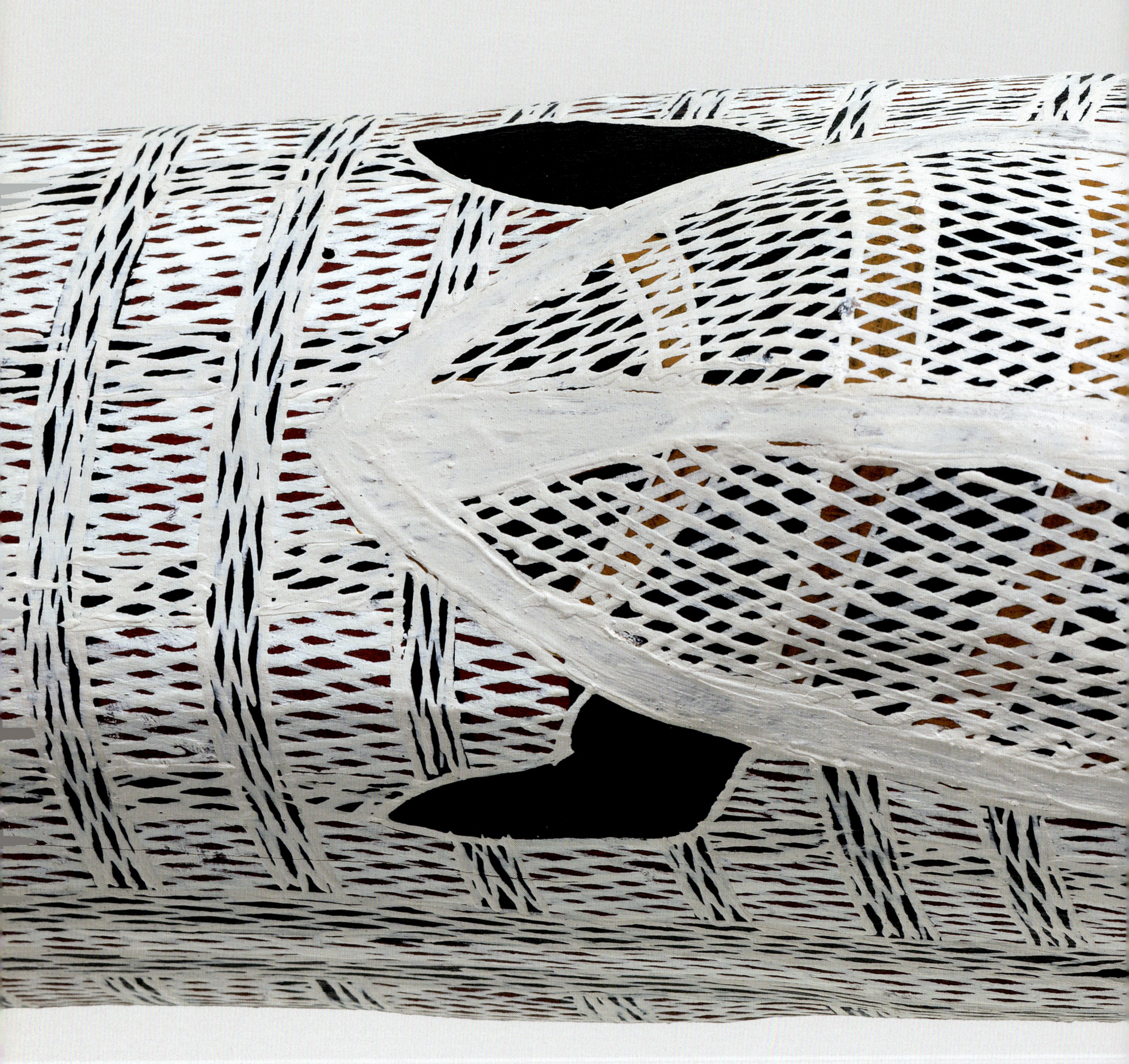

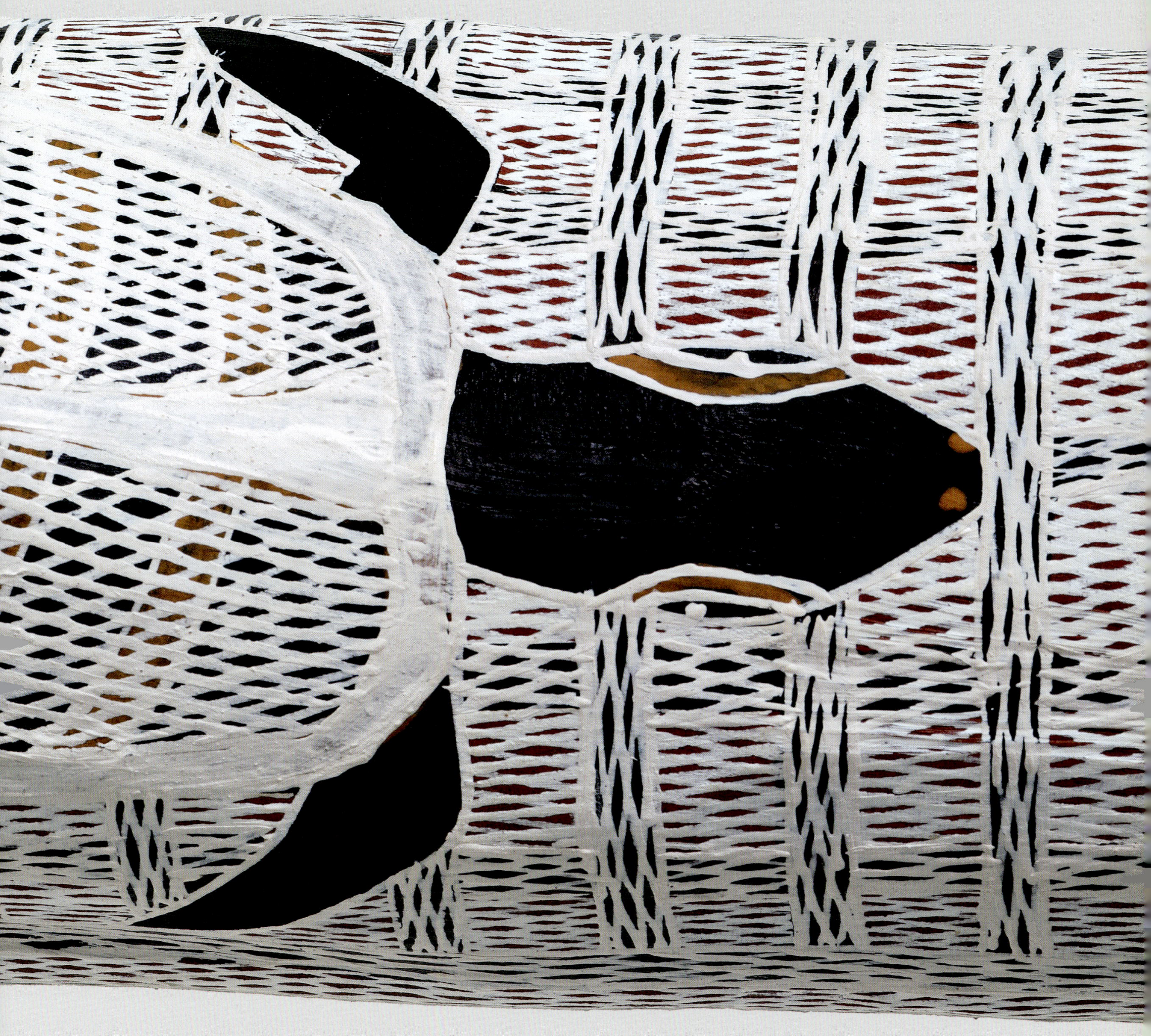

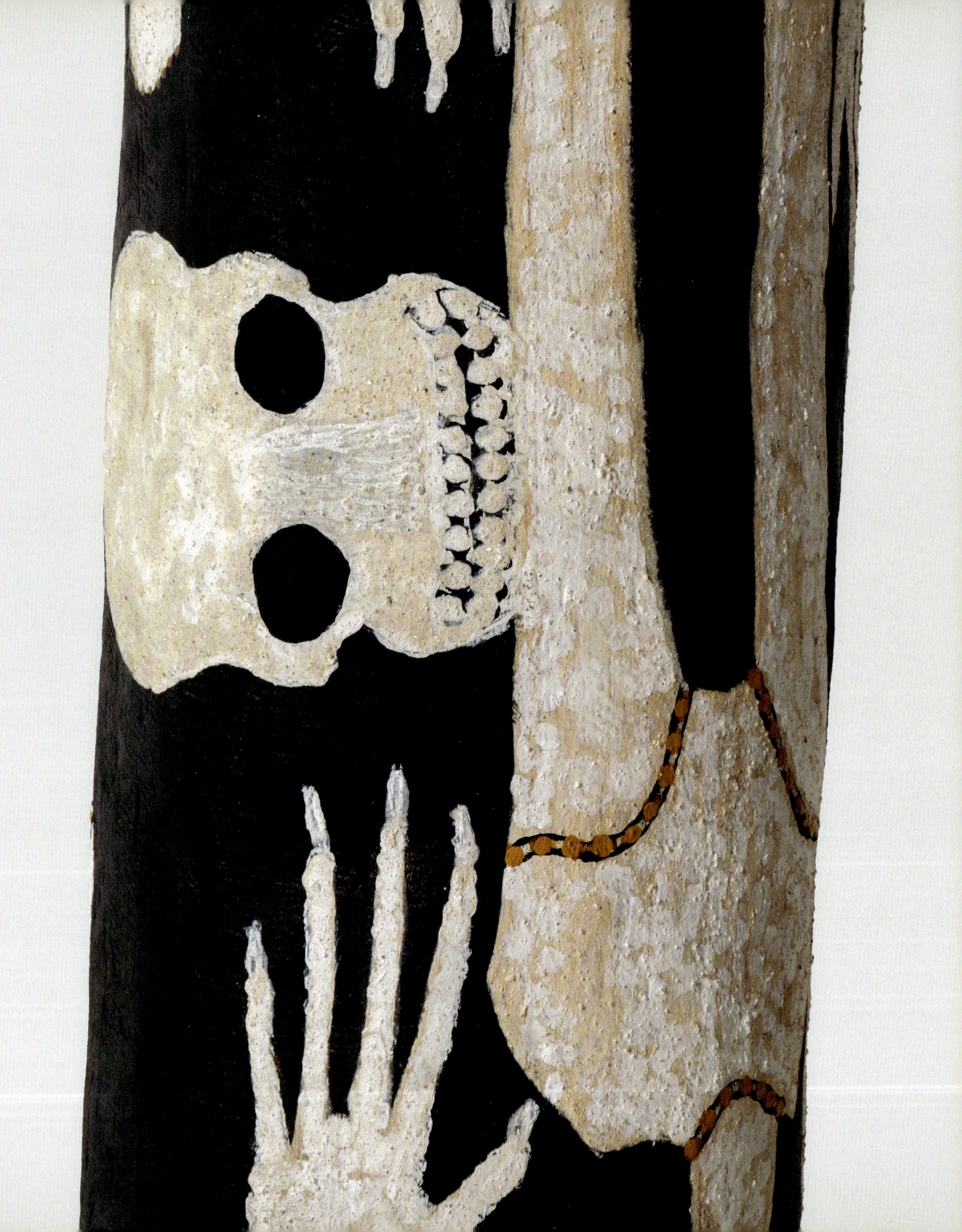

KUNBARRLLANJNJA (GUNBALANYA)

Joe Guymala
Gabriel Maralngurra
Joey Nganjmirra

Joe Guymala, *Lorrkkon Story* (detail), 2016 (see p. 52)

Nawarddeken Lorrkkon dja Injalak Arts
Stone Country Memorial Poles and Injalak Arts

David Wickens

In a busy shop in a small Aboriginal community, on a slight rise above a panoramic flood-plain of the Adjumarrllarl wetlands, a humble group of productive artists showcase their work, which employs traditions that have evolved over thousands of years of continuous creative practice. The community, Kunbarrllanjnja (Gunbalanya), is located around two hundred miles east of Darwin, in the stone country of western Arnhem Land. The busy little shop is part of the non-profit Aboriginal association Injalak Arts, which supports around three hundred artists in the region. The first white settlement at Kunbarrllanjnja was formed in 1906 by the buffalo hunter Paddy Cahill (1863–1923), who named it Oenpelli, confusing the name of the site with that of a local lagoon. The frontier outpost now known as Kunbarrllanjnja is located on the traditional lands of the Mengerrdji, whose descendents, the Gumurdul family, still reside in the community. With the establishment of the Oenpelli Mission in 1925, many neighboring clans began to settle in the community, and today it is home to around twelve hundred people, most of whom speak and identify as Kunwinjku.

> The paintings on my *lorrkkon* represent all the different types of animals that the people who passed away used to hunt for on my country. I painted them in that rock art style, same style like those old people. I painted *djenj* [fish], *burrar* [goanna] and *kedjebe* [file snake] because they live in that waterhole on my country in Kudjekbinj. When I paint these animals I think about my country, the songs and ceremonies those old people used to sing and dance, and when they would paint animals in the rock shelters.[1]
>
> Gabriel Maralngurra

Injalak Arts was established in 1989, primarily as a screenprinting workshop. The center quickly became a creative hub with arts and crafts being produced six days a week. In Kunwinjku culture, painting plays a significant educative role. This has made Injalak an important center for training in both art and cultural knowledge. Many artists choose to work onsite, with the men working on delicate figurative paintings of animals, plants, spirits and Dreaming stories (*djang*). The inspiration for these paintings comes from the extraordinarily rich rock-art tradition of the region. With controlled strokes of diagonal lines and shimmering cross-hatching applied with a locally sourced grass-brush, the artists participate in the continuation of one of the world's oldest artistic traditions. There are an estimated twenty thousand rock-art sites in the Arnhem Land plateau,

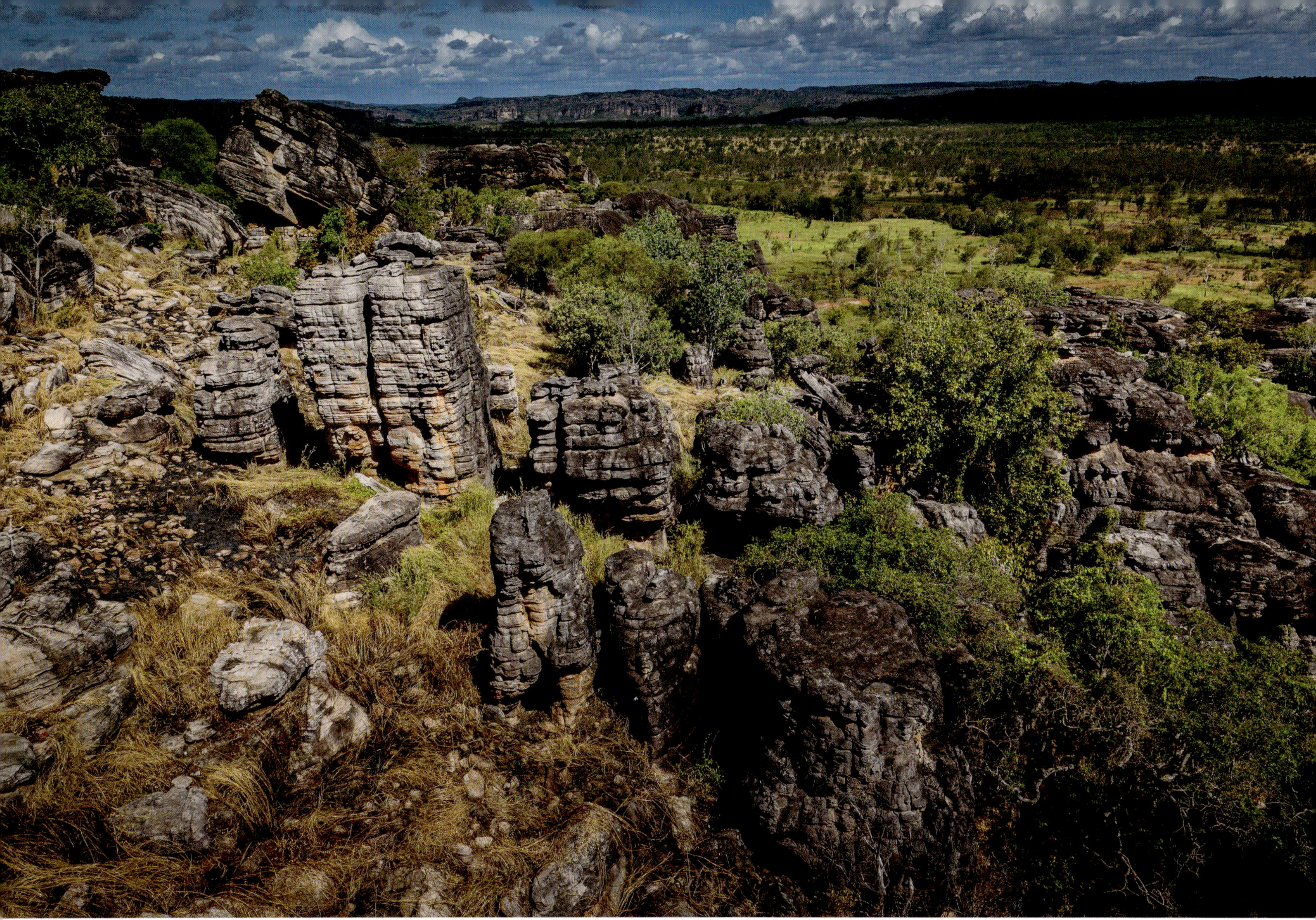

Fig. 1. The stone country of western Arnhem Land. Photograph courtesy of Injalak Arts

of which Injalak Hill—which overlooks the art center—is considered one of the most significant (Fig. 1). Injalak Hill features some of the oldest, most elaborate and breathtaking examples of rock-art on the planet (Fig. 2). Across its galleries are figurative paintings of ancient creation stories, educational diagrams, hunting tactics and an outstanding variety of native plants and animals, some of which have been extinct on the mainland of Australia for thousands of years. This elaborate palimpsest of images illustrates the continuous occupation of these lands over a period of more than fifty thousand years.

> The land and the country belong to my people. Stories stay in the country, in the land itself. Tradition is important. My uncle's [Thompson Yulidjirri (1930–2009)] way was to tell the stories, and he kept it in his mind for himself from his father who taught him those stories, kept not in books, but in our minds. We can still tell that same story to the young, the kids, and to the families so that they won't be forgotten. It will be kept in an archive or put in a place where it is kept safe. That's all. Now, these stories have to be written down and kept in a safe place. But the stories are still in our heads, our hearts and our minds. So the stories will never be forgotten. Paintings go away, but the stories always come back. So Dreamtime stories are like when the wind blows: it takes the smoke away, but it still comes back. The paintings hang in the galleries, but the stories stay in our country for our kids to learn.[2]
>
> Gabriel Maralngurra

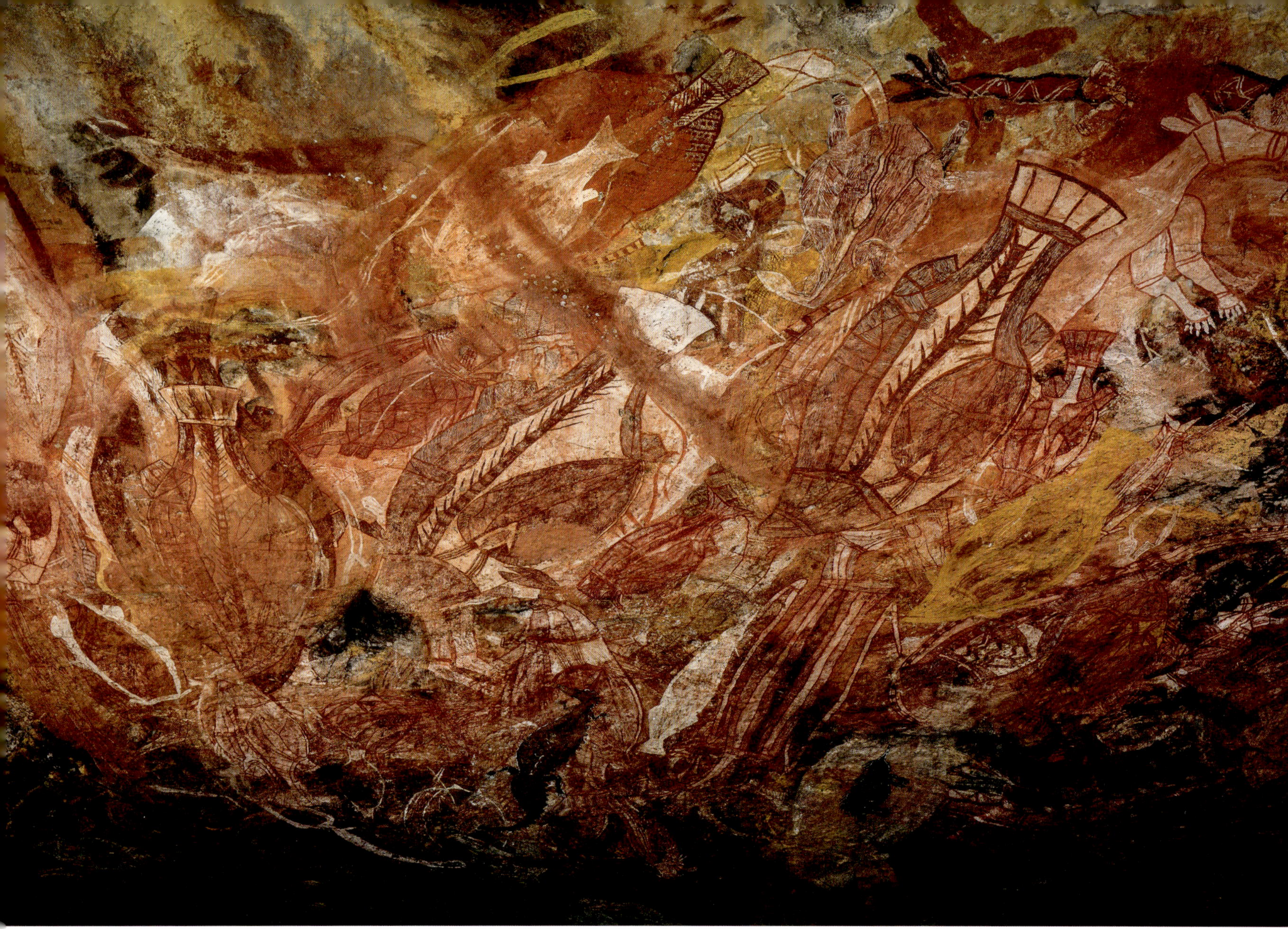

Fig. 2. Rock art on Injalak Hill. Photograph courtesy Injalak Arts

Maralngurra is a senior painter; he was among the founding members of Injalak Arts in the late 1980s and continues to be a driving force behind the art center today (Figs. 3, 4). Painting seven days a week, Maralngurra's artistic practice is reflected in the breadth and depth of the subjects he paints, his fluent line work, and highly original compositions. Maralngurra's work has developed over time, both in terms of style and subject matter, as he explores one artistic avenue after another. However, behind this tireless experimentation his own confident and fluid style is unmistakable, always balancing studied naturalism with a strong sense of design and stylization. He attributes much of his artistic education to senior painter Thompson Yulidjirri.

Maralngurra is continually inspired by the rock art of west Arnhem Land, always referencing it and working within this artistic tradition while pursuing formal innovations and new designs. His knowledge of stories, plants, and animals gives him a wide range of expressive material. He is an ambassador and mediator for Kunwinjku culture, having worked many years as a tour guide, Kunwinjku–English translator, Injalak board member and president, and screenprinter, as well as traveling widely around Australia for openings and launches. He is currently co-manager of Injalak. As a founder, it is in large part Maralngurra's vision and belief in the mission of the art center that has allowed it to carry on and thrive. He has helped create a place where the art history of western Arnhem Land can be

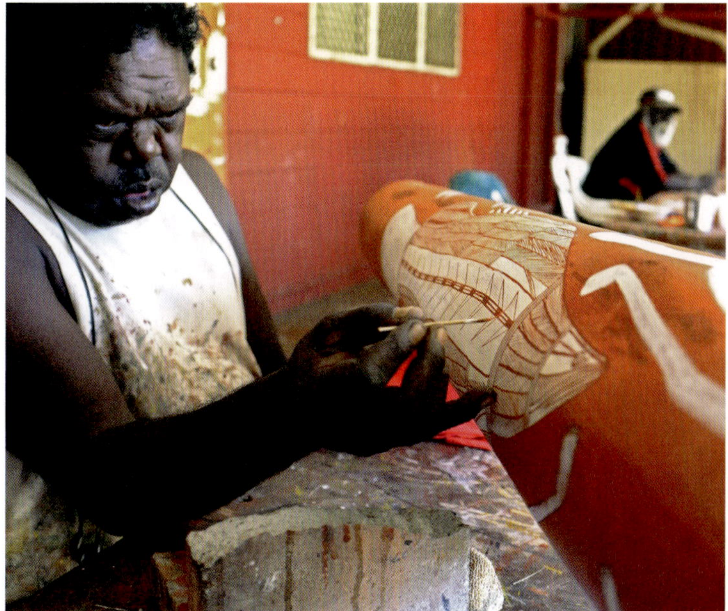
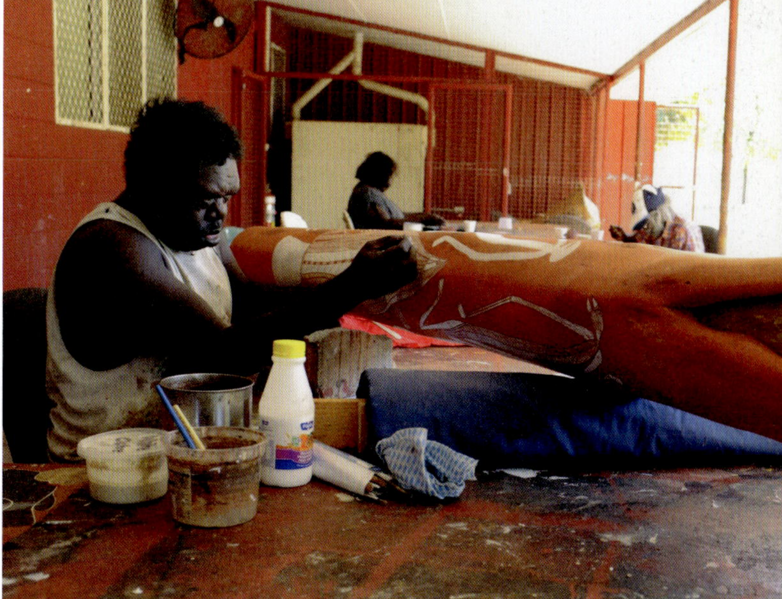
Figs. 3, 4. Gabriel Maralngurra at Injalak Arts working on *Mimih Spirit Hunting* 2017. Photograph by David Wickens

continued, developed, experienced by others and apprenticed to younger generations.

In western Arnhem Land, the passing of knowledge through generations is one of the primary catalysts for art making. By learning from senior artists in an informal system of apprenticeship, young people are gradually brought into an understanding of the "outside" and "inside" meanings of the world. The level of knowledge revealed is dependent upon an individual's maturity, moiety, gender, or homelands. Kunwinjku culture is made up of two complimentary halves, or moieties, called Duwa and Yirridjdja. These moieties are part of a larger kinship system that is divided into eight "skin" groups. Skin and kinship are central to all relationships between people and the natural world. For example, a Duwa person is the traditional owner of Duwa country, but is also responsible for the neighboring Yirridjdja country, and is described as a *djungkay* or manager for that country (and vice versa). The kinship system informs what and how an artist can paint: both Duwa and Yirridjdja can be identified by their style of *rarrk* (cross-hatching).

Although often innovative in design or subject matter, contemporary paintings follow age-old principles. After painting the background of the work, artists will usually start by painting the *waralno*, which is the "silhouette" of the object. *Warnalno* can refer to drawing in general, but also means shadow, reflection or spirit. Dan Kennedy notes that in western Arnhem Land, in the *Lorrkkon* mortuary ceremony, the hollow-log coffin would usually be painted exclusively with silhouettes of animals associated the clan of the deceased.[3] In contemporary works, such as the six *lorrkkon* in *The Inside World,* these silouettes are usually divided and filled with multi-colored *rarrk* using a grass brush or *manyilk*. Technically, *rarrk* refers to the cross-hatched designs painted on the body of initiates during ceremony. Today, however, it is also used to describe the simpler, parallel linework that is generally referred to as "single *rarrk*" or "rock art style." In considering the six *lorrkkon* from Injalak in *The Inside World,* it is notable that only those by Joey Nganjmirra contains cross-hatched *rarrk* (p. 57).

Harvesting *lorrkkon* is serious business. While the artists of Injalak have an in-depth knowledge of how to locate and prepare poles for painting, works of the scale included in *The Inside World* have rarely been produced for sale in the past. As a result, the exhibition offered an opportunity to reinvigorate the practice of producing *lorrkkon* at Kunbarrllanjnja. Putting out the call for major poles was met with much discussion about which artists would be interested in taking on such a task. After considerable discussion, three artists committed themselves to the project: Gabriel Maralngurra and Joey Nganjmirra from Kunbarrllanjnja, and Joe Guymala from Manmoyi outstation (around a hundred miles east of Kunbarrllanjnja).

> My style, it comes from rock art, really old style. I watched my uncle painting animals and I started to paint on bark and hollow-log. I like to teach the young ones, maybe they go out bush and collect the colors, maybe like new way with four

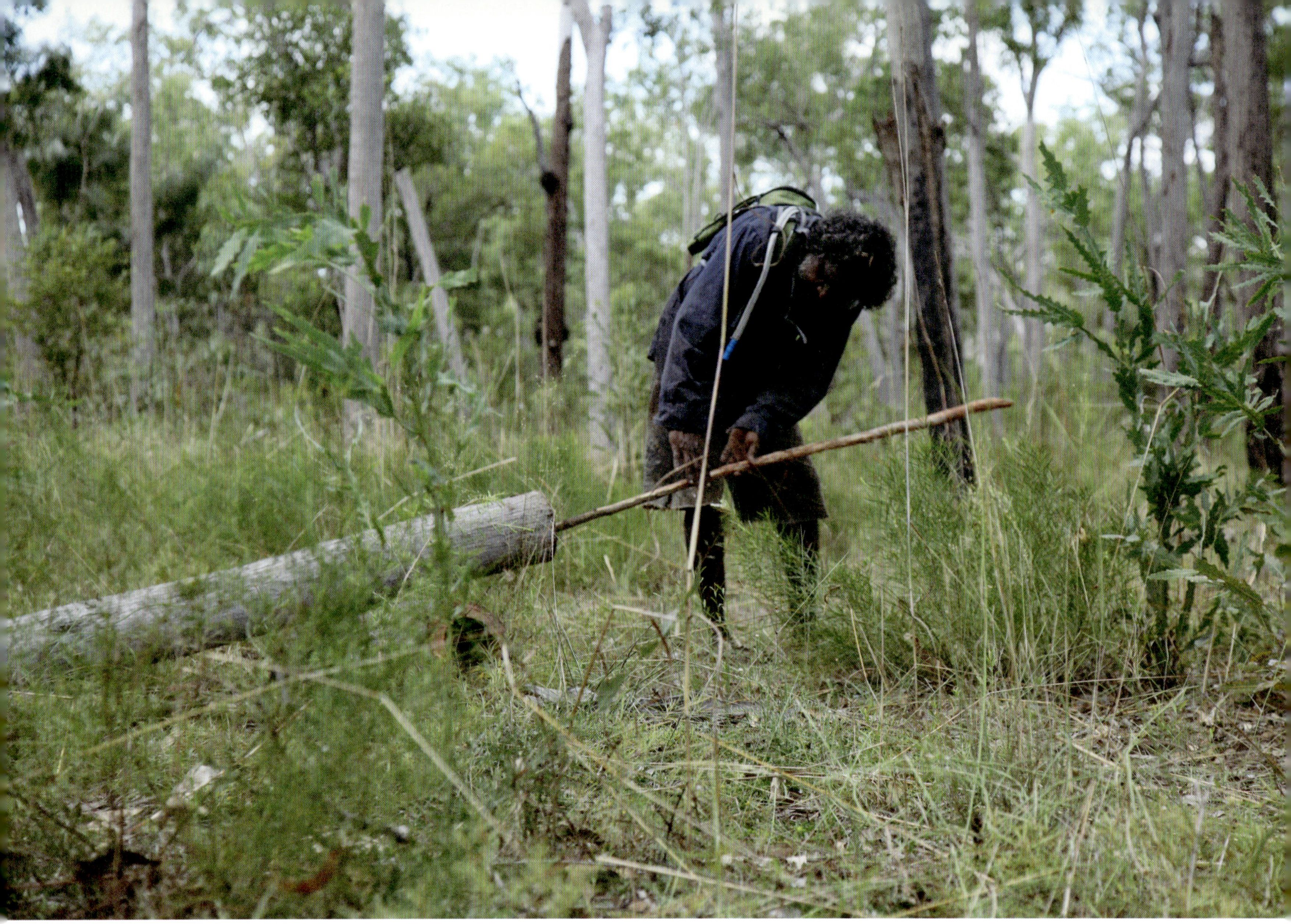

Fig. 5. Joe Guymala harvesting *Eucalpytus tetradonta* for *lorrkkon* at Namarnde Karni, Northern Territory, Australia. Photograph by David Wickens

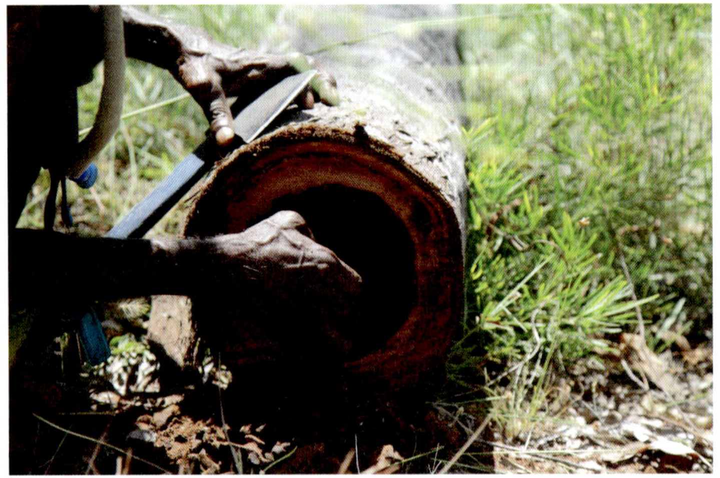

Fig. 6. Harvesting hollow logs for *lorrkkon.* Photograph by David Wickens

> colors: red and yellow, white and black. They can paint any style, rock art style or new way with all the colors, but I like to show them really old way like the old generation, with only one color.
>
> Joe Guymala

A field trip was organized to visit Guymala at his outstation, and we traveled east in the Injalak four-wheel-drive with all the tools needed to harvest poles. Joining us on the trip was Don Nakidilinj Namundja (b. 1954), the *djungkay* for Guymala's clan estate. Upon arrival we sat down with a fresh pot of tea and discussed the best places to look for *lorrkkon.* Guymala suggested that we visit Namarnde Karni, across the Liverpool River:

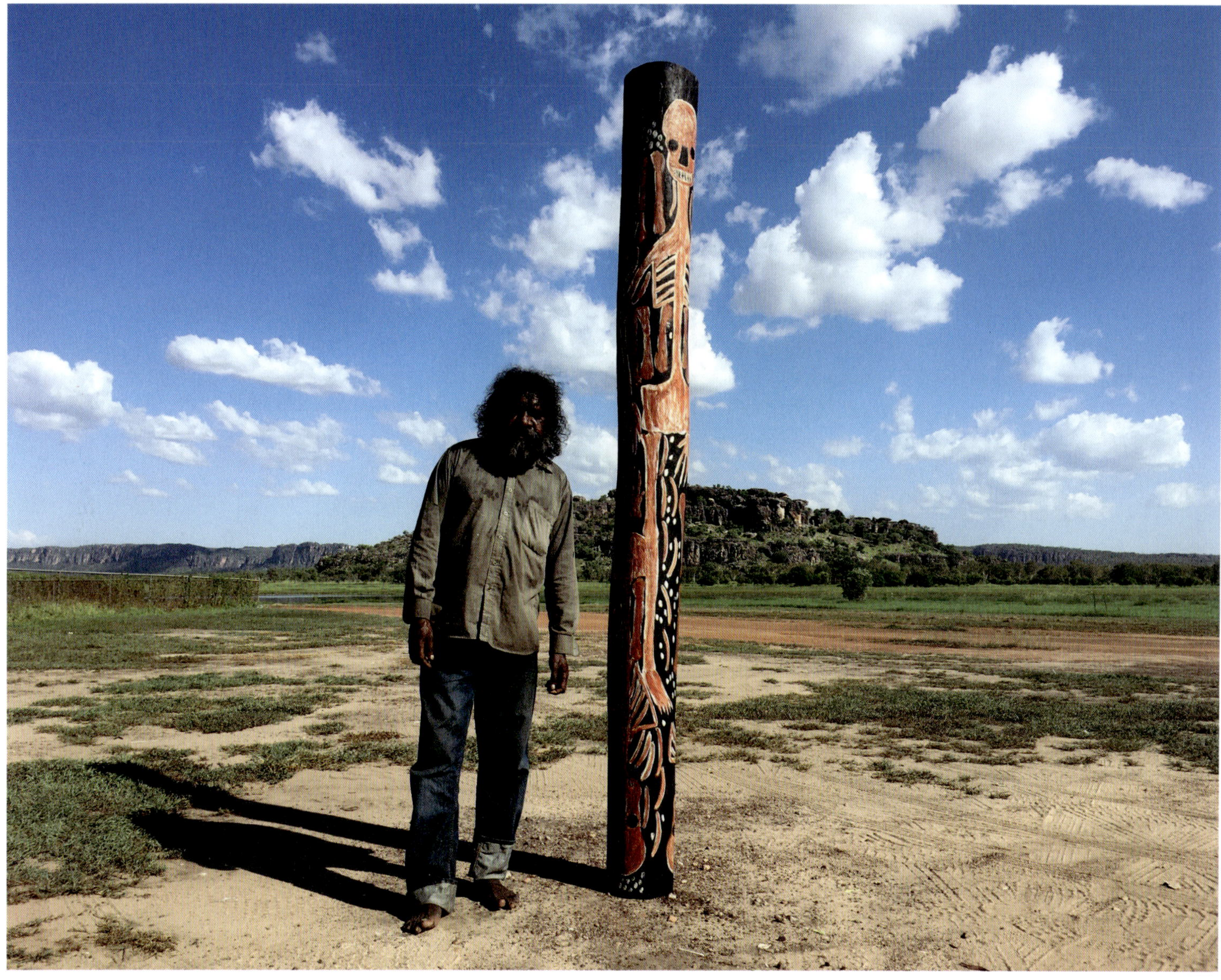

Fig. 7. Joe Guymala with *Lorrkkon Story*, 2016, in front of Injalak Hill. Photograph by David Wickens

a place well known for its quality *lorrkkon* and *dolobbo* (bark) (Figs. 5, 6). It is a dense stringybark forest, with large trees and ancient rocky outcrops. We parked the car and set out on foot looking for *lorrkkon*. Most *lorrkkon* are sourced from stringybark trees (*Eucalyptus tetradonta*), but any hardwood tree that has been hollowed by termites can be used for contemporary painted memorial poles. The trees are naturally hollowed by termites that leave only the hardest outer ring behind. To a trained eye, a suitable tree can be spotted from a distance, as there are often visible signs of hollowing in the branches and the tree can appear to be leaning or weakened by the hollowing. Joe explained his technique for locating a suitable tree for *lorrkkon*: "We look up at that tree and if we can see a hole from the termites then we know that tree could be ready for *lorrkkon*. I use my axe to hit the base of the tree, and if I hear the sound like rain inside, it's a cooked [ready] one."

Guymala is a humble man with an infectious laugh. He was born in 1969 and has spent most of his life living out in the bush on his outstation at Manmoyi. For many years, he was the bass-player and songwriter in the highly successful band Nabarlek, performing across Australia with groups such as Midnight Oil and Silverchair. His grandfather was the seminal artist Namerredje Guymala (c. 1926–1978), and Guymala recalls watching his grandfather paint on bark and rock shelters as a young boy. Joe also worked as ranger with the Warddeken Ranger group and spent time controlling feral animals, protecting rock-art sites and assisting in the controlled burning of his country. During this time, he would collect bark and visit rock-art galleries which he credits as a constant source of inspiration.

Guymala began painting around 2010, starting with small barks and works on found construction plywood left over from builders who had been working on his outstation dwellings. His early works were characteristic of Kunwinkju practice, using a mixture of rock-art style and crosshatching techniques to portray a variety of animals including *kunj* (kangaroo), *wak* (crow), *djenj* (fish) and *mimih* (spirit figures). Quickly, however, Guymala started experimenting with his style and technique, introducing more texture by not refining his ochres into a powder form, but by leaving a heavy and gritty surface, layering his paintings with thick lines in his own interpretation of the rock-art inspired single-line *rarrk*. He also experimented more with the use of watered-down loose brush strokes creating different shades and dimensions to his works. While Guymala holds deep knowledge of his cultural practices and stories, he often choses to create works that reflect his everyday life and allow us to see through the cultural boundaries. There is an innate naïvity and spontaneity to Guymala's work: a looseness that breaks away from the tight and steady practice of many contemporary Kunwinkju artists. This is well illustrated in the two monumental *lorrkkon* that Joe produced for *The Inside World* (Fig. 7).

> This *lorrkkon* is painted so you can see what *lorrkkon* is used for. I paint that skeleton to show *balanda* [non-Indigenous people] how we do traditional burial. My grandfather told me about that ceremony, but I've never been to one. They put the bones inside then paperbark on either side, we go there for ceremony to say goodbye, we miss you, *bobo* [goodbye]. This *lorrkkon* we still use sometimes but *balanda* brought more easy coffin box one with key.
>
> Joe Guymala

Once a suitable tree is located an axe is used to cut a hole at the base of the tree to check if it has been hollowed out enough for *lorrkkon*. If it is ready, a chainsaw is used to cut down the tree. It is important that the tree is still living, so that the timber is not dry or cracked. Once back at camp the outer bark is removed and the long task of filing the soft inner fiber from the tree begins. The objective is to leave only the hardest ring of tree behind. The trunk is sanded nice and smooth and round, and then it is ready to paint. It is incredibly labor-intensive, even with fancy *balanda* tools.

> In the early days before *balanda* harvesting *lorrkkon* was done with a *kundamal* [stone axe]. The size of the pole would need to fit all the bones of the deceased inside, including the skull. It would have taken a long-time. Now we have more modern tools like steel axes and chainsaws, but we still remember the old way and speak to those old people when we are looking for *lorrkkon*.
>
> Joey Nganjmirra

Lorrkkon have been a part of traditional burial ceremonies in lower western Arnhem Land for millennia. After a person has been buried for a number of years, Kunwinjku perform a *Bukkabud*, which involves the collection of the bones of the deceased, and cleaning and painting them with red ochre in preparation for the *lorrkkon* reburial. In the ensuing *lorrkkon* ceremony, the bones of the deceased are deposited in a hollow-log coffin. The log itself is constructed in seclusion over a number of days, firstly painted all over in red ochre and then transformed into a ritually powerful container through singing and being painted and repainted with white silhouettes of ancestral figures and animals related to the cultural identity of the deceased.

Joey Nganjmirra harvested his poles from a nearby outstation—Mekin Valley—on the traditional lands of the Nayingal family. His use of the Woollybutt tree (*Eucalyptus longifolia*) with its lumps and scars is a breakaway from the traditional straight pole favored by most Kunwinkju artists (p. 58). Nganjmirra is part of a richly artistic family and Djalama clan group. Among the younger generation at Kunbarrllanjnja, he is one of those who have taken responsibility for carrying on the stories and Dreaming for his ancestors. Many of his works are driven by narrative, with figures in different stages of a story compressed into a single scene. Others include strong graphic forms, often overlaid and woven into complex designs. His works are primarily figurative, but the interlocking figures sometimes tend towards abstraction and he also produces abstract works based on ceremonial patterns, such as the two works in this exhibition (pp. 56, 59). A look through his works reveals a broad range of stories and original compositions rivaled by few other artists at Injalak. He is a member of the Karrbarda dance troupe which often performs at festivals as well as local ceremonies. The two *lorrkkon* in this exhibition are a strong example of Joey's contact with his traditional cultural practice, each piece representing the two moiety groups Duwa and Yirridjdja and the *lorrkkon* ceremony that Joey has witnessed firsthand.

> When I was a young man, only eleven years old, I saw that *lorrkkon* ceremony for my uncle, old Bobby Barrdjaray Nganjmirra (1915–1992). It went for three months and started on Goulburn Island. The *lorrkkon* had the same design as my poles. The patterns represent water monitor lizards or *burrar*. It represents the patterns on his skin: one for Duwa and one for Yirridjdja. That design comes mainly from this Kunbarrllanjnja area. I was taught how to paint it from old Donald Gumurdul. This *lorrkkon* ceremony is the proper way for us Bininj. When we pass away, and when I go, I want to make sure my family make that ceremony and put my bones inside the *lorrkkon*.
>
> Joey Nganjmirra

The six *lorrkkon* from Injalak in *The Inside World* are historically significant as the first markers of the revival of an ancient cultural practice. Spurred on by this project, Joe Guymala, Gabriel Maralngurra, and Joey Nganjmirra have continued producing *lorrkkon*. In 2018, a *lorrkkon* by Joe Guymala was selected for inclusion in the prestigious National Aboriginal and Torres Strait Islander Art Awards, and another acquired by the Museum and Art Gallery of the Northern Territory in Darwin. At the same time, each one is a work of individual artistry reflecting the unique personalities, talents, and innovations of their creators. As such, these are layered works that demonstrate the ongoing engagement among the Kunwinjku on how to best represent and convey their traditional knowledge to the outside world. Harvested from the earth, they are a tool for teaching and learning, connecting the past, present, and future. As Gabriel Maralngurra declares: "Our art and our culture are not separate: they are part of us: one country, one skin, one blood."[4]

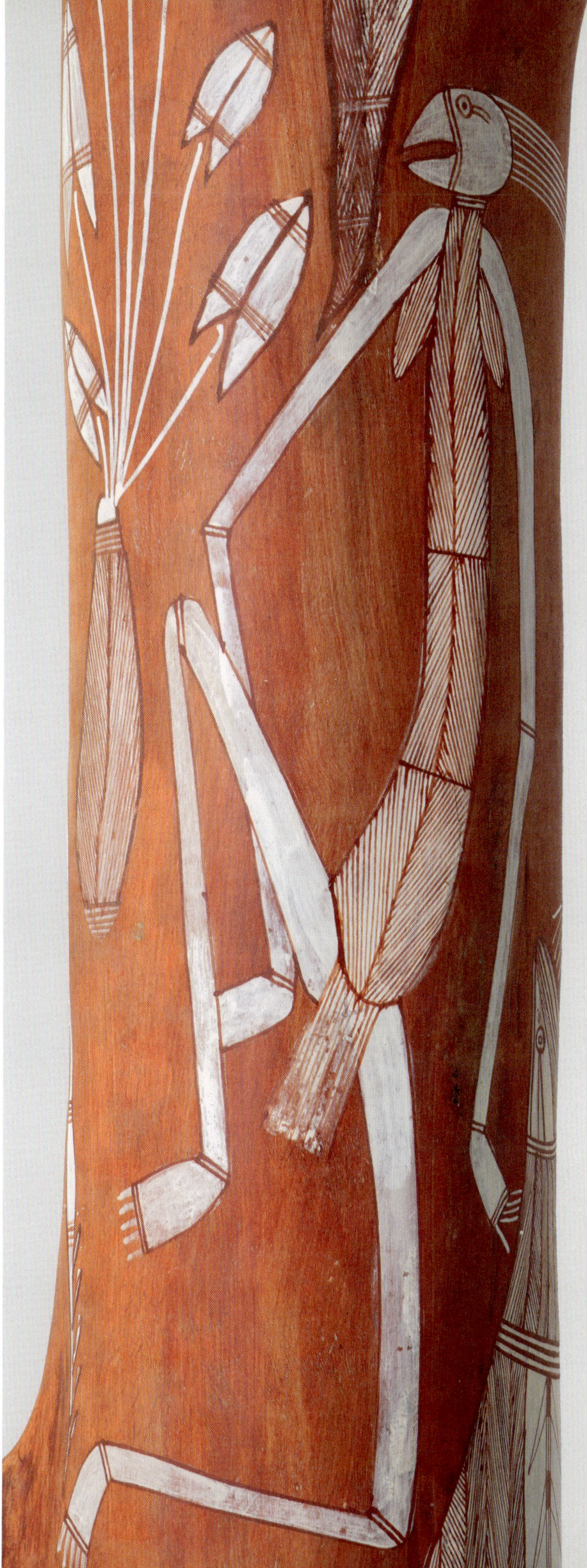

Fig. 8. Gabriel Maralngurra, *Mimih Spirit Hunting* (detail), 2017 (see p. 55)

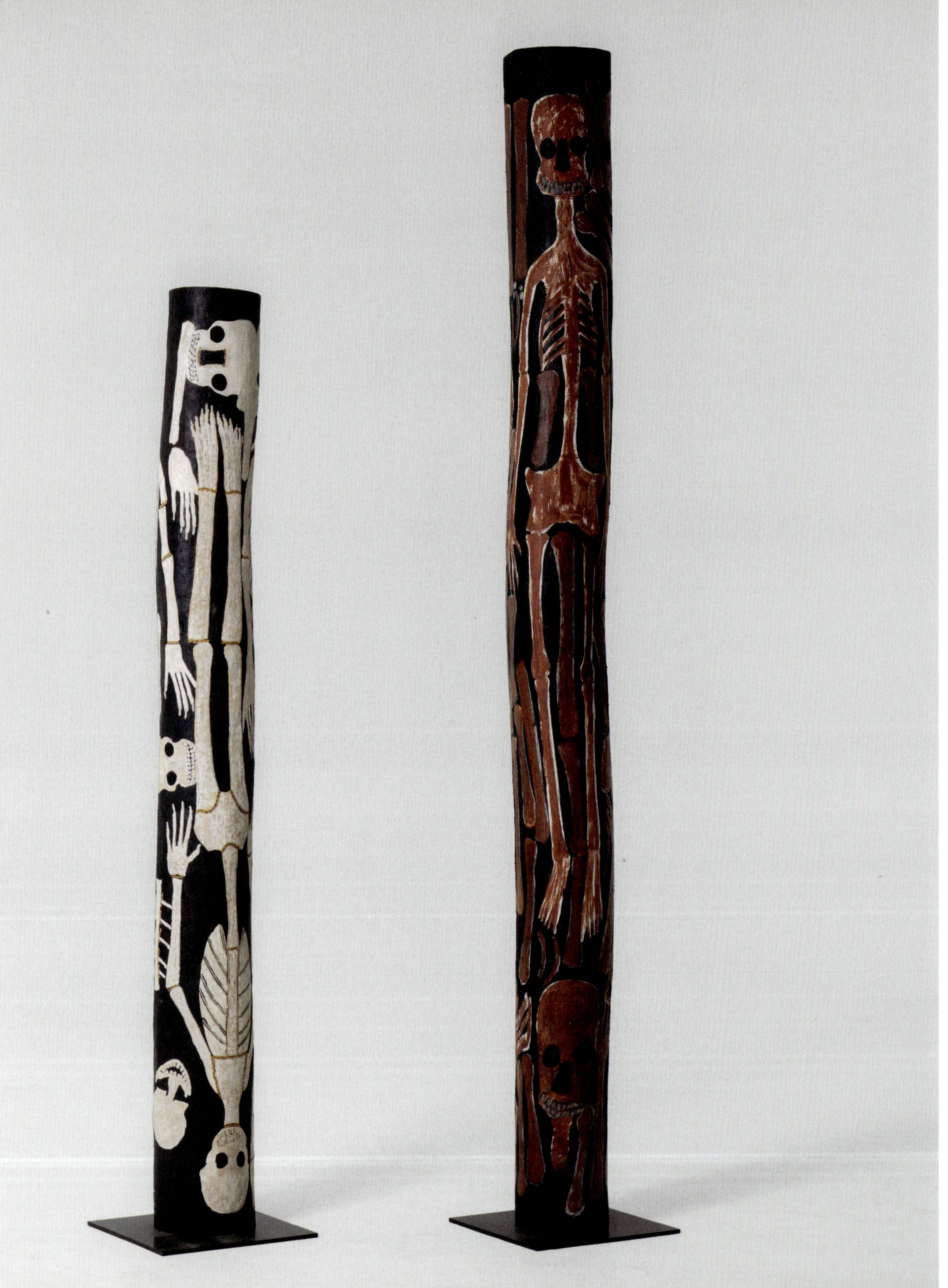

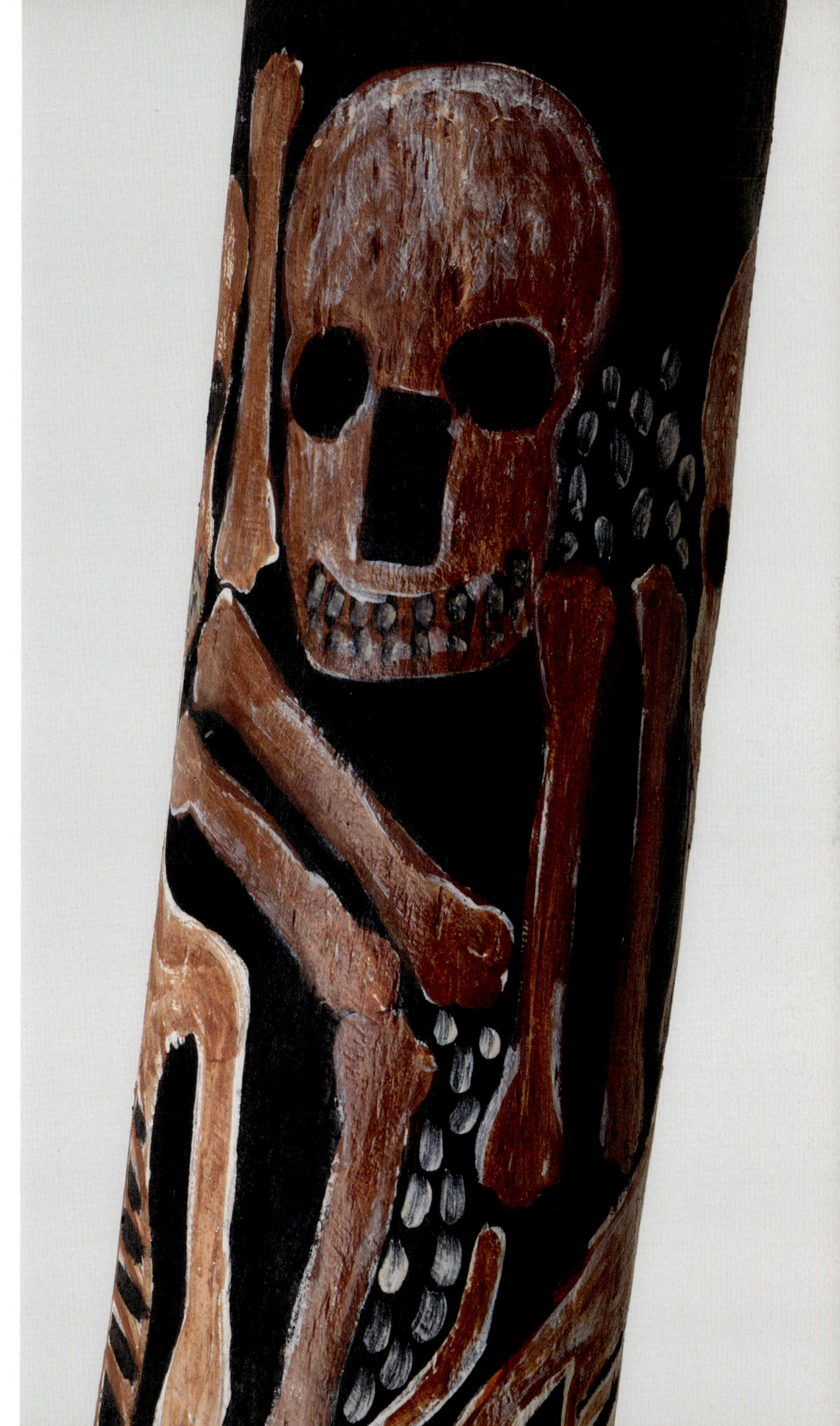

Joe Guymala, *Lorrkkon Story*, 2016. Earth pigments on wood, 84¼ in. (214 cm)

Joe Guymala, *Lorrkkon Story*, 2016. Earth pigments on wood, 106⅓ in. (270 cm)

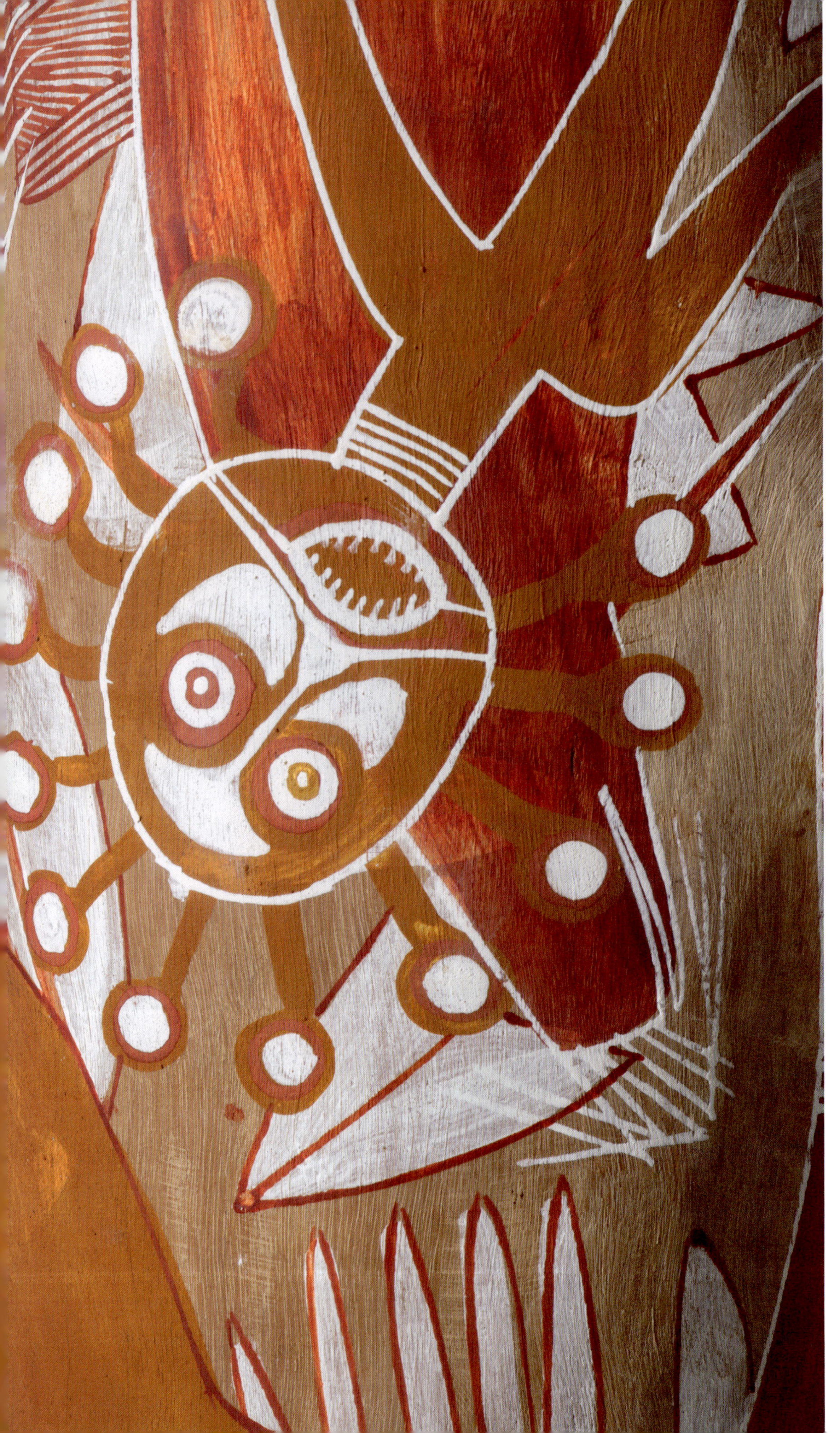

Gabriel Maralngurra, *Lorrkkon*, 2016. Earth pigments on wood, 86⅝ in. (220 cm)

Gabriel Maralngurra, *Mimih Spirit Hunting*, 2017. Earth pigments on wood, 89 in. (226 cm)

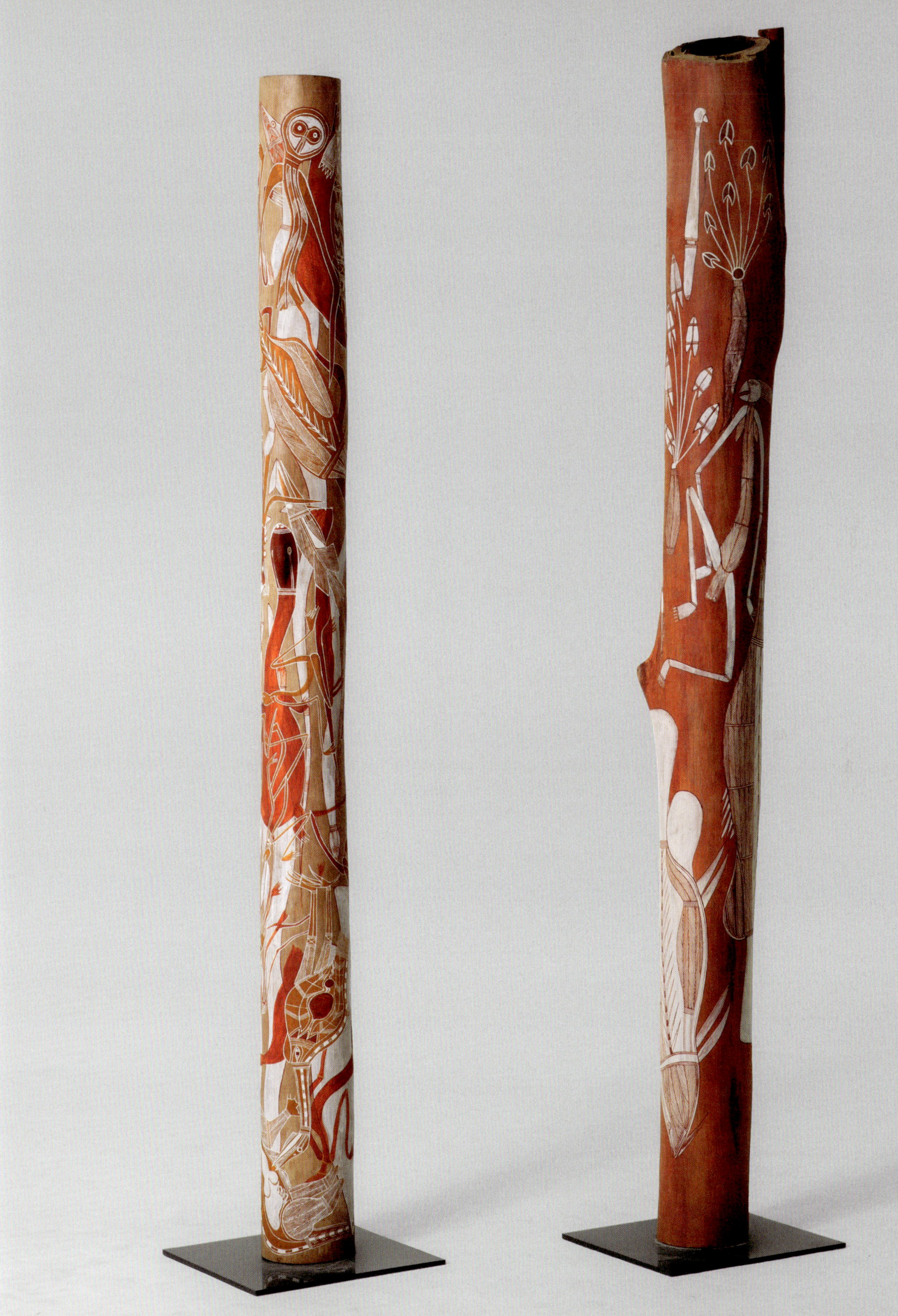

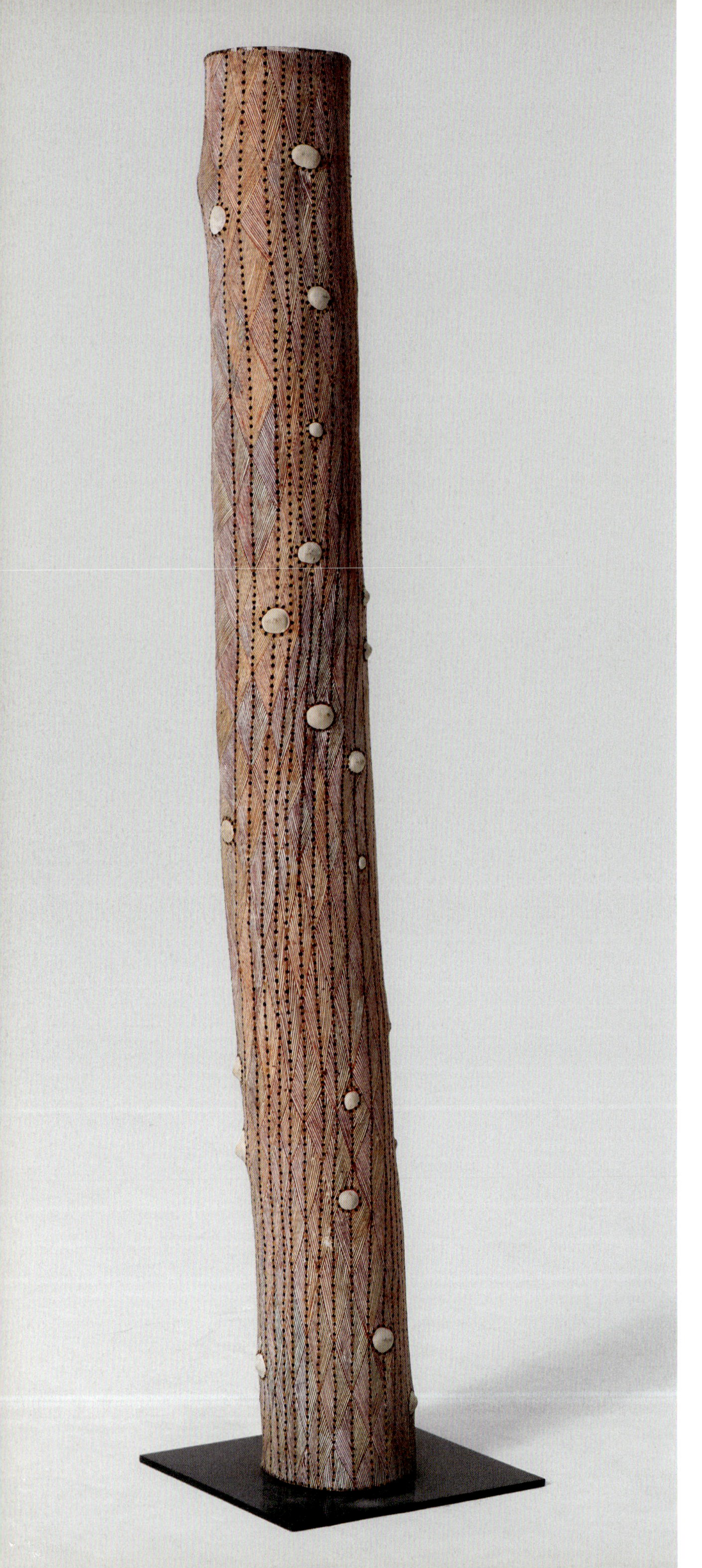

Joey Nganjmirra, *Burrar (Water Goanna) Lorrkkon*, 2016. Earth pigments on wood, 74⅛ in. (188 cm)

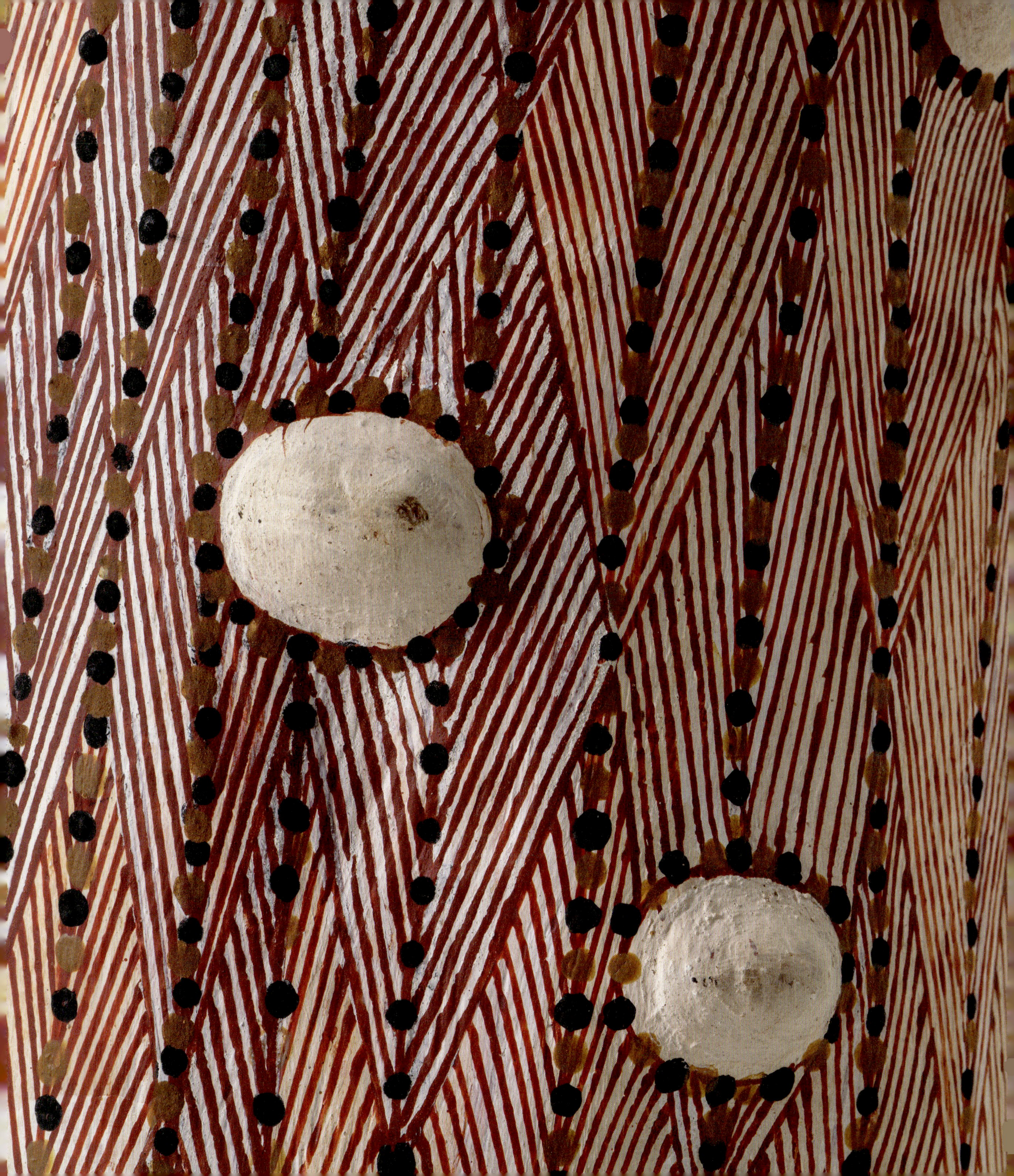

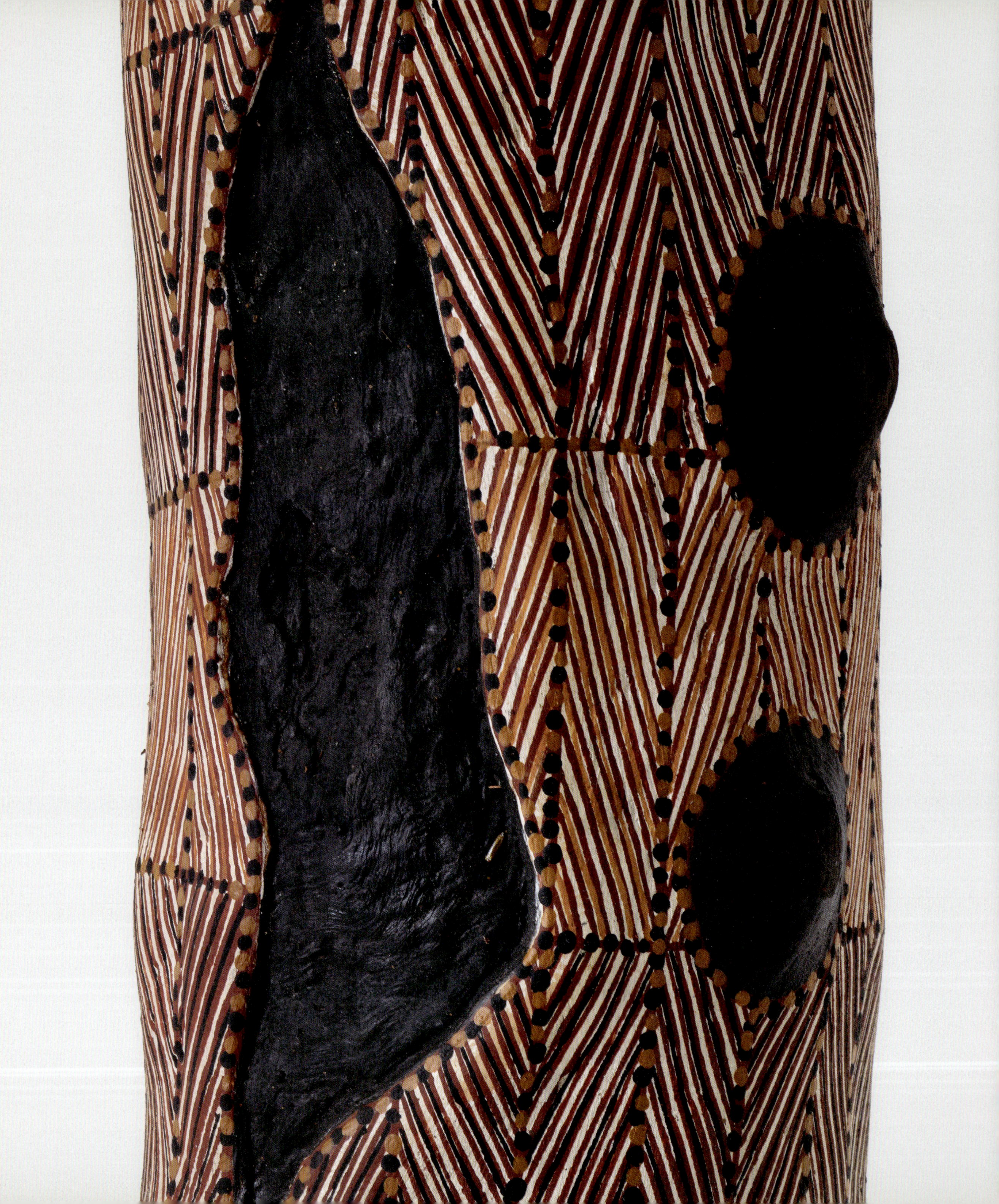

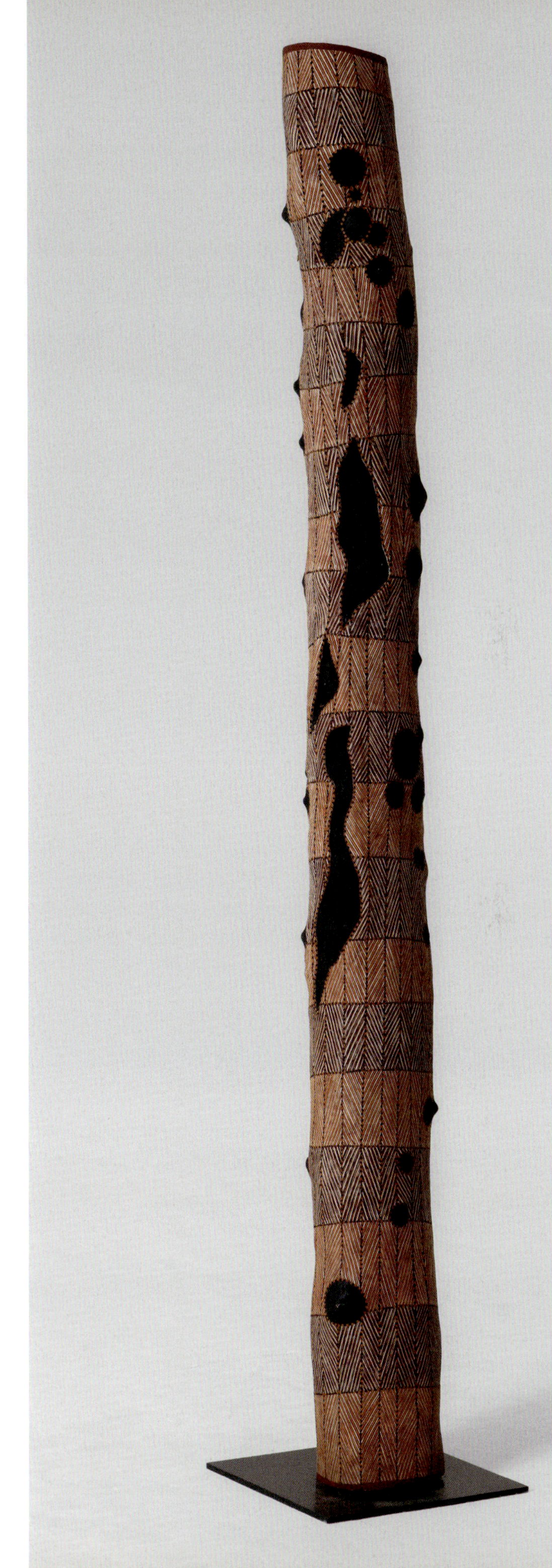

Joey Nganjmirra, *Burrar (Water Goanna) Lorrkkon*,
2017. Earth pigments on wood, 93¾ in. (238 cm)

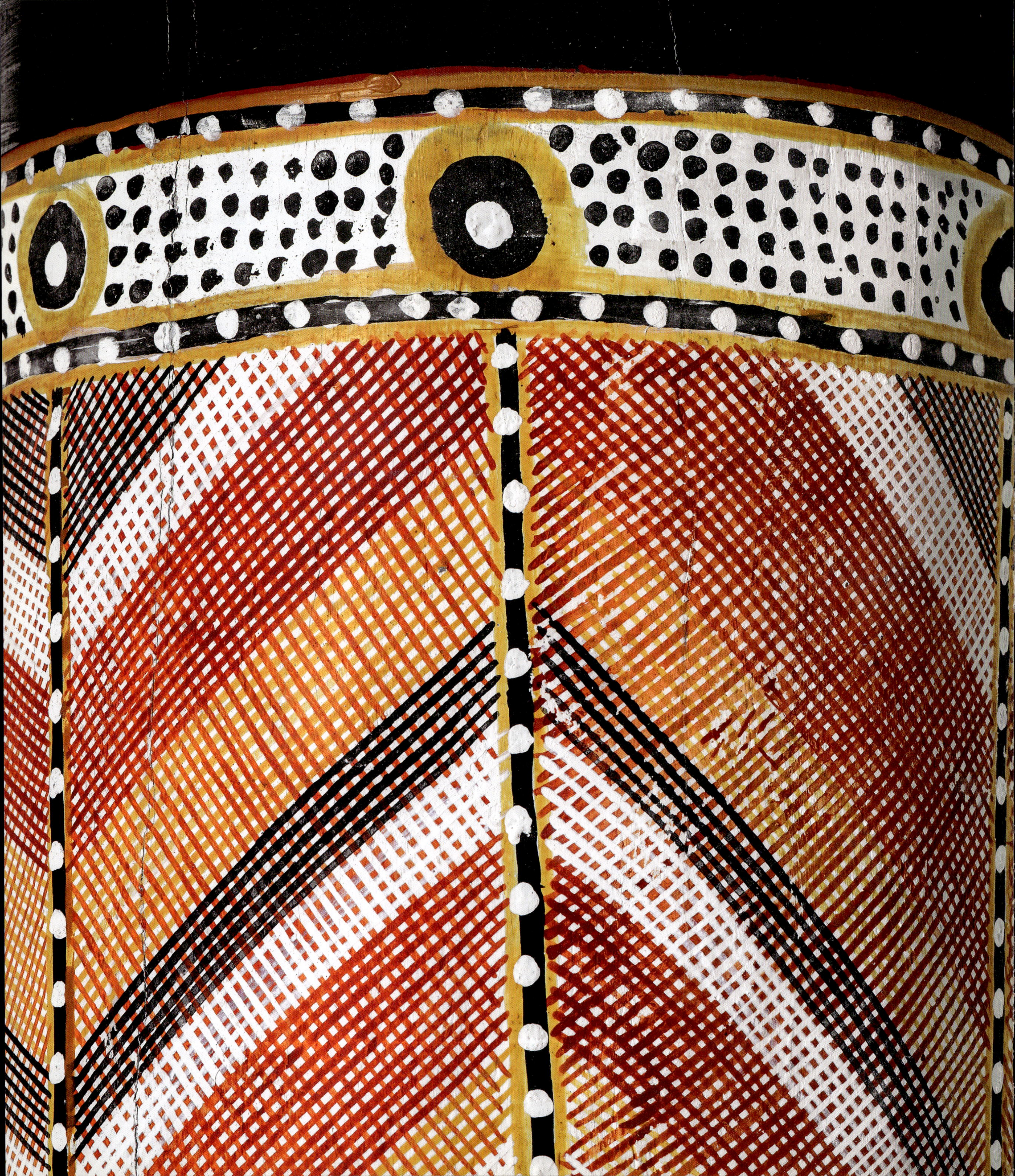

MANINGRIDA

Samson Bonson
Fiona Jin-majinggal Mason
Hamish Karrkarrhba
Kay Lindjuwanga
Susan Marawarr
John Mawurndjul
Ivan Namirrkki
Samuel Namunjdja
Deborah Wurrkidj
Owen Yalandja

Ivan Namirrkki, *Wubarr (A Ceremony)* (detail), 2017 (see p. 82)

Memories of a *Lorrkkon* Ceremony at Maningrida

Murray Garde

In 1988 I went to Maningrida in north-central Arnhem Land to work as a visiting homeland center teacher. My responsibilities included three Kuninjku-speaking communities; Mumeka and Yikarrakkal, both on the Mann River and Marrkolidjban near the lower reaches of the Liverpool River. As an Australian who had grown up in a capital city where most people are monolingual English speakers, I was impressed to finally meet Australians who spoke "Australian languages" as their mother tongue. I realized that if I was to be an effective educator, I would have to learn the first language of my students and their parents. It became clear to me that this was also the expectation of my new Kuninjku friends. This is a brief explanation of how I came to live with Kuninjku people and learn about the art of this part of western Arnhem Land.

In the late 1980s and early 1990s some of western Arnhem Land's most important artists were the parents of my students. We had a reciprocal learning relationship. I taught their children about *balanda* (non-Aboriginal) knowledge and they taught me about the Kuninjku world. These people included the four Kurulk clan siblings, John Mawurndjul (b. 1952) (Fig. 1), Jimmy Njiminjuma (1947–2004), James Iyuna (1959–2016), and their sister Susan Marawarr (b. 1967). At Marrkolidjban and Mankorlod outstations there was Ivan Namirrkki (b. 1961) and his brothers

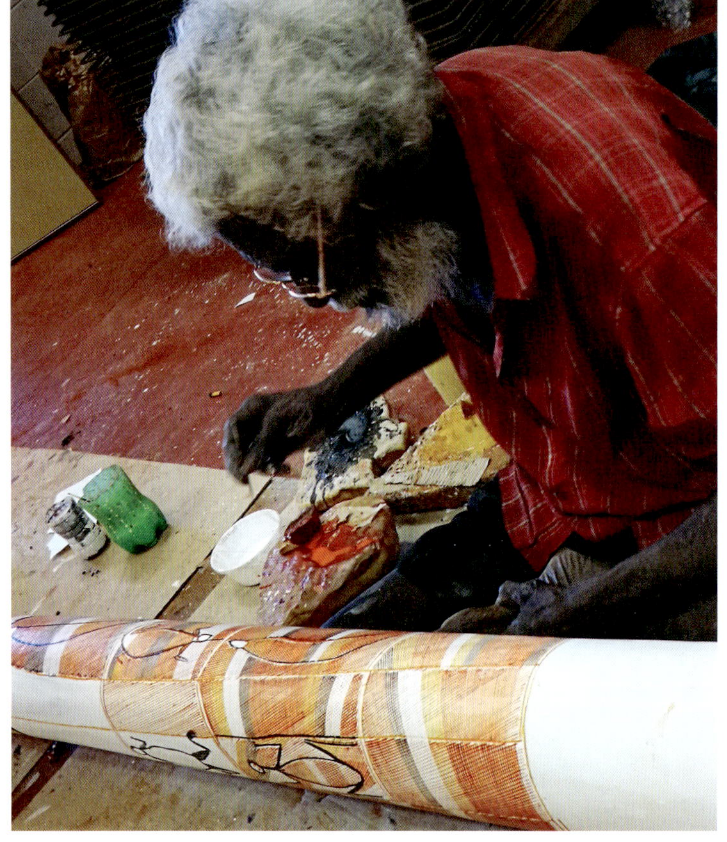

Fig. 1. John Mawurndjul working on *Mimih Spirit at Milmingkan*, 2017. Photograph courtesy of Maningrida Arts and Culture

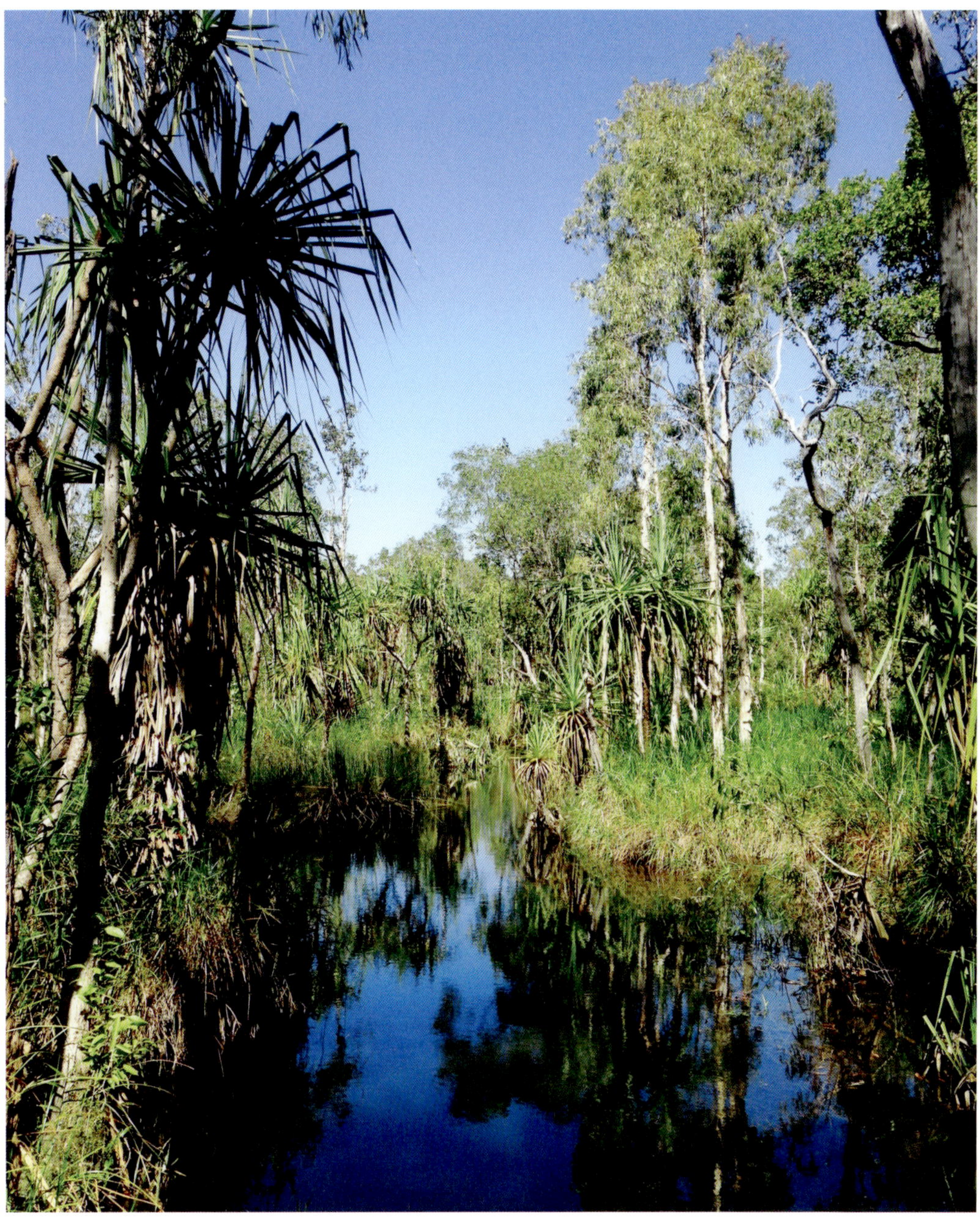

Fig. 2. Landscape around Maningrida. Photograph by Henry Skerritt

John Dalngadalnga (b. 1946) and Samuel Namunjdja (1965–2018). Further upstream on the Mann River in the rock country at Yikarrakkal, Mick Kubarkku (ca. 1925–2007) lived with his two wives Lulu Larradjbi and Edna Yiwuluma, and their nine children. Of course there were plenty of other artists at neighboring outstation communities as well. Women assisted their husbands with their artworks in many ways, but the women mostly specialized in creating art made from fiber such as string bags, fish traps, tightly woven dilly bags and items of adornment. Week by week I watched them produce exquisite paintings and other objects, some of which in later years I have recognized on display at prestigious state galleries in Australia and in other parts of the world.

After arriving in Maningrida I saw the impressively decorated hollow-log ossuaries or *lorrkkon* in the art center in Maningrida. I soon learned that their production for the art market was seasonal. In the wet season, stringybark from the *Eucalyptus tetradonta* trees was moist and easy to remove for bark painting but, from the start of *yekke* (the early dry season) in about April or May, this was no longer possible. This then became the time for making *lorrkkon* and wooden sculptures. The *lorrkkon* made for the art market however are quite different to those used in the actual ceremony. *Lorrkkon* are containers for human skeletal remains rather than the entire human body, so the term "hollow-log coffin" is not exactly the most accurate descriptor. The word *lorrkkon* is still partly semantically transparent in Kuninjku, where a related adjective *lorrkno* means "empty, hollow." In neighbouring languages such as Ndjébbana and Burarra, spoken at Maningrida and the Blyth River respectively, there is a vowel shift that results in the term for "hollow log" being *larrkan.*[1]

There is also regional variation in the way hollow-log ossuaries are made and decorated. The hollow logs to the east of Maningrida created by Burarra and Djinang speakers often have two extensions or spikes with serrated or zigzagged edges protruding from the top. As mentioned, these groups call their hollow logs *larrkan* and the main body of the log, together with the carved spikes at the top, are said to represent the body and long jaws of a barracuda. As the traditional story goes, a fisherman who fell out of his canoe when out at sea was devoured by a protean barracuda ancestor and his bones, now inside the fish, are equated with the bones of the dead inside the hollow log used in the ceremony. But on some occasions this eastern form of the *lorrkkon* is sometimes also used in the west by Kuninjku people who refer to the upper "jaws" of the hollow log as *djarrbirn.* I once recorded a text from the Kundedjnjenghmi elder and artist Kalarriya Jimmy Namarnyilk (ca. 1940–2012) who, in remembering a deceased relative, refers to him by the type of hollow log in which his skeletal remains were interred:

Ya, na-kka na-buyikahme na-Marrku na-yik-Bulanj
na-ni na-wu lorrkkon kalorrkkonyo ka-rri djarrbirn
nga-lorrkkon-kurrme-ng. Nani walem nawu
ngaburralkmi lorrkkon kondanj, anwandjad nahni . . .
Nungan mak nadjakerr nahni, Kamarrkawarn
Karrudjendi . . .

And another man, the late na-Bulanj subsection man of the Marrku clan
who is now in that hollow-log ossuary, the one with the spike motif
I put that hollow log there. The one in the south
I performed at that ritual, the hollow-log ossuary ceremony, along this creek . . .
and that one who is [your] brother [and my uncle], the one who
is buried at Kamarrkawarn

The ceremonial hollow logs which have been installed in the living areas of outstations in western Arnhem Land usually have less elaborate decoration in comparison to those made for the art market. There is often a raised ridge carved into the top of the log or a series of them. These are called *manbolidj* (cicatrice or scarrings) in Kuninjku. Usually the *lorrkkon* is painted with a red or yellow-ochre background and a smaller white section at the top. Solid white ochre images of natural species associated with the ceremony are then painted on the lower red or yellow background.

Lorrkkon made for the art market are innovative in that any subject matter can be represented within the same cultural constraints as those chosen for painting on bark. The logs are effectively painted sculptures or three-dimensional versions of bark paintings. When comparing the works of individual artists, similar (and in some cases the same) subject matter, infill techniques and color choices can be seen on both hollow logs and barks. For example, the Kuninjku artist Susan Marawarr uses a signature black and white cross-hatching on both her bark and hollow-log painting (pp. 74–5). It is again the same for another Kuninjku artist, Samuel Namunjdja. A common subject he paints is *kunkurra* (the wind): a religious emblem with associated sacred sites in his Kardbam clan country (pp. 84–5). The iconography he employs to depict this emblem involves patterns of cross-hatching that are the same on both his barks and hollow logs.

A further example of this preference for decorative non-representational infill on modern *lorrkkon* is shown by Owen Yalandja (b. 1962) (Fig. 3), whose other work has mostly focused on sculptures of the ethereal female spirit beings known in Kuninjku as *yawkyawk*. Yalandja covers the bodies of his *yawkyawk* sculptures with extremely tiny "u" shapes in white ochre (p. 87); they represent the scales of the fish-like bodies of these beings. Other parts of their bodies are covered in densely distributed minute white dots. The resulting effect is an analog to the expression of spiritual power effected by the use of *rarrk* or cross-hatching. These same infill designs, the scales and the tiny dots, sometimes completely cover his hollow logs. The infill is deceptively non-representational but it is indexical in the sense that anyone with the necessary background cultural knowledge will realize that the infill on Yalandja's *lorrkkon* points to his dominant religious emblem, the *yawkyawk* from the sacred site at Barrihdjowkkeng, east of the lower reaches of the Mann River.

On the other hand, traditional ceremonial poles feature representational artwork—goannas, praying mantis, fish and other natural species usually painted in solid-silhouette white ochre against a red or yellow ochre background. Maningrida artists have displayed innovation in the way they have created a new purpose and appearance for *lorrkkon* whilst retaining cultural continuity with the past. This is good evidence that their contemporary art practices are dynamic and evolving, as for any art tradition. The claims (thankfully now rare) that Aboriginal Australian art from Arnhem Land is "inauthentic folk art," as it was described by the organizers of Art Cologne in 1994 and 1998 (as grounds for rejecting it from exhibition) can be dismissed as unsubstantiated assertions.

Let us return now to some storytelling about the origins of this contemporary art form. In what follows, I describe what was probably one of the last performances of the hollow-log mortuary rituals. The first time I saw a *lorrkkon* ceremony was around the middle of 1988 at "Side Camp" on the western edge of the Maningrida township, where Kuninjku people camp. I remember being asked if I would like to witness this important event. It was the very first Kuninjku ceremony I attended and I was asked to join the other young initiates who had been assembled for induction. I remember the artist Balang James Iyuna explaining that this was the proper way to be inducted

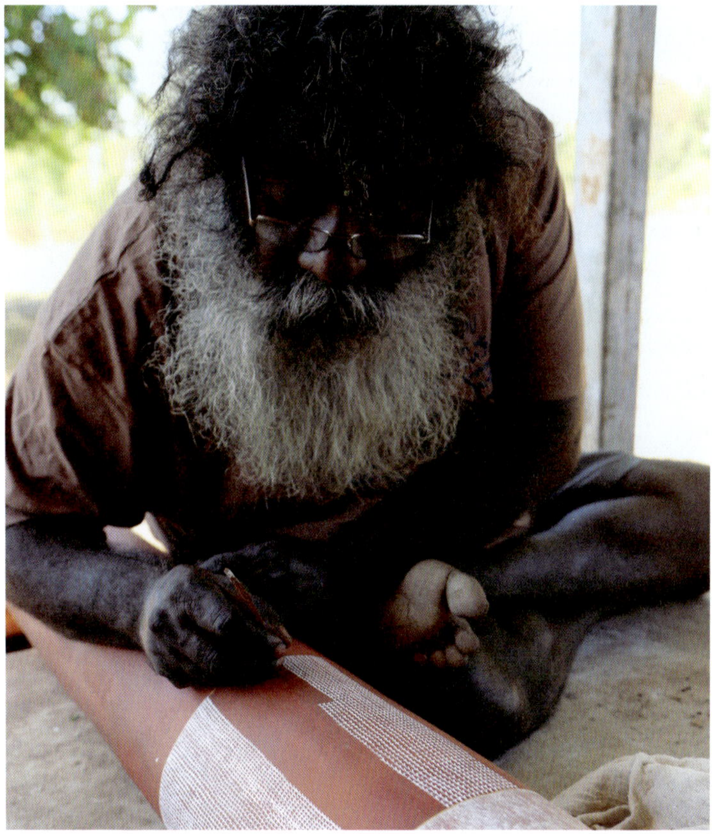

Fig. 3. Owen Yalandja. Photograph by Kate O'Hara

into the various regionally important ceremonies held each dry season throughout central-north and western Arnhem Land. Iyuna described the *lorrkkon* ceremony as *ngalbadjan*, "the mother one," and traditionally, a young man should witness a *lorrkkon* ceremony first, before being inducted into other regionally important cult ceremonies such as the Kunabibi or the Yabbadurruwa.

Later in 1988, the Kuninjku at Marrkolidjban performed another *lorrkkon* ceremony. I was staying at Marrkolidjban at the time, working as a teacher, so again I attended that ceremony. I recall it was for the remains of a woman of *Kalidjan* subsection who had died some ten years previously and whose bones had since been stored in a suitcase in one of the houses. There would have been a *bukkubud* disinterment ceremony at some stage many years earlier which would have allowed for the removal of her bones from a burial. The community made plans for the timing of the *lorrkkon* ceremony and other people from neighboring outstations started to arrive. The first task was to cut a suitable hollow log.

The cutting of the hollow log for the ceremony is organized by the senior men and is done privately. No women, children or uninitiated men or boys are present during the selection of a suitable hollow log. Once it is cut, the log is taken to a private men's camp where it is prepared and cleaned. In the case of the 1988 ceremony at Marrkolidjan, this was located on the opposite side of the airstrip to where the community was located. The bark on the log is stripped off and it is set up at a low angle off the ground, supported by a Y-shaped post, so the log can be decorated. It was then taken back into the public camp ready for the evening performances of the *lorrkkon* song series. Then in the late afternoon before sunset, the men assembled and commenced singing segments of a long series of songs that make up the *lorrkkon* song canon. They are not sung in a cycle and so should not really be referred to as such but perhaps a better term would be "song series." The singing takes place each afternoon and into the night over a period of a week or two. Everyone—men, women and children—assembled to listen to the songs, and the young men who were watching for the first time—the initiates—stood in a line, side by side for an hour or two of the performance, just before sunset. The young men have a line painted across their knees in white ochre to mark their new status as *limbidj*, "initiates of the *lorrkkon* ceremony." In Kuninjku this knee painting is called *kabirribarddjobke* "the cutting of the knees." After the young man has completed the full observation of his first *lorrkkon* ceremony, he can no longer be addressed by his usual name. He will be referred to as *limbidj* until he has seen a second ceremony.

The songs of the *lorrkkon* ceremony are called *karreno* or *mankarre* in Kuninjku. This word also means "lower leg" (below the knee) and more generally it means "cultural practice, way of doing things." The verb *-wayini* (to sing) is not used to refer to the singing of these kind of songs but rather another verb, *-kadjung*, is used instead, which means "to follow." This may reflect the requirement to "follow" the songs in a series over some days. The historical stories about the origins of the *lorrkkon* ceremony also include the travels of ancestral beings who feature in segments of the song series. By "following" the songs, the singing also follows the path of those ancestral heroes who instigated the first hollow-log ceremony. More specifically, the verb to sing *lorrkkon* songs in Kuninjku has a special prefix *-wanda* (to give) *-wandakadjung* (to sing, i.e. follow) songs of the *lorrkkon* ceremony.

> *Kabirriwandakadjung.*
> They are singing *lorrkkon* ceremony songs.

The songs for the *lorrkkon* ceremony tell of the adventures of the creator ancestral beings and the landscapes they traversed as they brought the *lorrkkon* ceremony to the various peoples of central and western Arnhem Land. Each song is very brief and has two lines—an A and a B part—and they are repeated many times before the group moves on to the next "leg." The language of the songs is often semantically opaque and may in fact be in the language of a neighboring group such as Dalabon or Ngalakan. Typically the ancestral beings sang in the language of the territory they passed through, switching to each new language as they entered new linguistic regions.

Back at Marrkolidjban in 1988, I recall how one afternoon during the preparations for the ceremony, Charlie "Shotgun" Namurludda walked over to a shade shelter in the middle of the outstation, to join a group of us sitting there waiting. He carried a suitcase and then proceeded to open it and take out the contents. Inside were the skeletal remains of the woman who had died a decade ago and who would be placed into the *lorrkkon* as part of the ceremony. The task now was to cover them completely in *yamidj* (red ochre). Several men started grinding the ochre on a stone palette and adding water. The paint was smeared over all the bones. I remember the atmosphere being both solemn but also an enjoyable moment. There was occasional light banter and good humored conversation as the bones changed from white to their new bright-red ochre patina. With everyone handling the bones of a woman who was once alive as we were at that moment, I recall someone reflecting on the inevitability that we too will one day be as she is now.

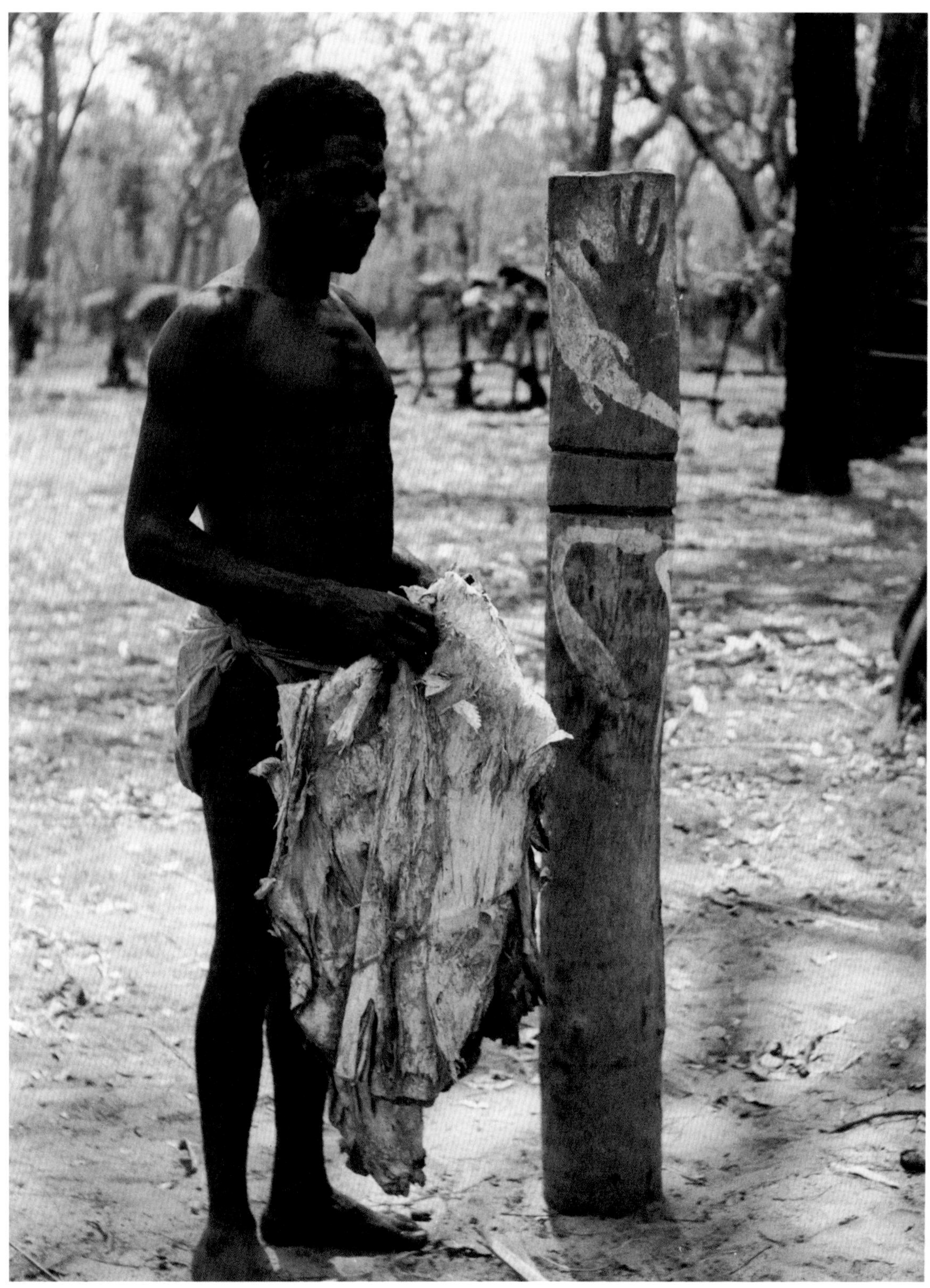

Fig. 4. Rríngkidj renews the designs on a *lorrkkon* containing the bones of his father, and replaces the bark covering, 1952. Photograph by Axel Poignant. National Library of Australia, Canberra

Such profound encounters and conversations are never forgotten. But that is the purpose of the *lorrkkon,* to cause us to remember. With the task completed, the bones were wrapped up again in cloth, carefully placed back into the suitcase and taken away to the men's camp on the other side of the airstrip.

In the afternoon the singing started up again. It would be better described as chanting and is accompanied by the clapping of pairs of boomerangs called *barlkkan* or *kalikali,* the latter being a name that has clearly been loaned from desert languages far away to the south. Several men standing near the hollow log (one of them I recall being Earl Namadburrundul) also held short sticks and they pounded the ends of them on the *lorrkkon* which produced a regular beat for the singing. Once the chanting warmed up, the voices of the twenty or thirty men present seemed to create a hypnotic unison that pulled you in and created the feeling that something powerful with a life of its own was in train. The men leading the songs are also the ones who decide when to move on to the next "leg" of the series. Once reminded of the text being sung by the older song leaders, the rest of the group join in and the chanting takes off again. I recall the two Kurulk clan brothers Jimmy Njiminjuma and Kevin Djimarr (b. 1955) being lead singers or *mankarlangkarl* directing the group and I can clearly hear their voices on the audio recordings I made at the time. Those recordings are now lodged with the Australian Institute of Aboriginal and Torres Strait Islander Studies in Canberra.

Each language group that performs the *lorrkkon* ceremony in Arnhem Land has its own key emblems which feature in the song series and also sometimes in the artwork on the log itself. For the Kuninjku these include *marlinjdji* (the praying mantis), *burarr* (Merten's water monitor) and *karrkkanj* (the brown falcon or fire hawk). The praying mantis is associated with death. The Kuninjku say this is because the insect has the appearance of a living skeleton without flesh and a large skull-like head. In the *lorrkkon* ceremony *marlinjdji* the praying mantis has a different ceremonial name—*rumburre.* This is the song of the praying mantis in the *lorrkkon* ceremony (the words are archaic and cannot be translated into English):

kanan ngadjburru, ngadjburru ngadjburru
kanan rumburre, rumburre rumburre

The appearance of *marlinjdji* can sometimes be associated with an auspicious moment indicating the recent death of a family member. In 2007, I was in Sydney accompanying the Kunwinjku artist Don Nakardilinj Namundja (b. 1945) for an exhibition of his art together with paintings of his classificatory brother Bob Wanurr Namundja (ca. 1922–2007). Don and I were in the house of our good friends, the musicologists Allan Marett and Linda Barwick, whilst we waited before traveling to the exhibition opening. At some point a praying mantis found its way into the lounge and Don had no doubt as to the meaning of its presence. Sadly, Bob died a few days before the show opened.

Perhaps the most spectacular part of the *lorrkkon* ceremony relates to the segment that celebrates *karrkkanj,* the fire hawk. This ritual is performed on the last night that the *lorrkkon* remains in the public camp. The performing fire hawk men take the hollow log away, together with the soul of the deceased and carry it off to the men's secret camp where the ceremony continues out of view of the women and children. *Karrkkanj,* "the brown falcon," is a special bird in the Top End and when in human form in the period of creation, he was skilled at burning the country. This is the same tradition that continues to this day with the important greenhouse gas abatement work of Indigenous land-management groups across the Top End of Australia. Bininj say that *karrkkanj* will not only find food amongst the fleeing insects and small animals flushed out by a fire, but that the bird will also grab burning embers from the ground and fly away with them to other areas of unburnt bush where they are dropped into the grass in order to spread the fire. This characteristic of brown falcons is celebrated in the *lorrkkon* ceremony.

On the last night of the public section of the ceremony, all of the men of *kodjok* and *bulanj* subsections glue decorative cottonwool down known as *buluk* to their bodies. The down is white, but some of the cottonwool is rubbed with ground charcoal turning it a black colour. Creating a highlight against the white cotton down, the men placed the wide black strips of *buluk* from their necks down to their waists on both chest and back. They then make torches from long rolls of stringy-bark and set fire to the ends. In two lines representing the pale and dark morphs of the brown falcon—one being *kodjok* subsection and the other *bulanj*, the men hold aloft their burning torches and sing the songs of light and dark morphs of the fire hawk as they move off out of the public camp into the darkness.

For the dark morph:

> *Yikarrkkanj marnda, karrkkanj marnda*
> *Walinjanboro linjanboro*

And for the pale morph:

> *Bambidj korna, bambidjko*
> *Bambidj korna, bambidjko*

I recall everyone warning me that this was a dangerous ritual as there was a real chance of embers falling from the torches into their body down which could burst into flames and cause serious burns. The sight of the men holding aloft their firebrands whilst chanting these beautiful songs as they carried off the hollow log into the darkness is something I have never forgotten. Likewise there were further rituals that continued in the men's camp on the other side of the airstrip at Marrkolidjban but these are not in the public domain and I cannot describe them here. The singing of the men throughout the night continued until dawn. It could still be heard by the women and children in the public camp on the other side of the airstrip and both groups periodically made ritual calls to each other. By first light the men had filled the *lorrkkon* with the remains of the deceased and the log was carried back over to the public camp. A hole in the ground had been prepared and the *lorrkkon* was erected in the middle of the camp. Women of certain kinship relationships to the deceased then danced in a shuffling movement around the *lorrkkon* until finally the ceremony was completed. Many of the older people then cried as they remembered the woman who had died all those years ago.

I attended another performance of the ceremony at Kurrurldul outstation in 1990 and there was another at Bolkdjam south of Maningrida in 1994. That was, I believe, the last full performance of the *lorrkkon* ceremony, at least in the Maningrida region. It is unlikely that this ceremony will be performed again, but the new brilliantly decorated *lorrkkon* made for the art market remain a testimony to this stunning mortuary ritual. These objects have always been about remembering those held dear. At the same time, the *lorrkkon* ceremony places their passing into a grander perspective, surrounded as we are by other species with whom we should all have an important connection if the planet is to be properly sustained. Each *lorrkkon* has its own story and a connection to its maker. In some ways they will never be "hollow," filled as they are with memories of love, loss, and the connections we the living, have with each other.

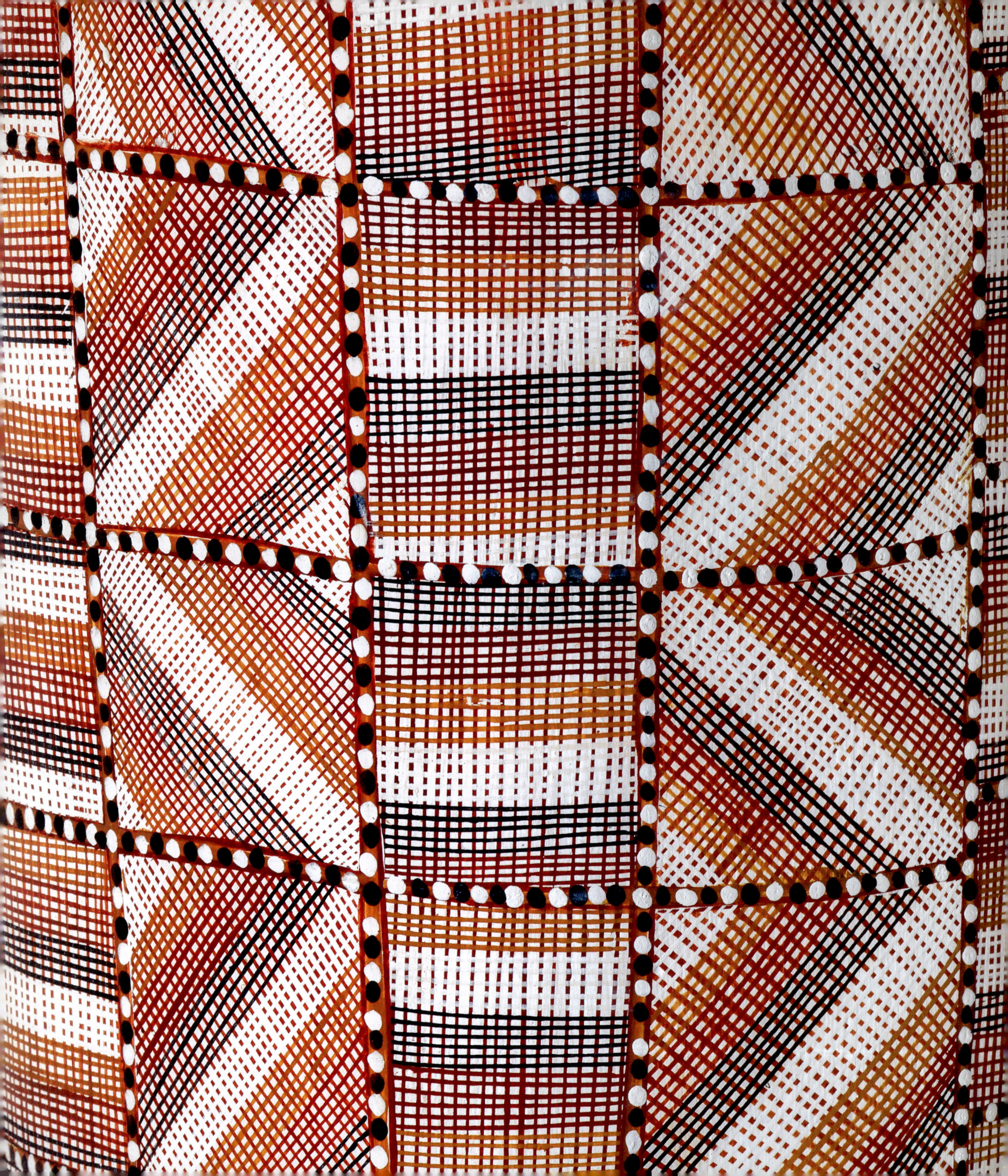

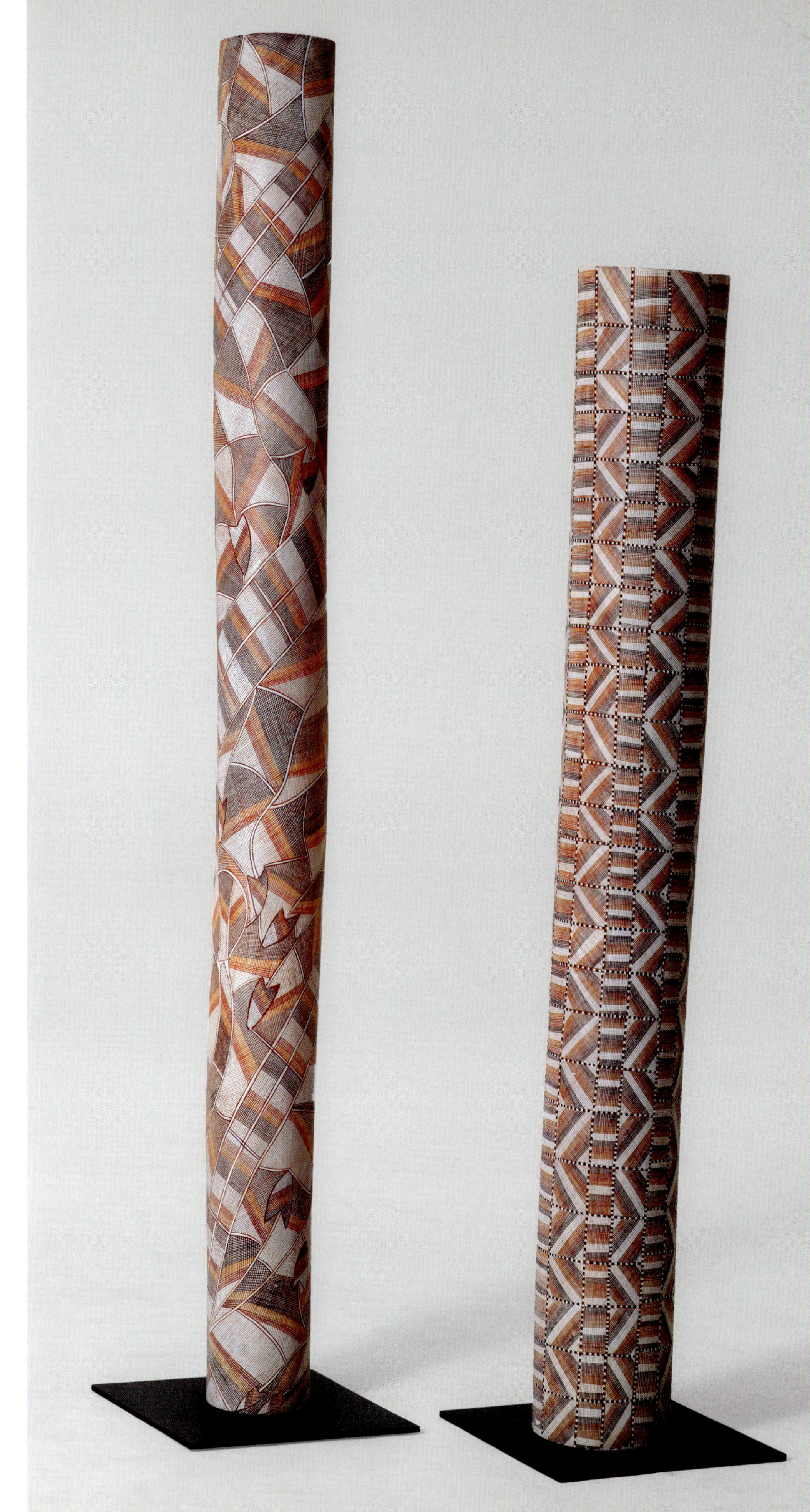

Hamish Karrkarrhba, *Ngalyod (Rainbow Serpent)*, 2017. Earth pigments on wood, 83½ in. (212 cm)

Deborah Wurrkidj, *Wak*, 2017. Earth pigments on wood, 69⅝ in. (177 cm)

Owen Yalandja, *Ngalkodjek Yawkyawk*, 2017. Earth pigments on wood, 60 in. (152 cm)

Samson Bonson, *Lorrkkon*, 2017. Earth pigments on wood, 79⅛ in. (201 cm)

Owen Yalandja, *Ngalkodjek Yawkyawk*, 2017. Earth pigments on wood, 64 in. (162.5 cm)

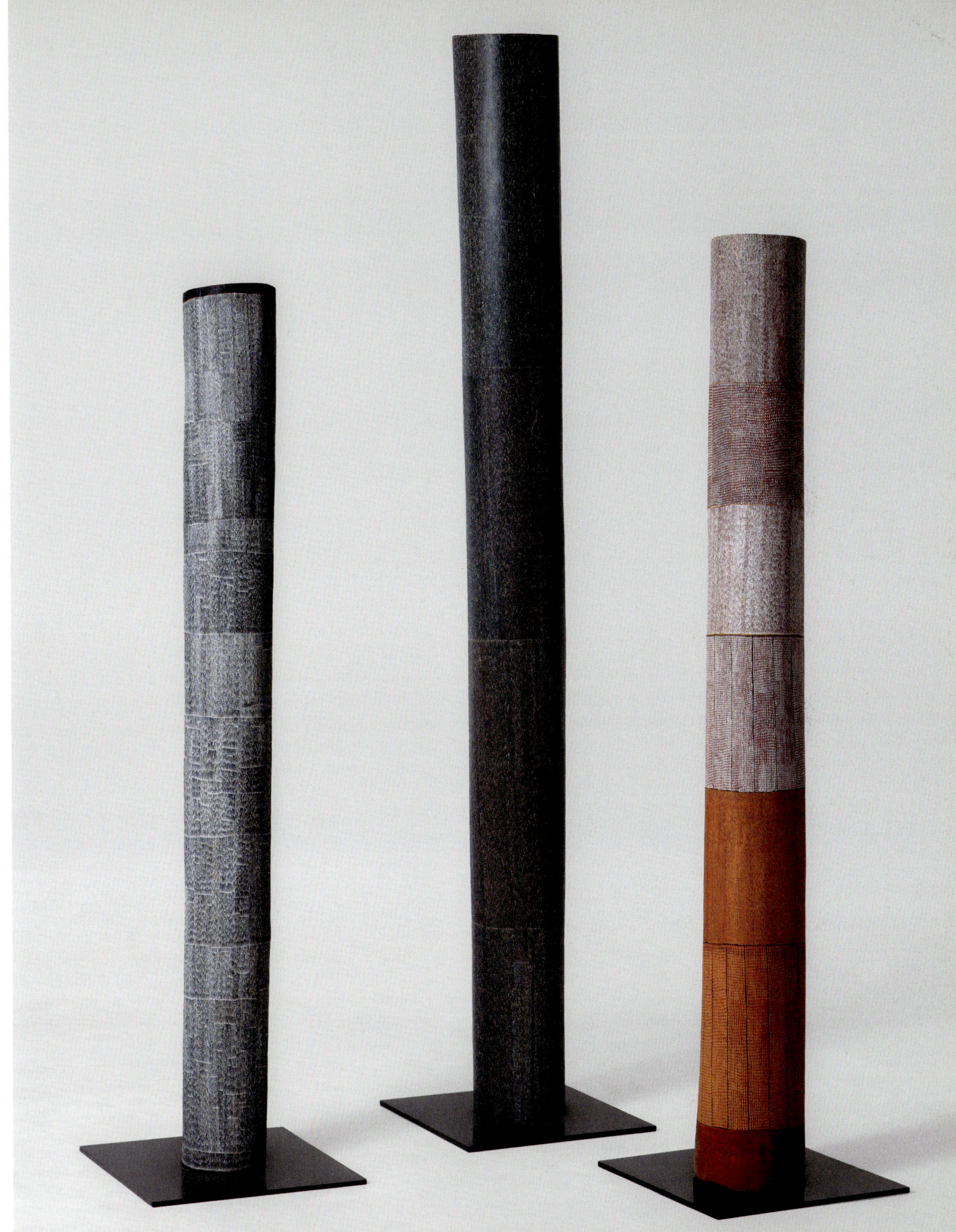

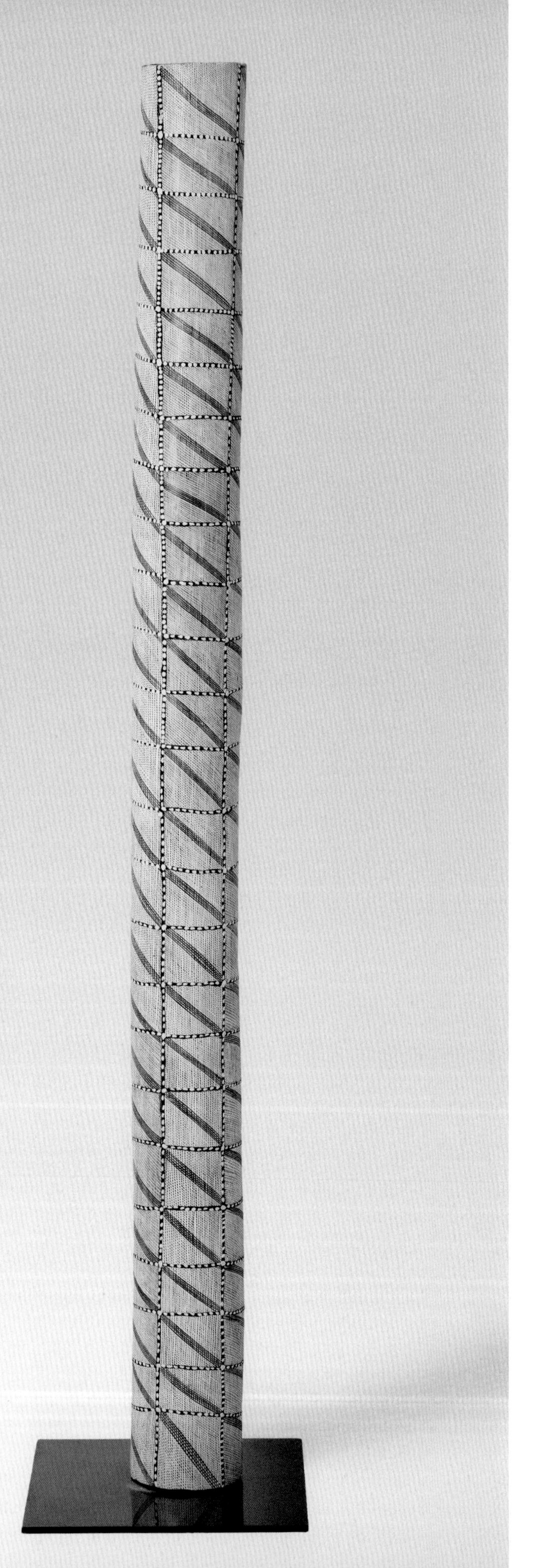

Susan Marawarr, *Wak Wak*, 2017. Earth pigments on wood, 81⅛ in. (206 cm)

Opposite:
Susan Marawarr, *Wak Wak*, 2017. Earth pigments on wood, 86 in. (218.4 cm)

Susan Marawarr, *Wak Wak*, 2017. Earth pigments on wood, 79⅞ in. (203 cm)

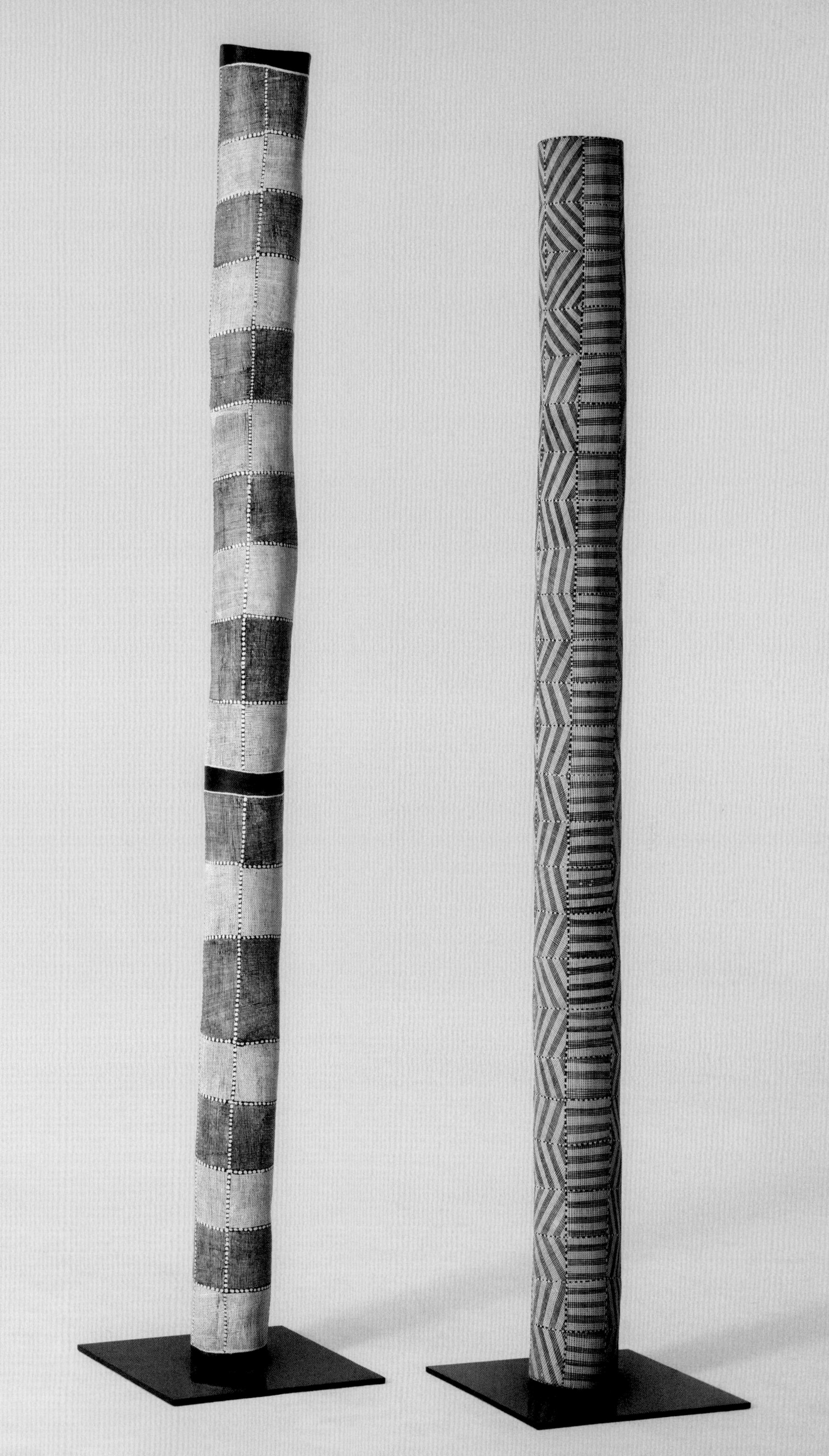

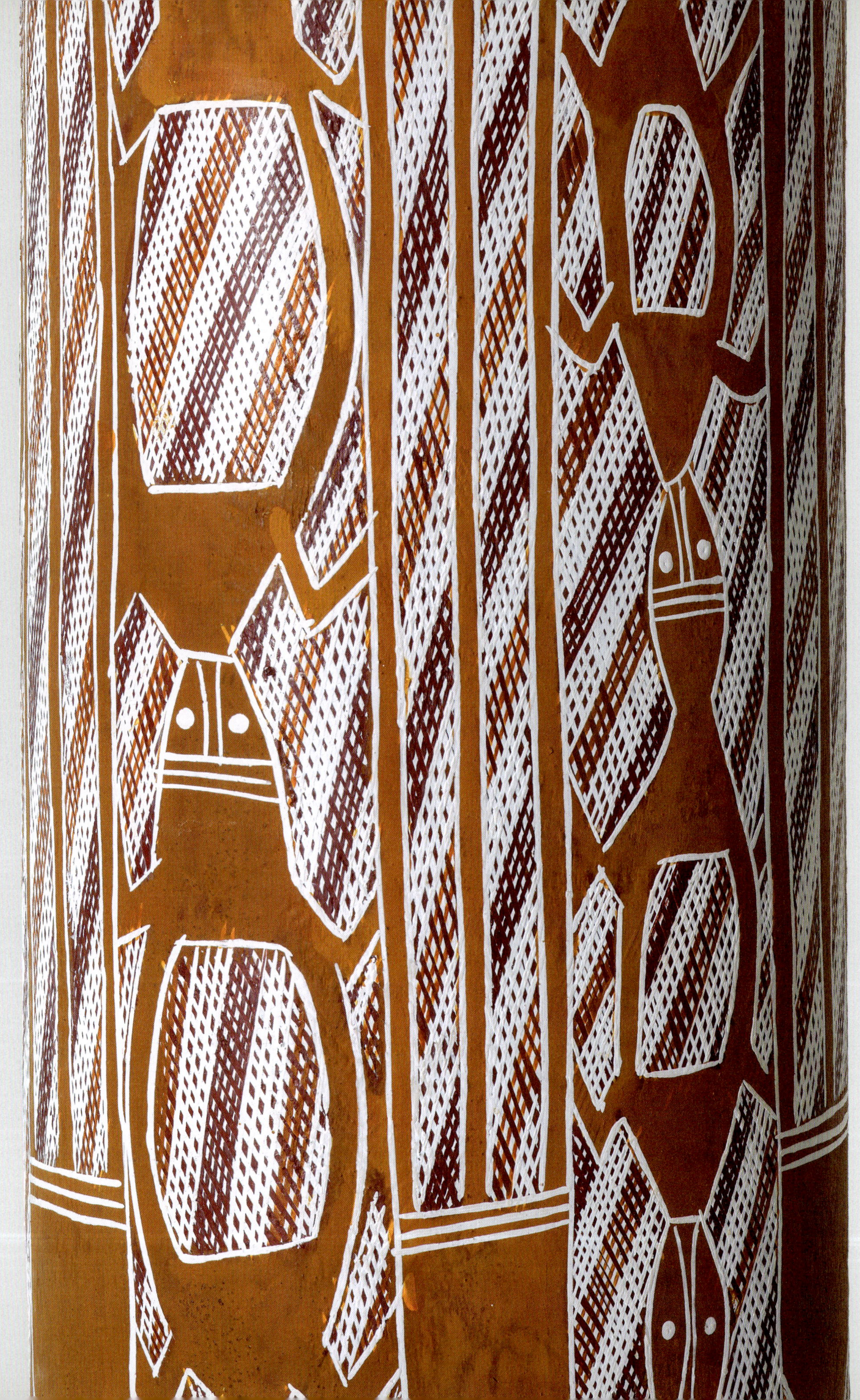

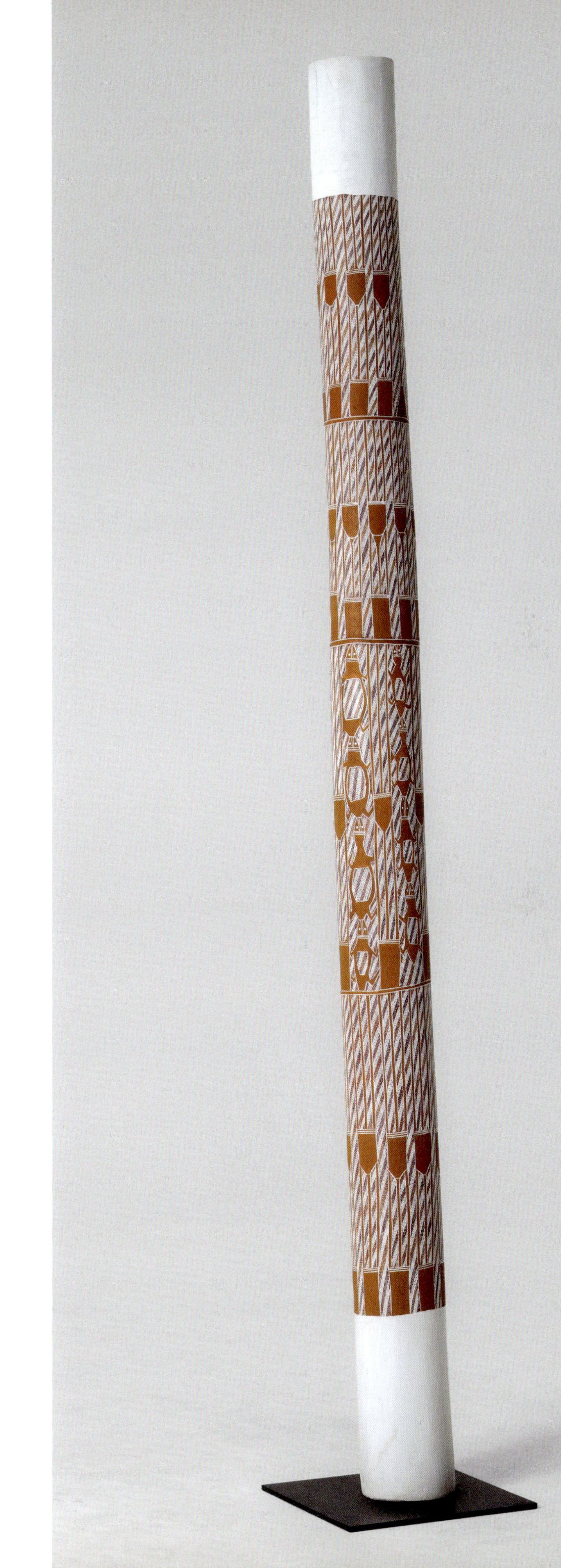

Fiona Jin-majinggal Mason, *Garnawarra (Frog) and Jima Jima (Waterlilly)*, 2017. Earth pigments on wood, 108 in. (274.3 cm)

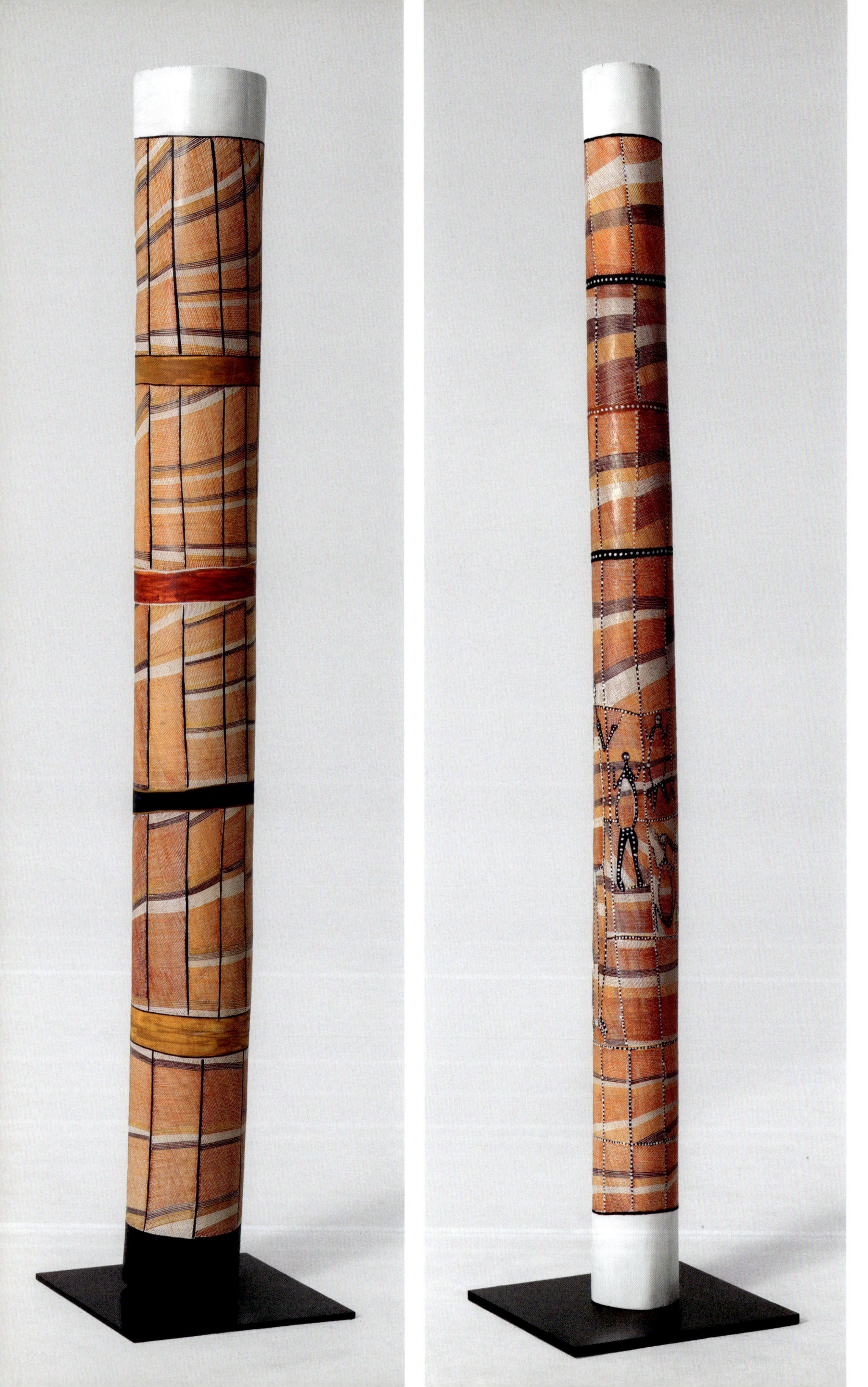

John Mawurndjul, *Lorrkkon*, 2009. Earth pigments on wood, 77¼ in. (196 cm)

Kay Lindjuwanga and John Mawurndjul, *Mimih Spirit at Milmingkan*, 2017. Earth pigments on wood, 86¼ in. (219 cm)

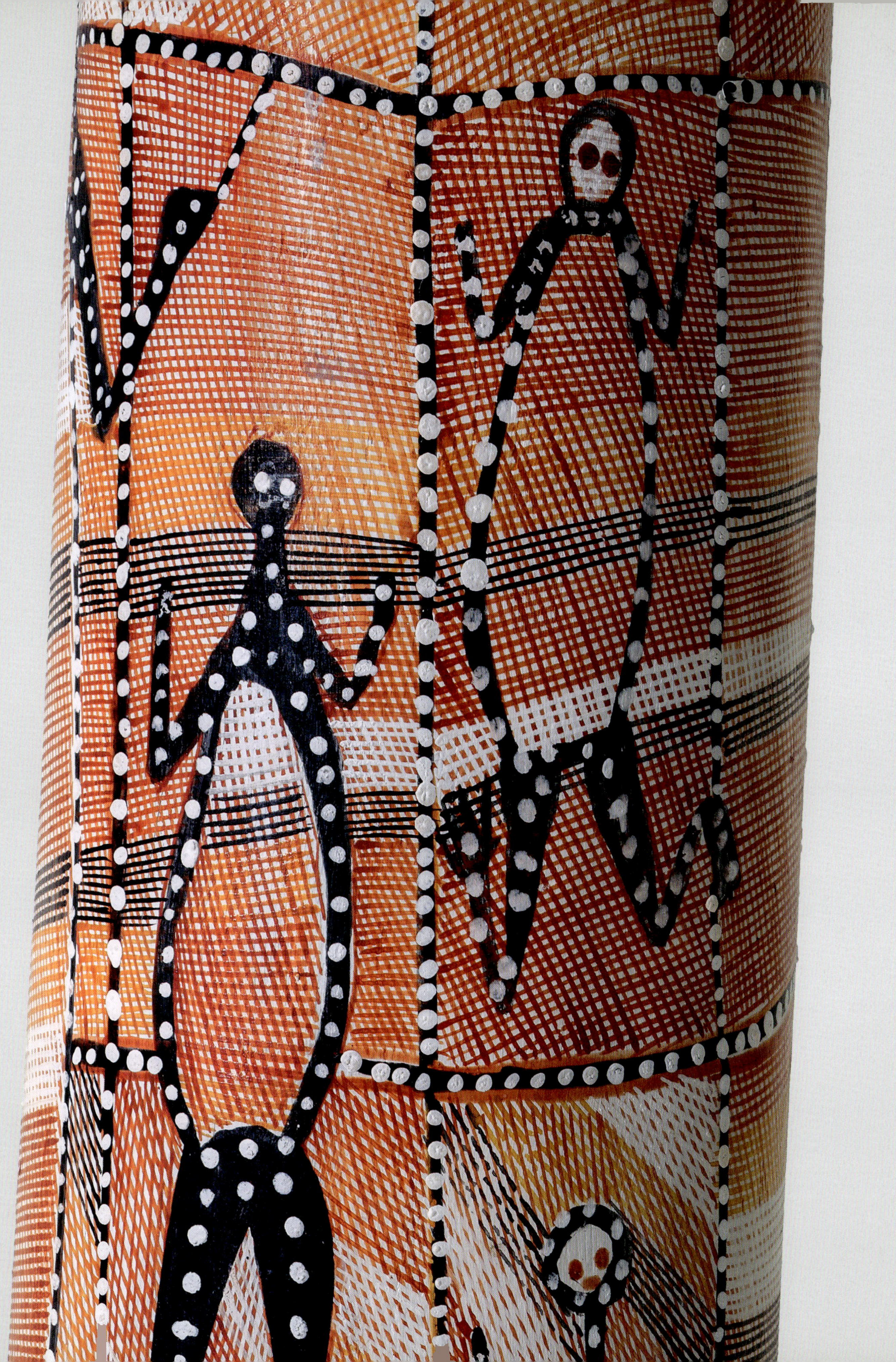

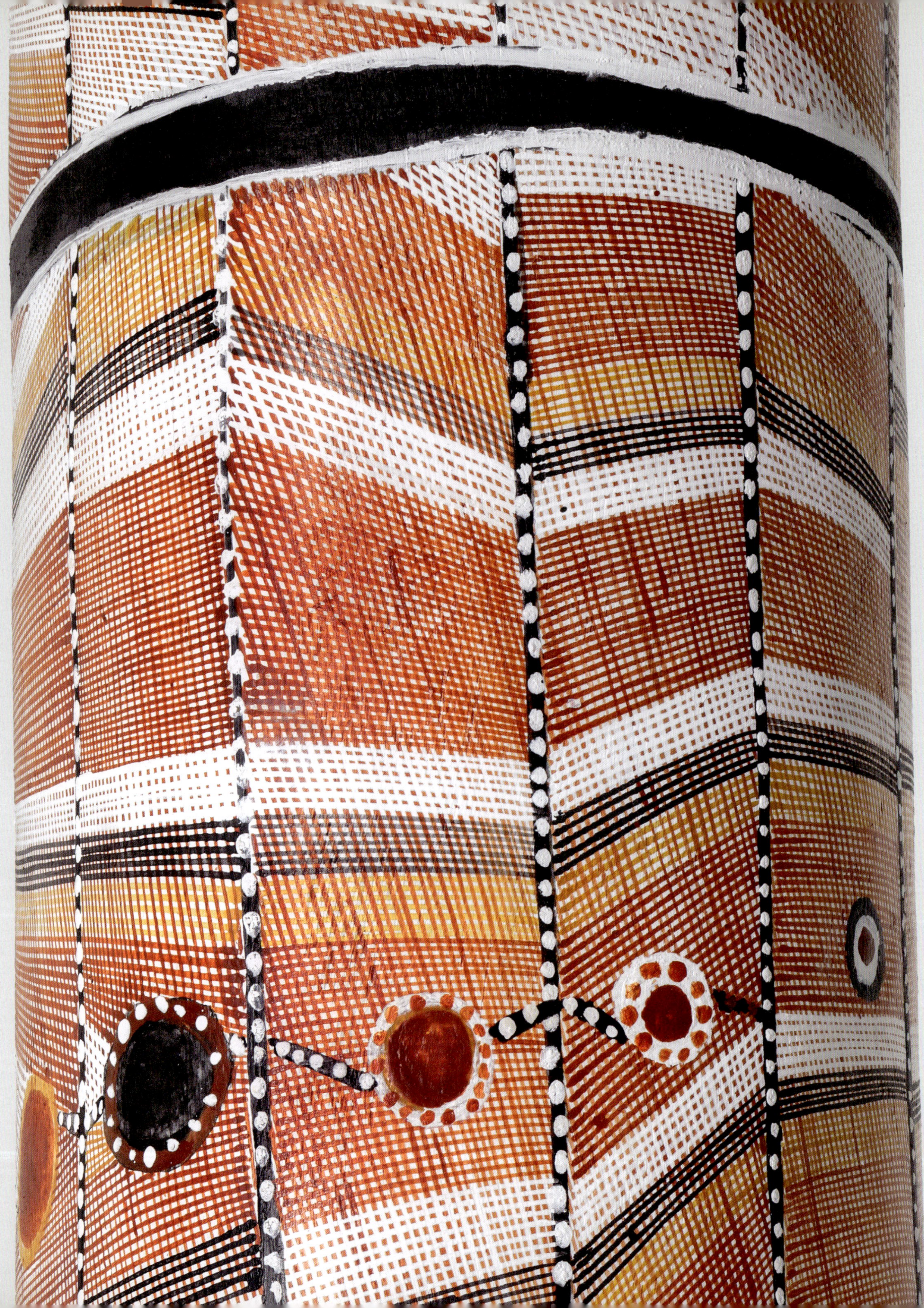

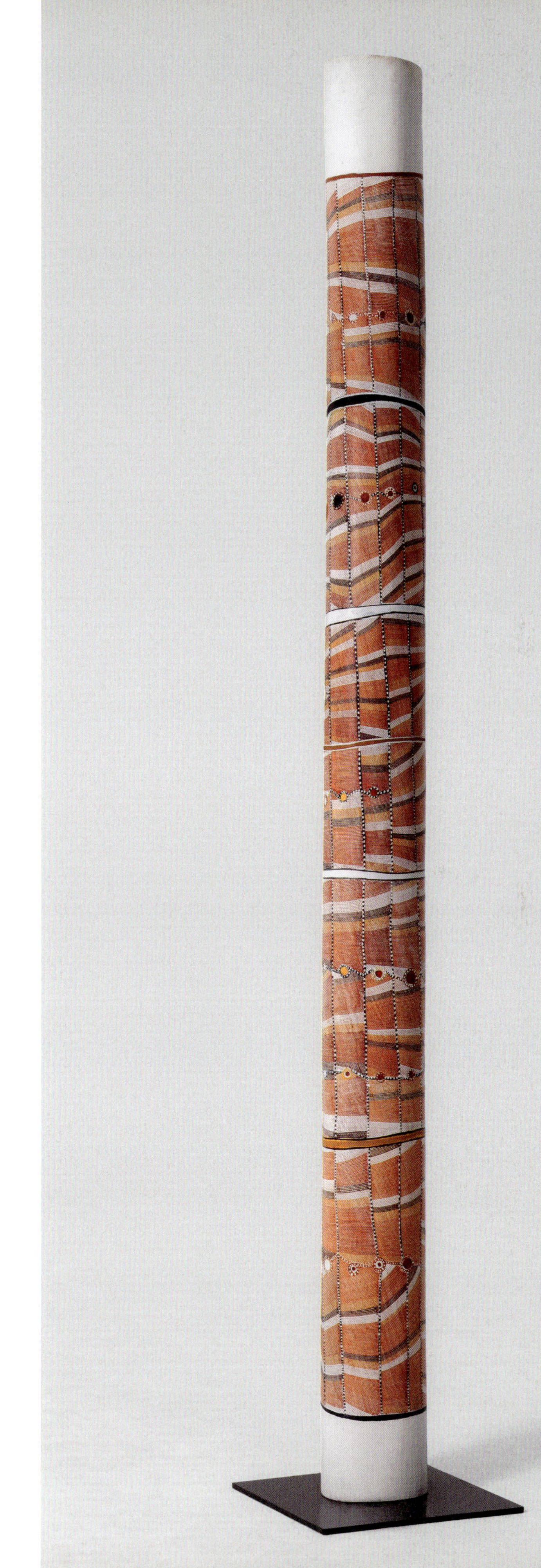

John Mawurndjul, *Mardayin Design at Dilebang*, 2017.
Earth pigments on wood, 101⅜ in. (259 cm)

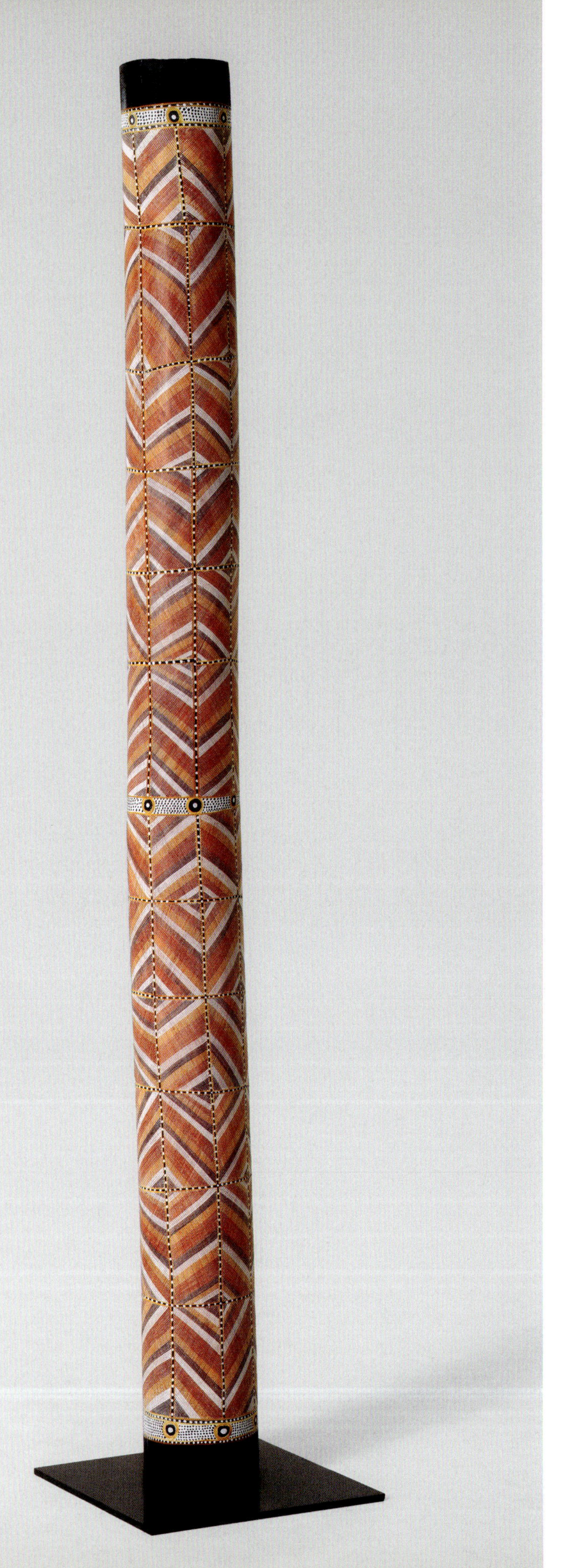

Ivan Namirrkki, *Wubarr (A Ceremony)*, 2017. Earth pigments on wood, 82⅝ in. (210 cm)

Opposite:
Ivan Namirrkki, *Morak (A Ceremony)*, 2017. Earth pigments, feathers and wax on wood, 85⅜ in. (217 cm)

Ivan Namirrkki, *Nayungki Namomoyak* (The First People, The Earliest Ancestors), 2017. Earth pigments, feathers and wax on wood, 96 in. (244 cm)

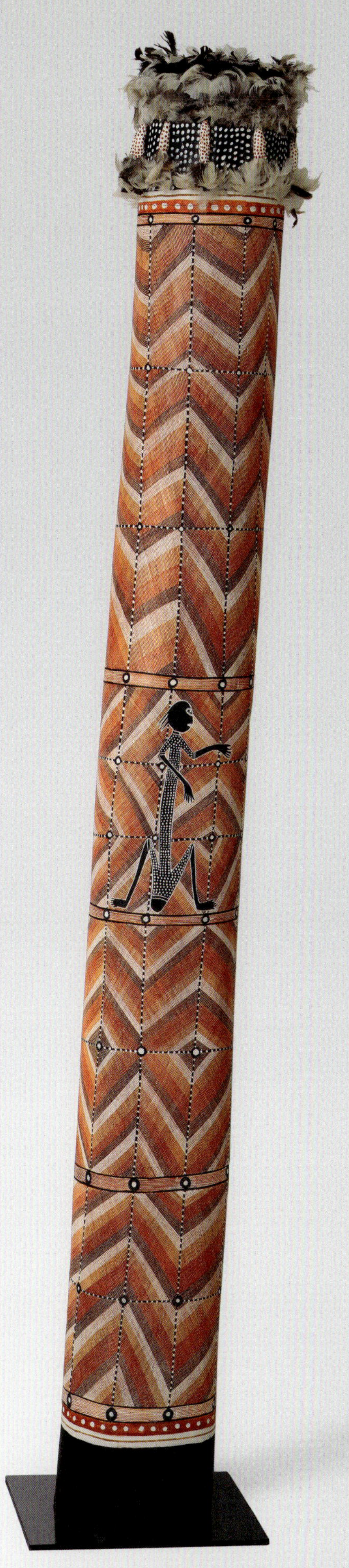

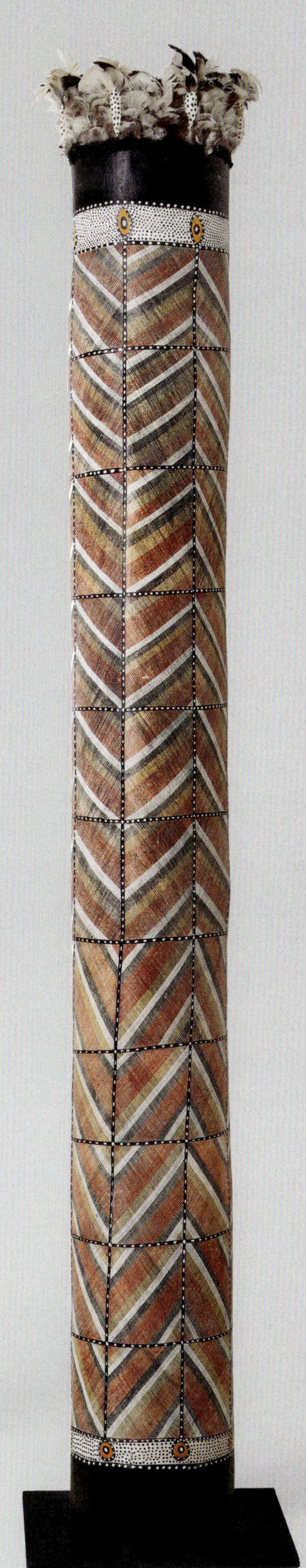

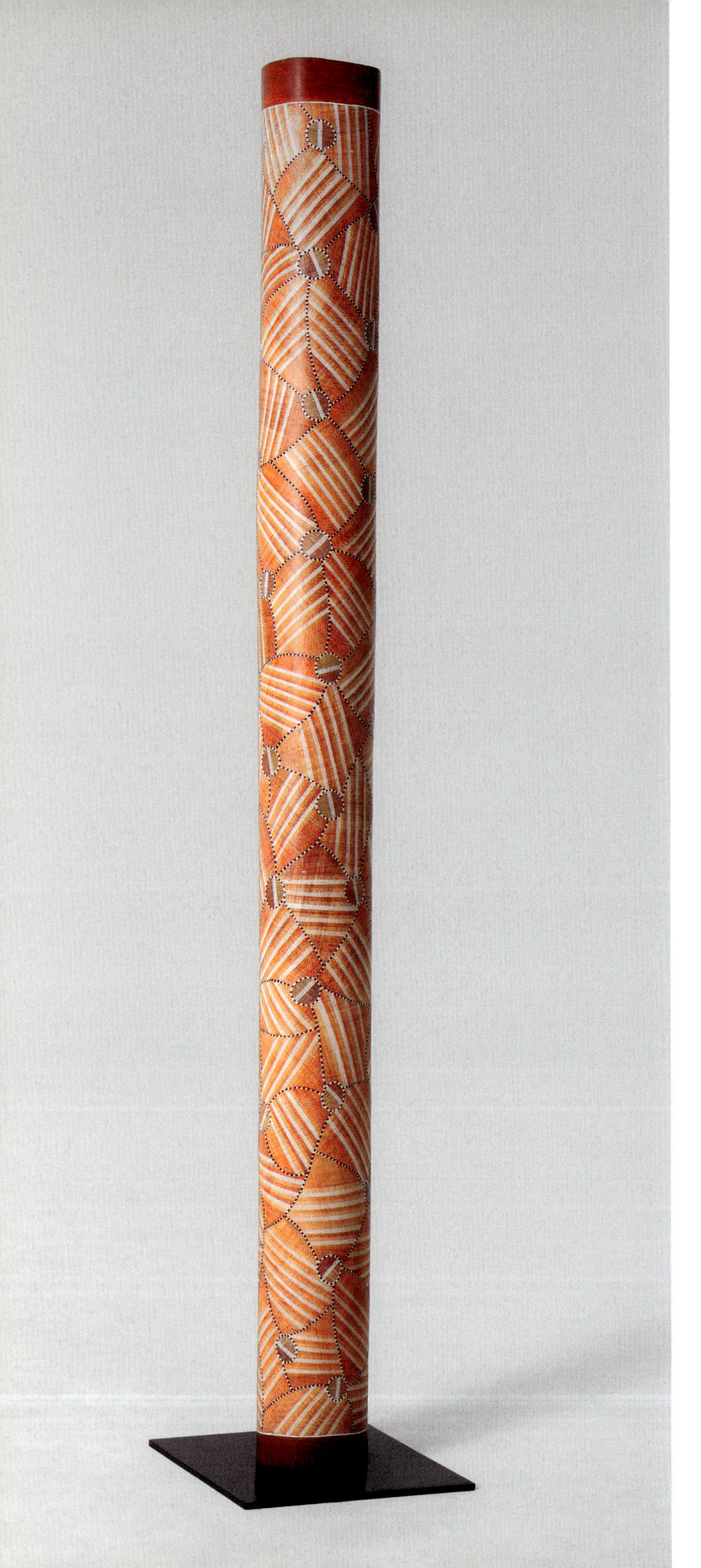

Samuel Namunjdja, *Kunkurra (The Wind)*, 2017.
Earth pigments on wood, 87 in. (221 cm)

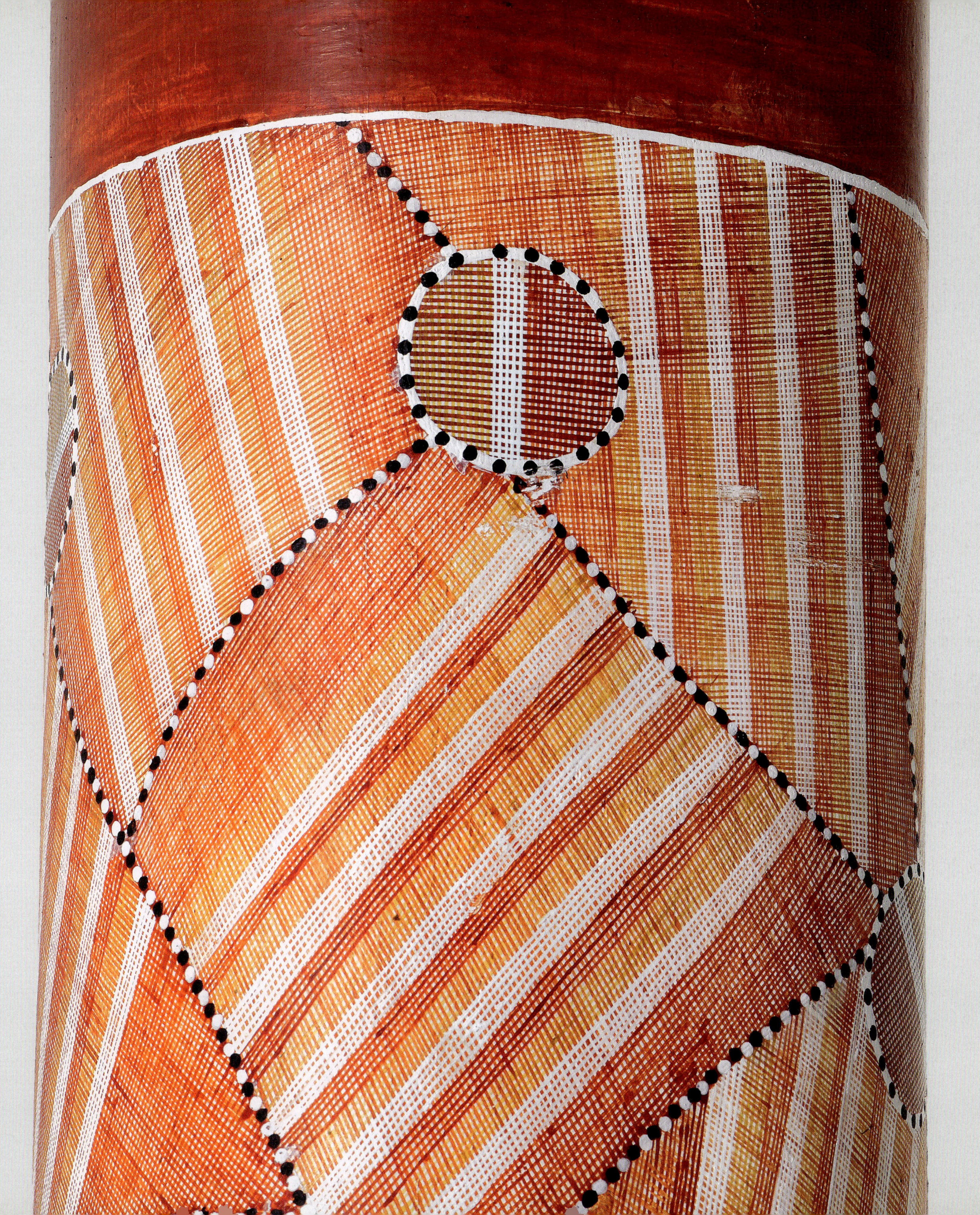

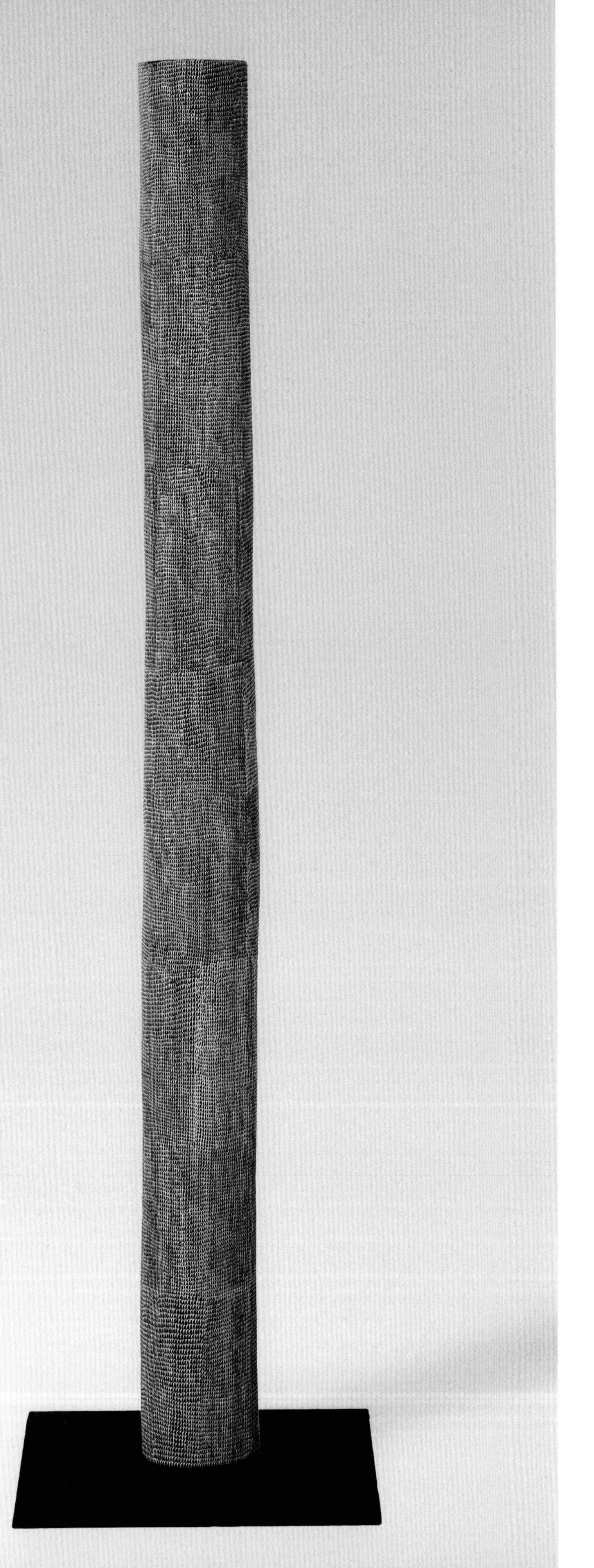

Owen Yalandja, *Ngalkodjek Yawkyawk*, 2017. Earth pigments on wood, 61⅞ in. (157.5 cm)

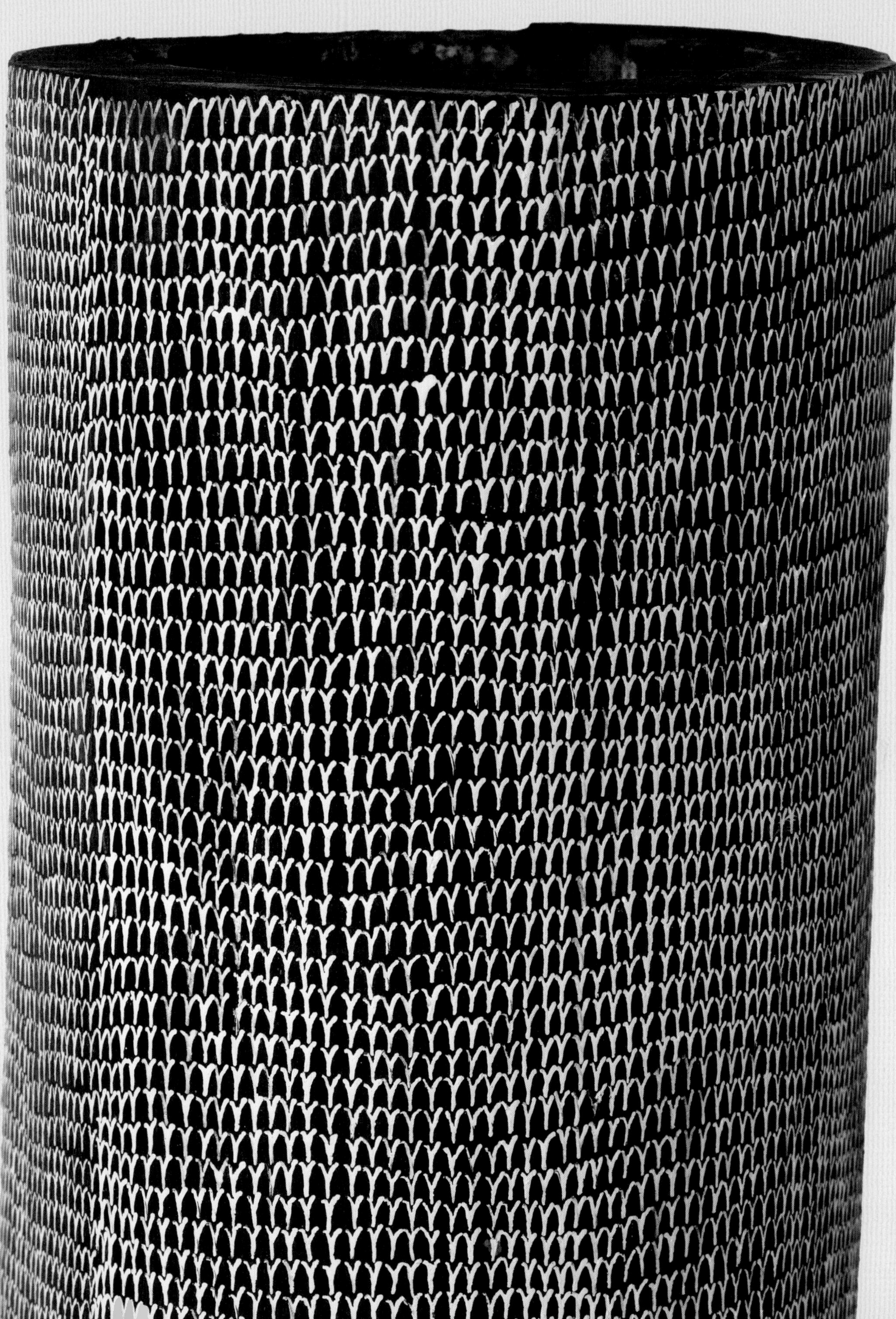

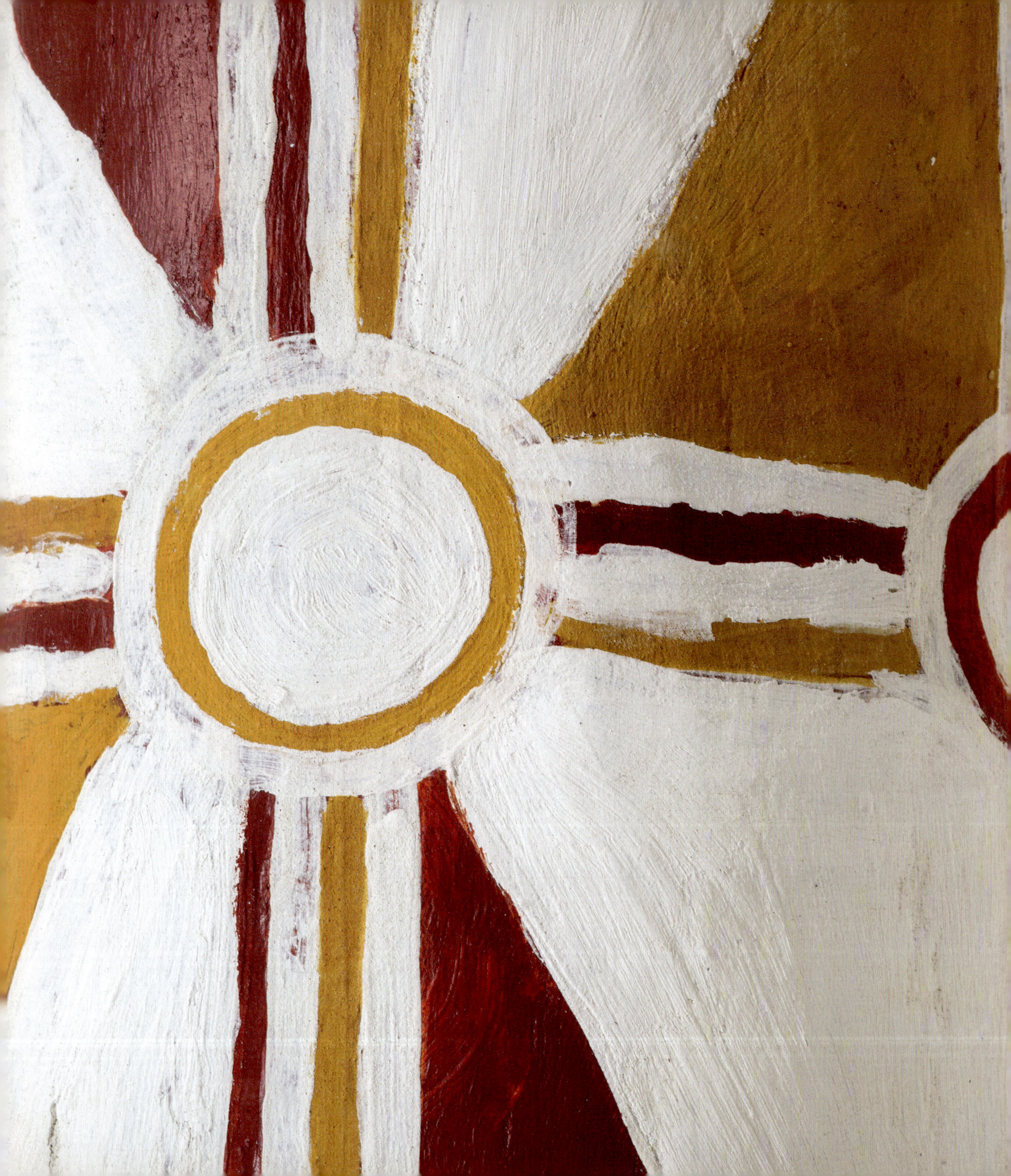

MILINGIMBI

Nicky Djawutjawuku
Helen Ganalmirriwuy
Mandy Batjula Gaykamuŋu
Jocelyn Gumirrmirr
Helen Milminydjarrk
Margaret Rarru

Margaret Rarru, *Garrawurra Body Paint Design* (detail), 2016 (see p. 101)

Garrawurra Ḏupun

Louise Hamby

Memorial poles (known as hollow logs) from Yurrwi (Milingimbi) play an important role in the reconciliation of outsiders with people from Milingimbi and forming relationships between people today. This circumstance has developed from their role in the ancestral past, not only in Yurrwi but also in other locations in Arnhem Land. The memorial poles from Yurrwi that are presented in *The Inside World* are a group that honors and recognizes the Garrawurra family of the Liyagawumirr clan. This clan group is from coastal country connected with the ancestral Djan'kawu Sisters who traveled from the east giving people their language, ceremony, kinship, and designs. The Garrawurras were given the distinctive striped body design composed of three colours: red, white, and yellow. Kinship or *gurrutu* links me, the artists and the works to the stories that the hollow logs tell, from their naming, and their ownership, to the changing role of women in the community.

NAMING

As with many material culture objects in Arnhem Land the sculptural pieces in this exhibition are known by many different names. In English they are known as hollow logs, hollow-log coffins, burial coffins and memorial poles. The same is true in the different languages from Arnhem Land. The American William Lloyd Warner was the first anthropologist working at Milingimbi to name these items in Yolŋu language: "The log of each moiety has a different name. The Dua call theirs dai-mer-i, and the Yiritja, char-lum-bu."[1] Ian Keen reiterates these names for hollow logs at Milingimbi seventy years later in their contemporary spellings, *daymirri* and *djaḻumbu*.[2] Some refer to the hollow logs as *lorrkkon*, particularly west of Milingimbi.[3] To the east many use the term *ḻarrakitj* for a decorated hollow log.[4] In the 1970s Ads Borsboom referred to them as *doban*, "the bones are kept in dillybags for years until the Doban ceremony when they are broken up and put in a hollow log called doban."[5] A current spelling for *doban* is *ḏupun*.[6] The Garrawurra people at Yurrwi call the poles *ḏupun* or hollow logs.[7]

HISTORY ASSOCIATED WITH GARRAWURRA PEOPLE

The ceremonies surrounding *ḏupun* are intimately linked not only with mortuary customs but with the creator ancestors. Howard Morphy elegantly describes this process and connection: "It was a ritual to celebrate the final separation of the soul from the body and its return to the spirit world, but it was also a process of reaffirming the ancestral connections that were manifest in the person's life."[8]

Yolŋu believe that in the past hollow logs had the capacity to perform actions and make changes in the lives of people. For example a hollow log created Lake Evella,[9] and the country around it is associated with the hollow log and the ancestor Murayana in ancestral times.[10] These important items are also intimately connected with the creator ancestors known as the Djan'kawu Sisters. These two sisters traveled from the east carrying sacred objects with them in their canoe, creating people and features of the landscape. At one point their canoe turned into a hollow log.[11] The Sisters traveled to Garrawurra country starting at Dhambala on the southern end of Galiwin'ku (Elcho Island). They stopped near Howard Island and created a number of waterholes at Garriyak on the mainland of Australia between Elcho Island and Howard Island.[12] Garriyak and Djiliwirri (two outstations with no current residents) were visited by many Garrawurra and Gupapuyŋu people in 2004 and 2005. "The importance of Garriyak is that it is the place at the end of the Sisters' travel by canoe (Guluwurru) where their sacred *Rangga* were stolen by men (and to this day it is men who predominate in sacred ceremonies and who hold the most sacred items)."[13]

Since the influx of explorers, anthropologists, and missionaries to Yurrwi, a written history of the use of hollow logs has developed. Amy Corfield, Goulburn Island missionary, records the following in her diary:

> October 26, Saturday, 1916
> Men busy working in the morning and then went to Illalari to take pictures of a corroboree in the afternoon. I stayed here with the children. The ceremony was the putting of bones in a bamboo of an old man who was buried in a tree 12 months ago.[14]

Sir Hubert Wilkins was the first to record seeing one on the mainland near the Goyder River:

> A wooden platform on which a body had been placed was still standing about twenty yards from where a hollow tree, about ten inches in diameter and eight feet high, was placed on end in the ground. About two feet from the top two rings had been cut round the post and two holes an inch in diameter were cut and placed to face north-east and south-west. A parcel of bones wrapped in paper-bark was to be seen in the hollow log.[15]

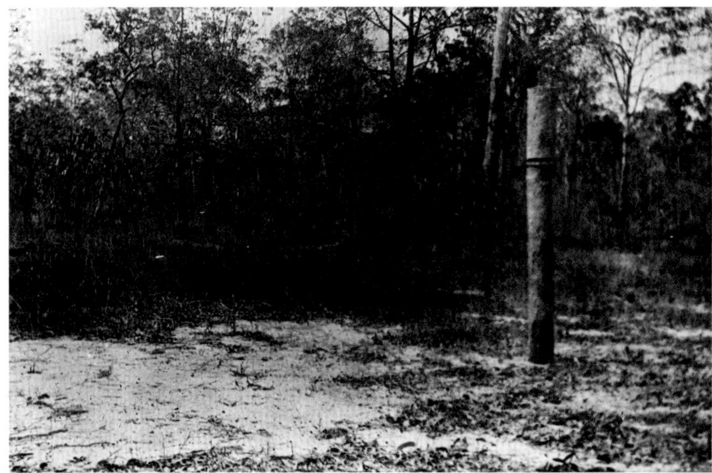

Fig. 1. A hollow-log coffin near the Goyder River, central Arnhem Land, 1924. Photograph by George Hubert Wilkins. The Ohio State University, Byrd Polar and Climate Research Center Archival Program, Sir George Hubert Wilkins Papers

A photograph that Wilkins took of this hollow log is in the Byrd Polar Research Center at Ohio State University. It is difficult to ascertain the clan identity of the hollow log, as the painting on it is unclear in the photograph (Fig. 1).[16] A few years later Lloyd Warner described the incised lines typical of these early hollow logs. "A foot below the 'eyes' a band a half-inch wide is incised around the cylinder to represent the cicatrice [scarring] on a native man or woman's body."[17] Wilkins did not collect this log, but he was the first to collect a *yiḏaki* (didjeridu), a close relative to the hollow log but different in purpose, at Milingimbi in December 1924. It is now in the British Museum in London, unfortunately sawed into two pieces.[18]

Lloyd Warner, who worked at Milingimbi between 1927 and 1929, also collected *yiḏaki* and the first hollow-log coffin from Milingimbi, now in the National Museum of Australia (Fig. 2).[19] The late Dr. J. N. Gumbula viewed this log in July 2014. He thought it could possibly have been made for Burinjiŋu, the father of the late Laurie Baymarrwaŋa from Murrunga Island, east of Milingimbi. The top projections from the pole he identified as being barracuda and the log could have been made for a ceremony performed for Warner. Jack Roy (b. 1971), a Malarra artist, today makes hollow logs with the same type of top projections as this older one. Around the same time as Warner was working in Milingimbi, Herbert Read, a missionary at Goulburn, photographed a man between two hollow logs.

This early documentation sets the scene for the development of an art market and subsequent art center at Milingimbi. The arrival of the missionary Edgar Wells in 1949 began the belief among outsiders that Milingimbi was a center where Aboriginal art flourished. During Wells' decade of service art was promoted. He set a path for interested anthropologists and collectors who followed him, including Ronald and Katherine Berndt, Karel Kupka and Ed Ruhe.[20] The mission appointed David Morgan as art and craft advisor in 1972. Before that time Alan Fidock took this role with the first art shop underneath his house. After David Morgan, the position was held by Jurgen Groneberg during the mid-1970s. Djon Mundine came to this position at Milingimbi in 1979 and the title was changed to art adviser.[21] Susan Jenkins's discussion of the most famous installation of hollow logs, *The Aboriginal Memorial* (p. 37), brings them into the realm of the art centre.[22] This collection has had the most publicity; it was put together in 1988 by Mundine for the Bicentennial celebration to commemorate Aboriginal people who had died since the arrival of British colonists. It includes logs by two Garrawurra artists, Tony Dhanyala (1935–2004) and Mick Daypurryun 2 (1929–1994).

GARRAWURRA KINSHIP

The Garrawurra *ḏupun* in *The Inside World* are linked through kinship and ancestral knowledge to a long line of artistic Garrawurra people. Nupurra Garrawurra and his brother Madaŋgala, were the fathers of many of the artists both in the past and the present ones at Yurrwi. Nupurra was identified by the Garrawurra sisters as a young man in a photograph with William Lloyd Warner in 1928. In more recent times the late Yolŋu artists Mickey Durrŋ (1940–2006) and his brother Tony Dhanyala, Garrawurra men of the Liyagawumirr clan, were the best-known artists using classic Garrawurra designs that

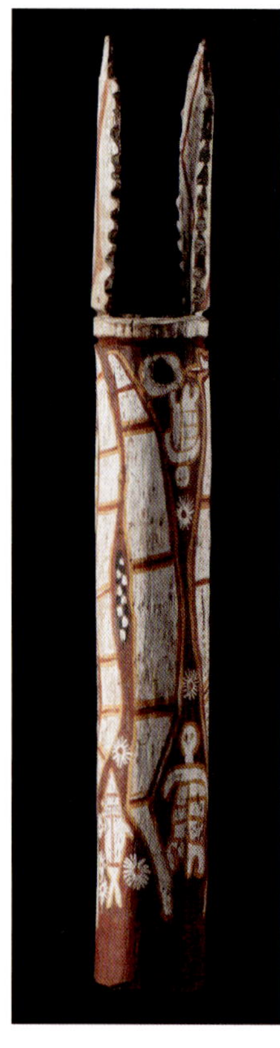

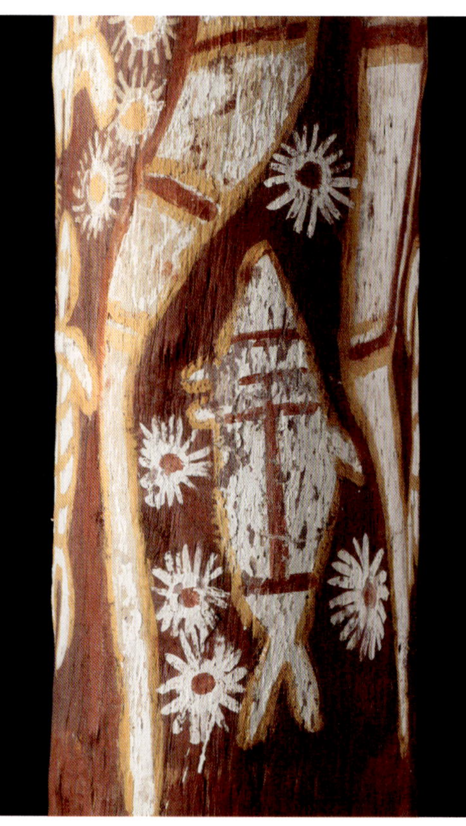

Fig. 2. Hollow-log coffin collected by William Lloyd Warner at Milingimbi, c. 1927–9. Earth pigments on wood, 69 11/16 x 9 7/16 x 9 7/16 (177 x 24 x 24 cm). National Museum of Australia, Canberra

include bush turkey and the classic body-painting striped design known as kingfisher. These are found on the logs in the exhibition. Their homeland was Laŋarra on Howard Island but they lived and died at Yurrwi.

My association is with the current generation of Garrawurras at Yurrwi, although some spend much of their time at Laŋarra. Through my adopted *yapa* (sister), Ruth Nalmakarra Garrawurra (b. 1954), I have been introduced to the family. Nalmakarra's father was Madaŋgala, but she was raised by Durrŋ's father, Nupurra, after the death of her father. She and her sisters are strong women who have been given the authority to paint their ancestral stories. Traditionally the role of painter has been the domain of men. The authority was given to Nalmakarra and her sisters by her late brother Durrŋ.[23] When discussing the poles at Milingimbi with a group of women, Joyce Naliyabu (1956–2017) told me information that she had learned from talking to the Garrawurra women. "They put their own body painting, their own totems. But they should not paint sacred ones unless they

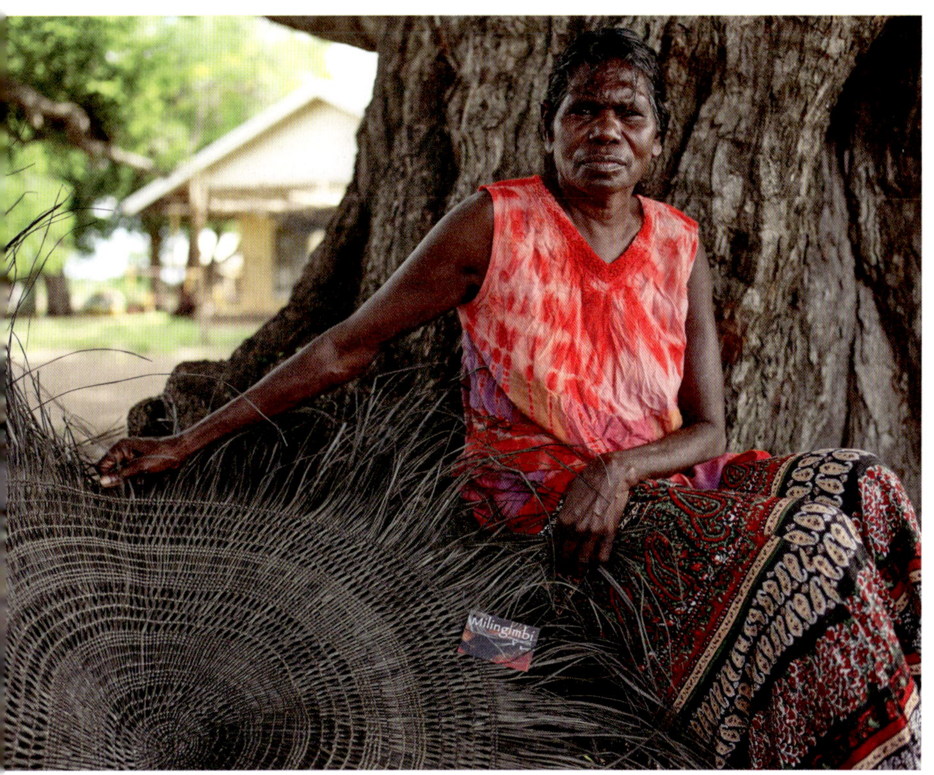

Fig. 3. Helen Ganalmirriwuy with her woven artwork at Yurrwi (Milingimbi), 2018. Photograph by Ben Ward

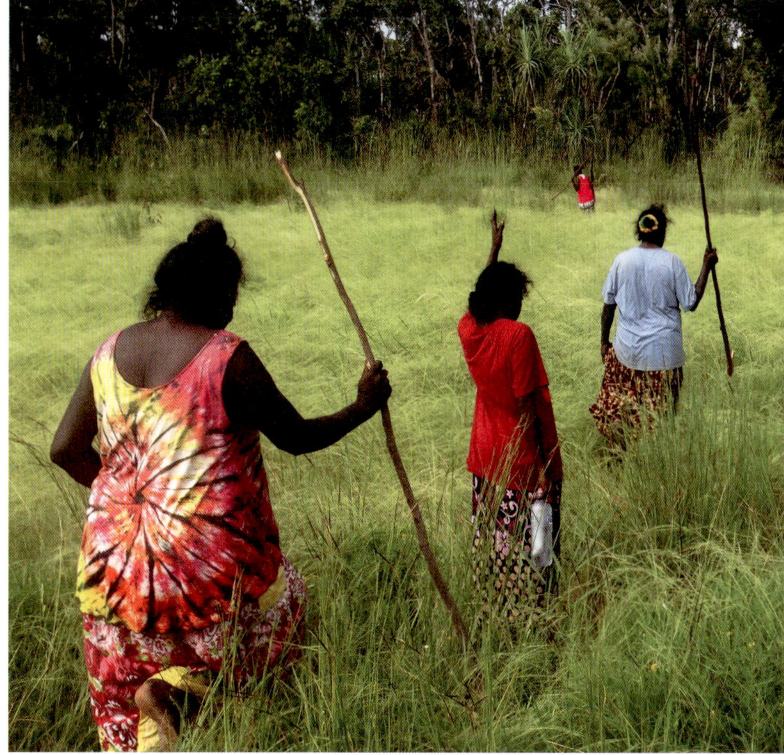

Fig. 4. Margaret Rarru, Priscilla Gapirriwuy and Mandy Batjula Gaykamuŋu setting out to harvest *gunga* (pandanus) at Yurrwi (Milingimbi), 2017. Photograph by Rosita Holmes

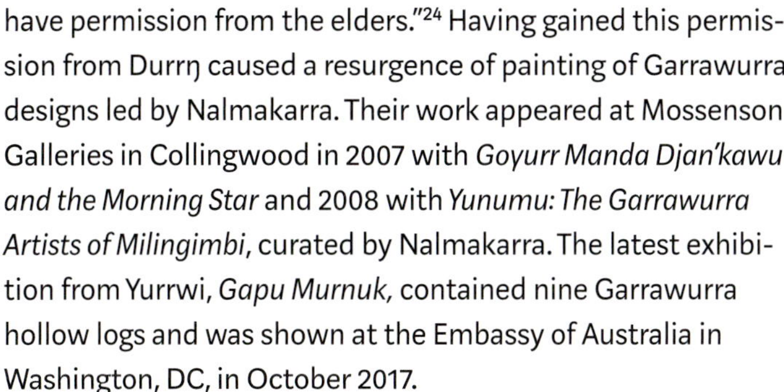

have permission from the elders."[24] Having gained this permission from Durrŋ caused a resurgence of painting of Garrawurra designs led by Nalmakarra. Their work appeared at Mossenson Galleries in Collingwood in 2007 with *Goyurr Manda Djan'kawu and the Morning Star* and 2008 with *Yunumu: The Garrawurra Artists of Milingimbi*, curated by Nalmakarra. The latest exhibition from Yurrwi, *Gapu Murnuk,* contained nine Garrawurra hollow logs and was shown at the Embassy of Australia in Washington, DC, in October 2017.

Six related Garrawurra artists feature in the exhibition *The Inside World*. Although Nalmakarra does not have work in this exhibition I have connected with the artists through her. All are women except for Robert (Nicky) Djawutjawuku (b. 1971), son of Durrŋ. Nalmakarra calls him *gurruŋ* (son-in-law): "He is the right person to paint. He is Garrawurra."[25] He is married to the daughter of the Garrawurra artist Helen Milminydjarrk (b. 1959), Mandy Batjula Gaykaymaŋu (b. 1980) also one of the artists. Milminydjarrk is the younger sister of Nalmakarra. Helen Ganalmirriwuy (b. 1955) is the younger sister of Margaret Rarru (b. 1940) (Figs. 3, 4). Jocelyn Gumirrmirr (b. 1974) is the daughter of the late Jeffery Walkundjawuy, Nalmakarra's youngest brother. She has also inherited rights to paint from him.

THE ART

Having younger artists in the family continues the tradition but as Henry Skerritt notes, "Not only has this kept the designs strong within the Liyagawumirr, but it has provided an important economic and cultural outlet at Milingimbi."[26] In my opinion Garrawurra women have always been "strong" in many ways including their fiber-art practice. The right to do this work and carry cultural knowledge to the outside world did not need the sanction of men nor did they need to be told the stories of the Djan'kawu Sisters. This was manifest in the artwork of their baskets, mats, and string bags. The materials of the *ḏupun*—the *gaḏayka* stringybark *(Eucalyptus tetradonta)* and the ochres, *ratjpa, miku, buthalak*, were not new. Women used to dig and search for these to paint their twined baskets and knew their significance. For both their fiber work and their poles they employ the same

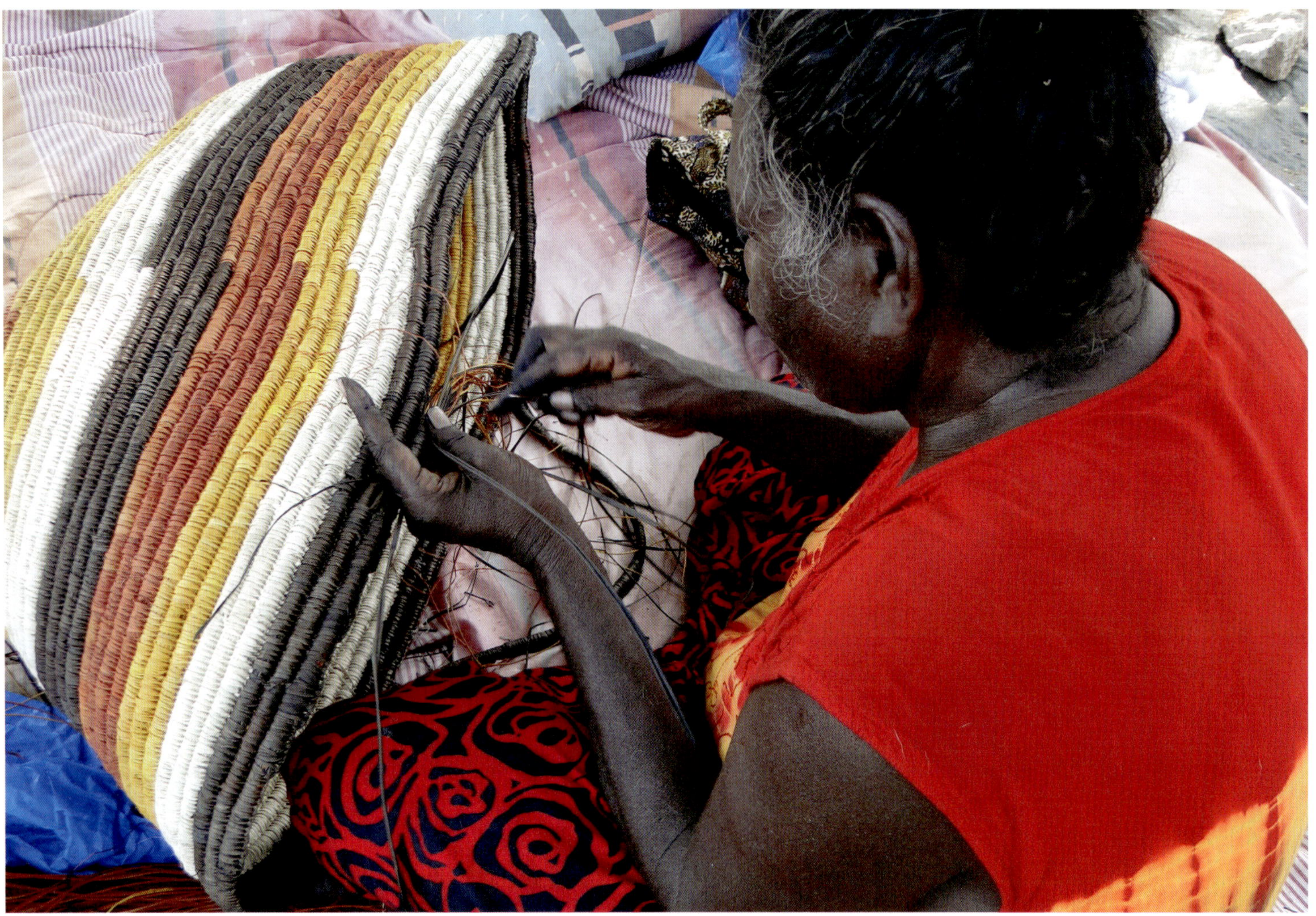

Fig 5. Margaret Rarru working on a coil *bathi* (basket) at the Milingimbi Art and Culture center, 2016. Photograph by Zanette Kahler

color palette and the same stripes (Figs. 5, 6) In Skerritt's interview in 2009 with Nalmakarra she said, "There are different ways of painting and different patterns, but they mean the same thing. We know the stories, so we know which ones to chose."[27]

In August 2017 the current manager of Milingimbi Art and Culture center, Chris Durkin, and I were discussing the preparation of poles with many of the Garrawurra women including Milminydjarrk, Ganalmirriwuy, Rarru, and Batjula, as they and other women were working on their latest fiber commission for Koskela, an Australian object and furniture design company in Sydney. Durkin recounted how he had tried to get the men motivated to go out and collect *gaḏayka* and they responded with all the things they needed or wanted before that would happen. He went to the strong Garrawurra women with the same request. "That same afternoon they came back from the bush with these big *larrakitj* over their shoulders. They just went and got it straight away."[28] The rangers (with chainsaws) went out to Laŋarra with the women (with hand saws) to help them harvest logs. They also got ochre, *gunga* (pandanus), and dyes. Durkin reiterated the generosity of the women in their consistent working to make sure that the art center remained viable.

When asked about how and what they painted, Naliyabu translated, "Hollow logs—what they are going to paint. They talk about it first what designs. Then they paint it. The *miny'tji* (designs) that they paint the most often on the Garrawurra *ḏupun* are the body painting stripes or *djirriḏiḏi*." Westley and Westley note

> *Djirrididi* can express many things: the azure kingfisher bird, the shining rays of the sunrise; the shadows of the sunset; the sacred body designs worn at men's *Ngarra* and men's business ceremonies; or the stripes on the Two Sisters' bodies.[29]

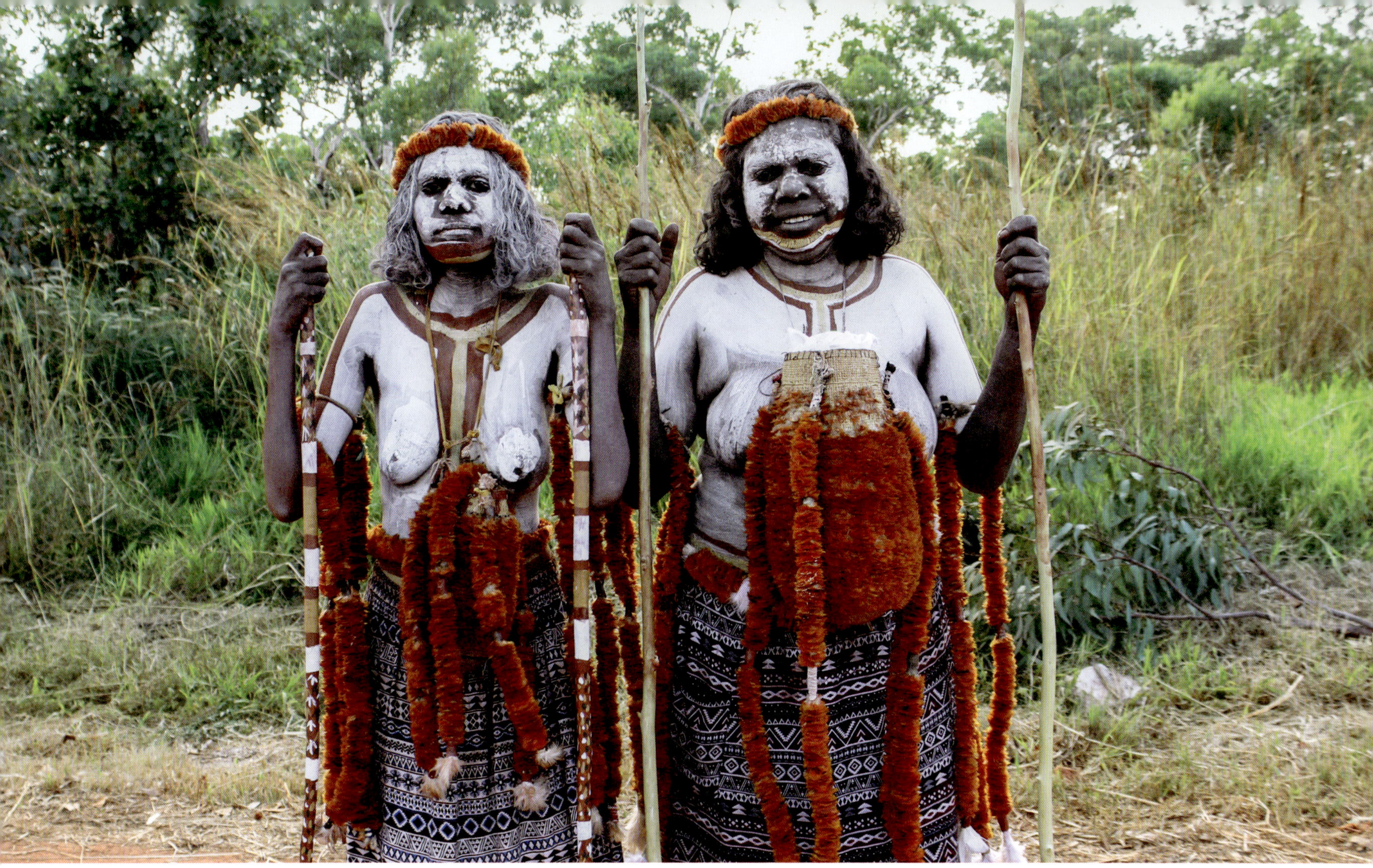

Fig. 6. Elena Ŋulumay and Marayetta Nulgurr Ŋawuy wearing *maḏayin mindirr* (sacred conical baskets) decorated with feathers for Djan'kawu *buŋgul* (ceremony) during *bäpurru* (funeral), Bodiya, 2018. Photograph by Rosita Holmes

All of the Garrawurra related artists use this design on their *ḏupun* to some extent. The majority of Margaret Rarru's works feature these Djan'kawu body-painting designs on the entire surface (pp. 100, 103). One is more complicated and includes the waterhole design as well as *djirriḏiḏi* (p. 101). Full horizontal stripes across the chest in a ceremony signifies the end of men's business.[30] Jocelyn Gumirrmirr's *ḏupun* has alternate blocks of five stripes with broad bands of *miku* (p. 102). *The miku* or reddish-brown ochre is associated with Garriyak.

The bush turkey, *buwaṯa,* design is described as a keyhole design in yellow and red surrounded by white, *gamunuŋu.* Milminydjarrk, Ganalmirriwuy and Djawutjawuku all use this design (p. 99). It is seen at the top and/or bottom of the *ḏupun* and the amount of white surrounding it varies. The most complex designs associated with the Djan'kawu Sisters are the waterholes found at Milminydjarrk at Garriyak (p. 97). Djawutjawuku uses this design, sometimes referred to as the Union Jack, of intersecting diagonal lines with a circle in the center. His *ḏupun* also contain *buwaṯa, and djirriḏiḏi.*

The Garrawurras are united in their cultural heritage from their ancestral creators, the Djan'kawu and their kinship through earlier members of their Liyagawumirr clan like Nupurra and Madaŋgala. This is manifest in their creative work today both in fiber and in the *ḏupun* represented in *The Inside World.* The women are strong and so is their story.

Mandy Batjula Gaykamuŋu, *Milminydjarrk at Garriyak (Sacred Waterholes)*, 2016. Earth pigments on wood, 63⅜ in. (161 cm)

Nicky Djawutjawuku, *Milminydjarrk at Garriyak (Sacred Waterholes)*, 2016. Earth pigments on wood, 62⅝ in. (159 cm)

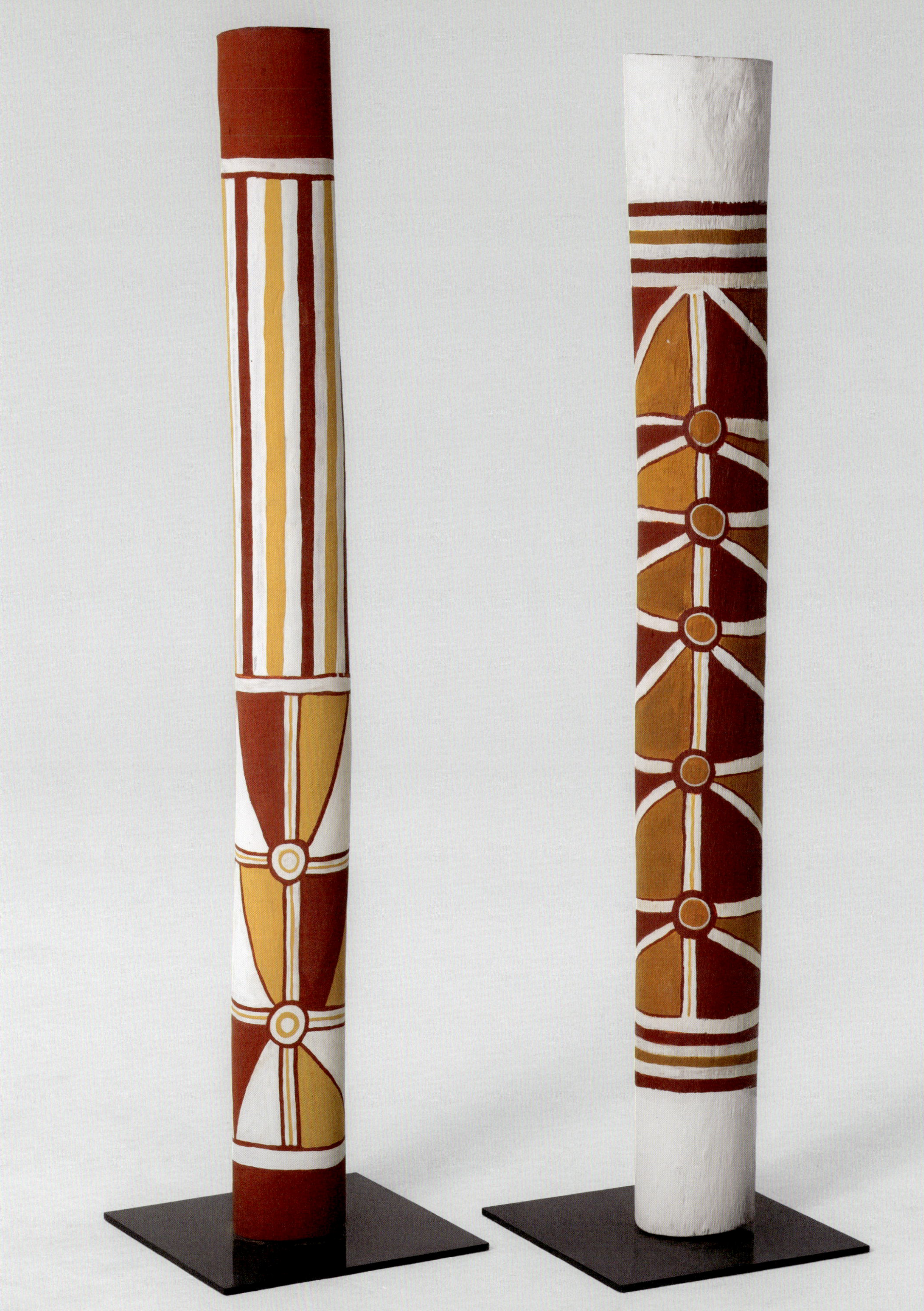

Nicky Djawutjawuku, *Garrawurra Body Paint Design*, 2016. Earth pigments on wood, 59⅞ in. (152 x 20 cm)

Helen Ganalmirriwuy, *Garrawurra Body Paint Design*, 2016. Earth pigments on wood, 77½ in. (197 cm)

Helen Milminydjarrk, *Garrawurra Body Paint Design*, 2016. Earth pigments on wood, 61⅛ in. (155 x 20 cm)

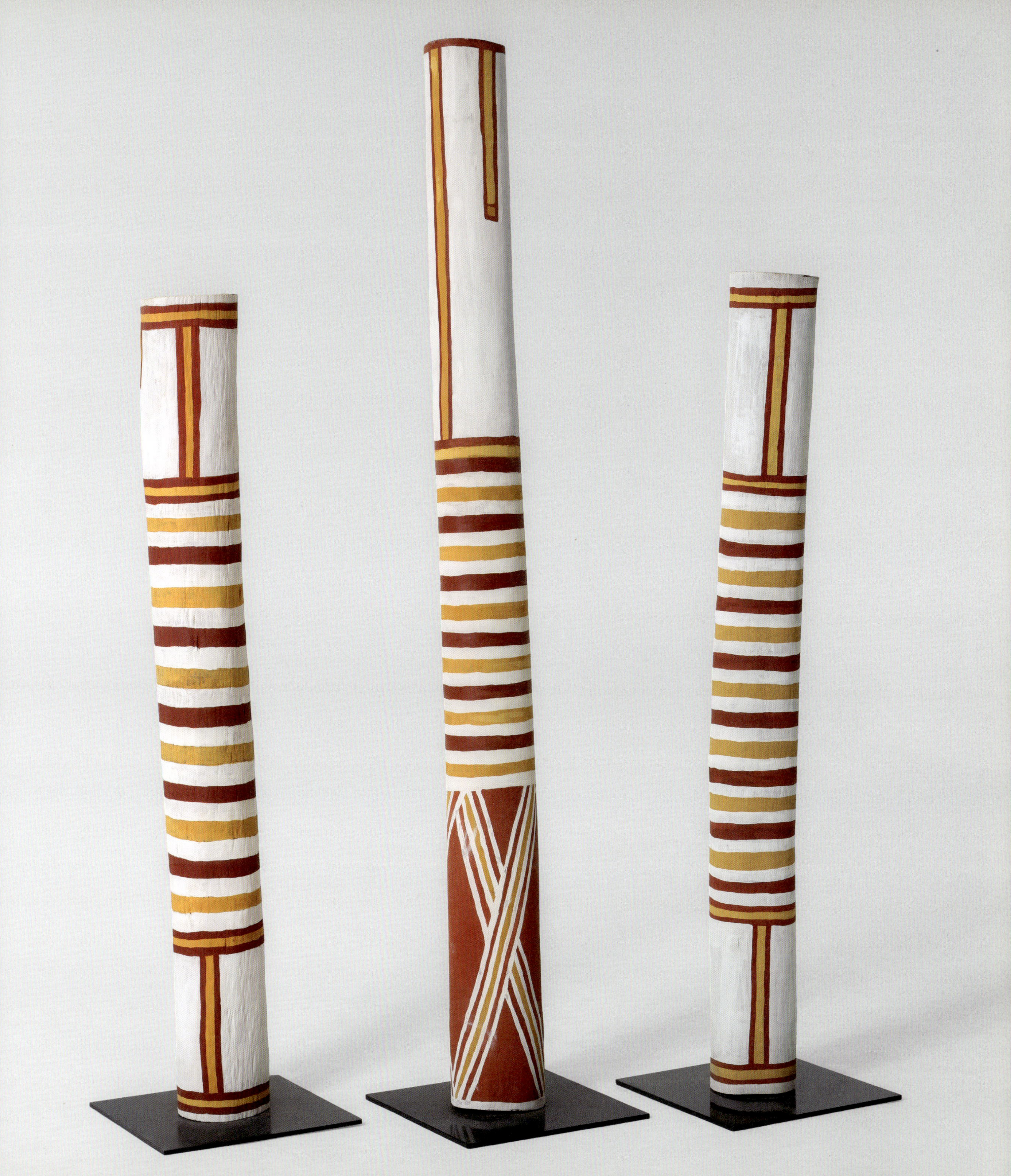

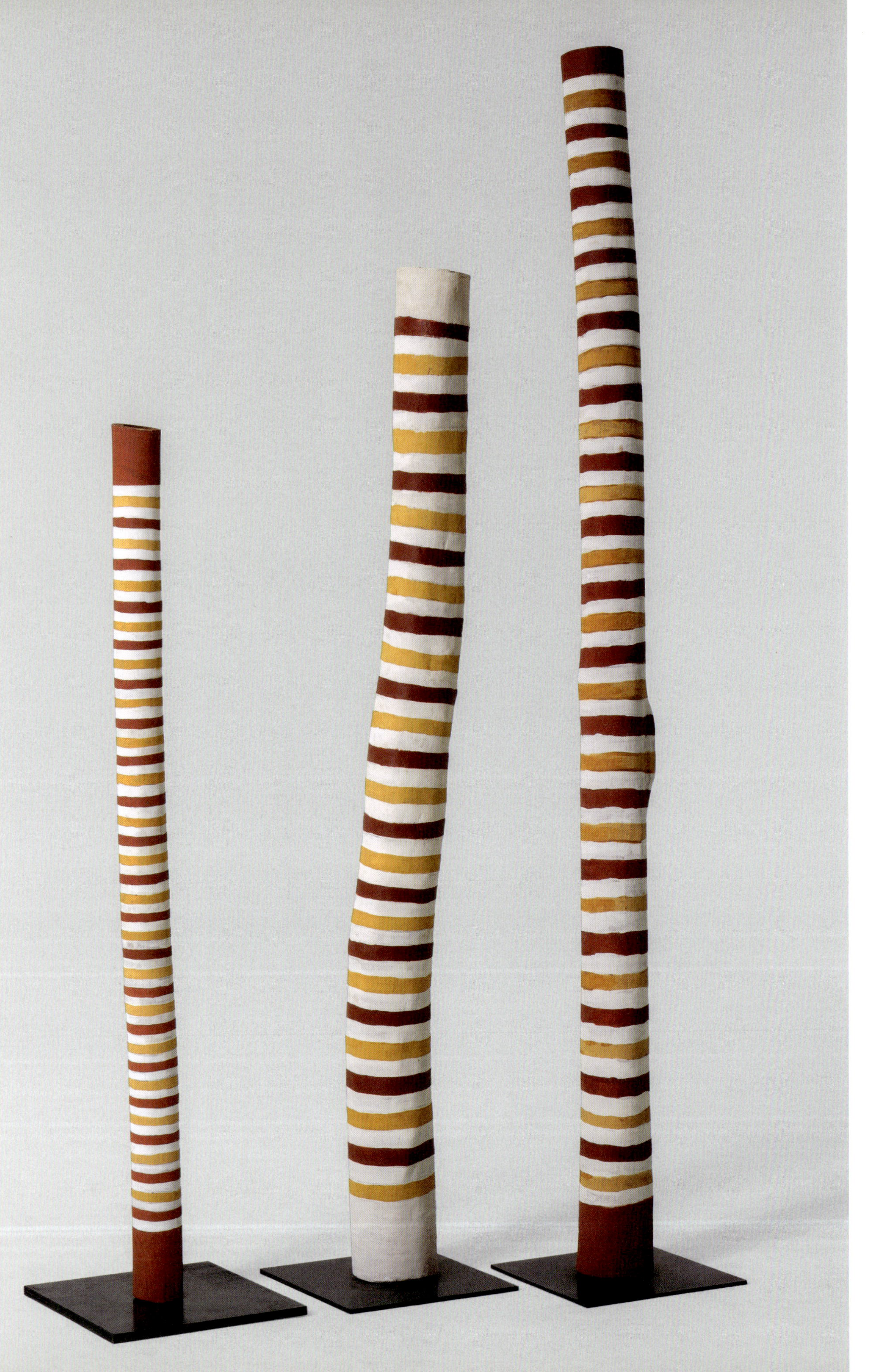

Opposite:
Nicky Djawutjawuku, *Garrawurra Body Paint Design*, 2016. Earth pigments on wood, 67⅜ in. (171 cm)

Margaret Rarru, *Garrawurra Body Paint Design*, 2016. Earth pigments on wood, 80⅜ in. (204 cm)

Helen Milminydjarrk, *Garrawurra Body Paint Design*, 2016. Earth pigments on wood, 98⅞ in. (251 cm)

Margaret Rarru, *Garrawurra Body Paint Design*, 2016. Earth pigments on wood, 139 in. (353 cm)

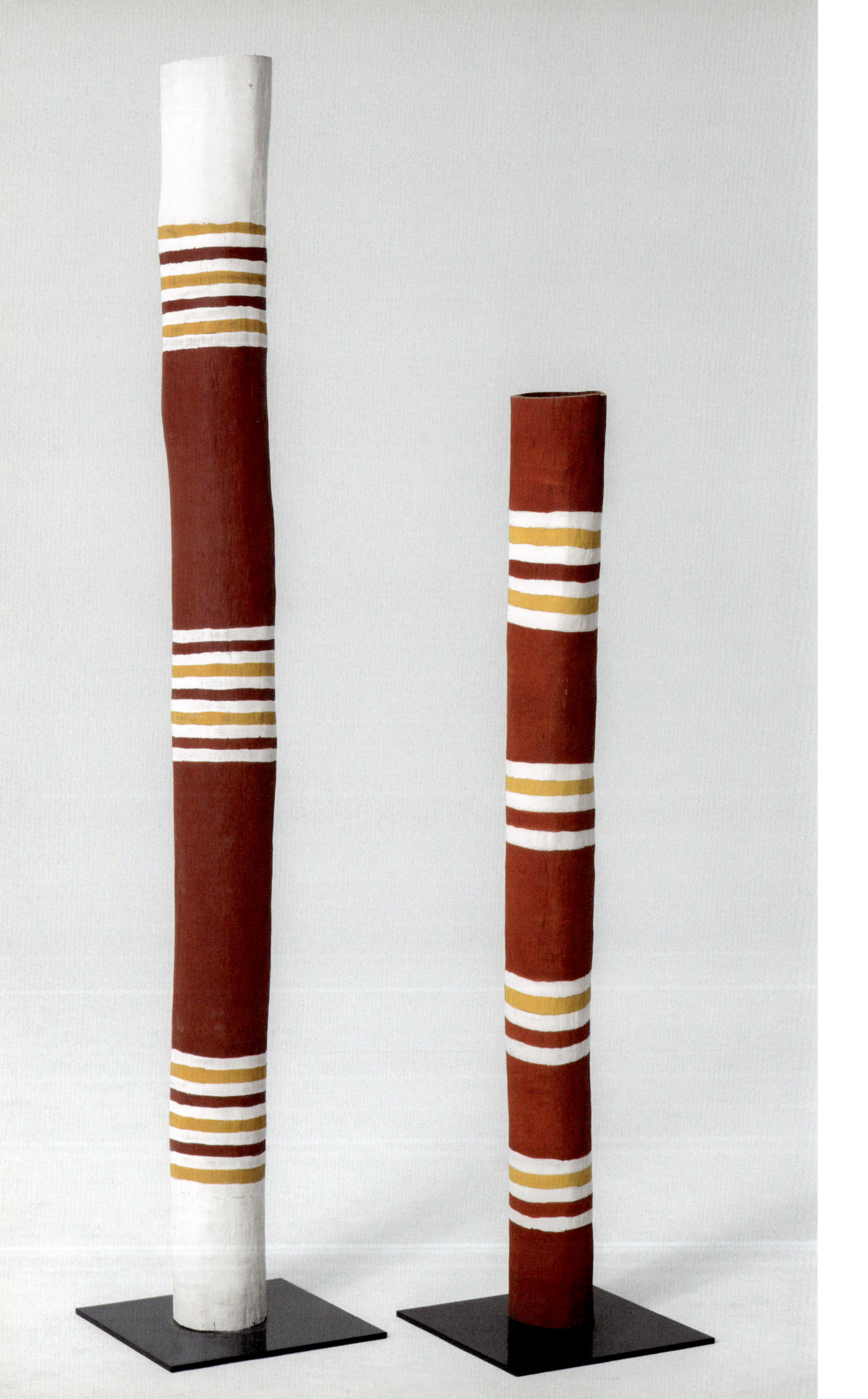

Opposite:
Helen Ganalmirriwuy, *Garrawurra Body Paint Design*, 2016. Earth pigments on wood, 79⅛ in. (201 cm)

Jocelyn Gumirrmirr, *Garrawurra Body Paint Design*, 2016. Earth pigments on wood, 61¾ in. (157 x 14 cm)

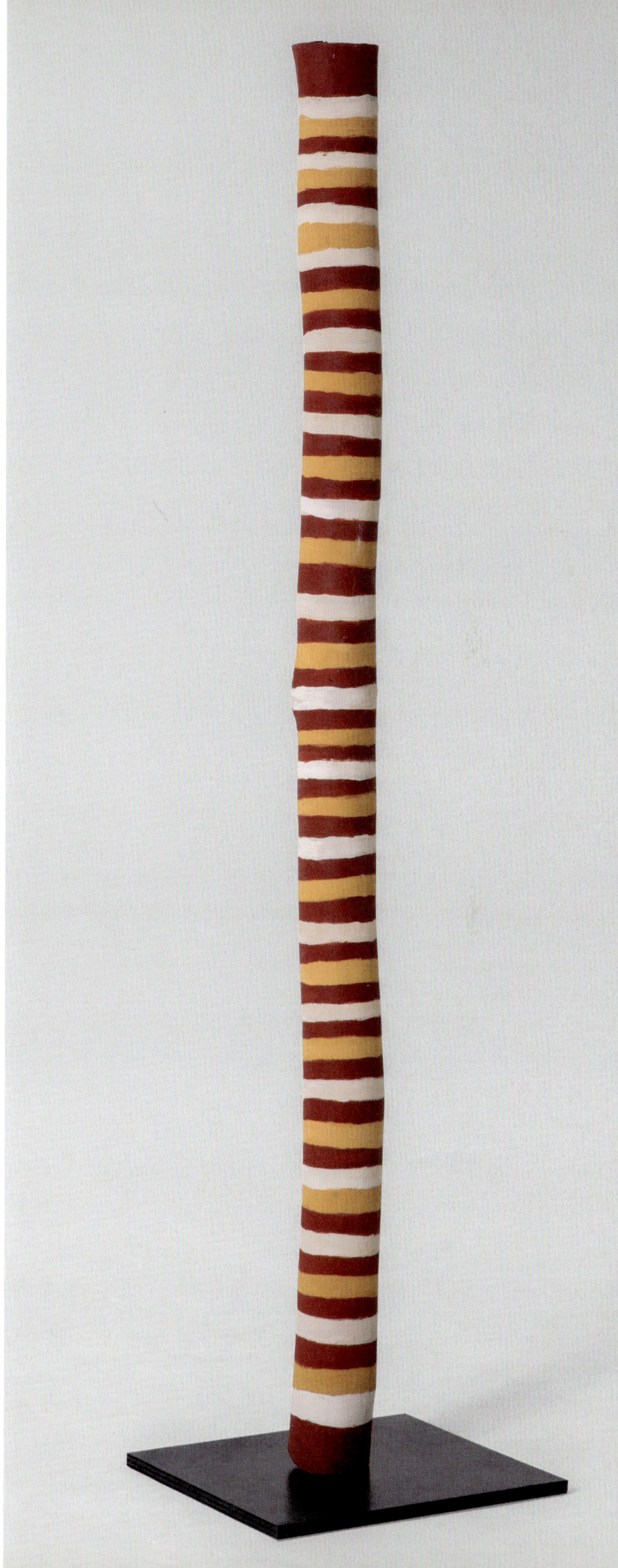

Margaret Rarru, *Garrawurra Body Paint Design*, 2016. Earth pigments on wood, 74⅛ in. (188 cm)

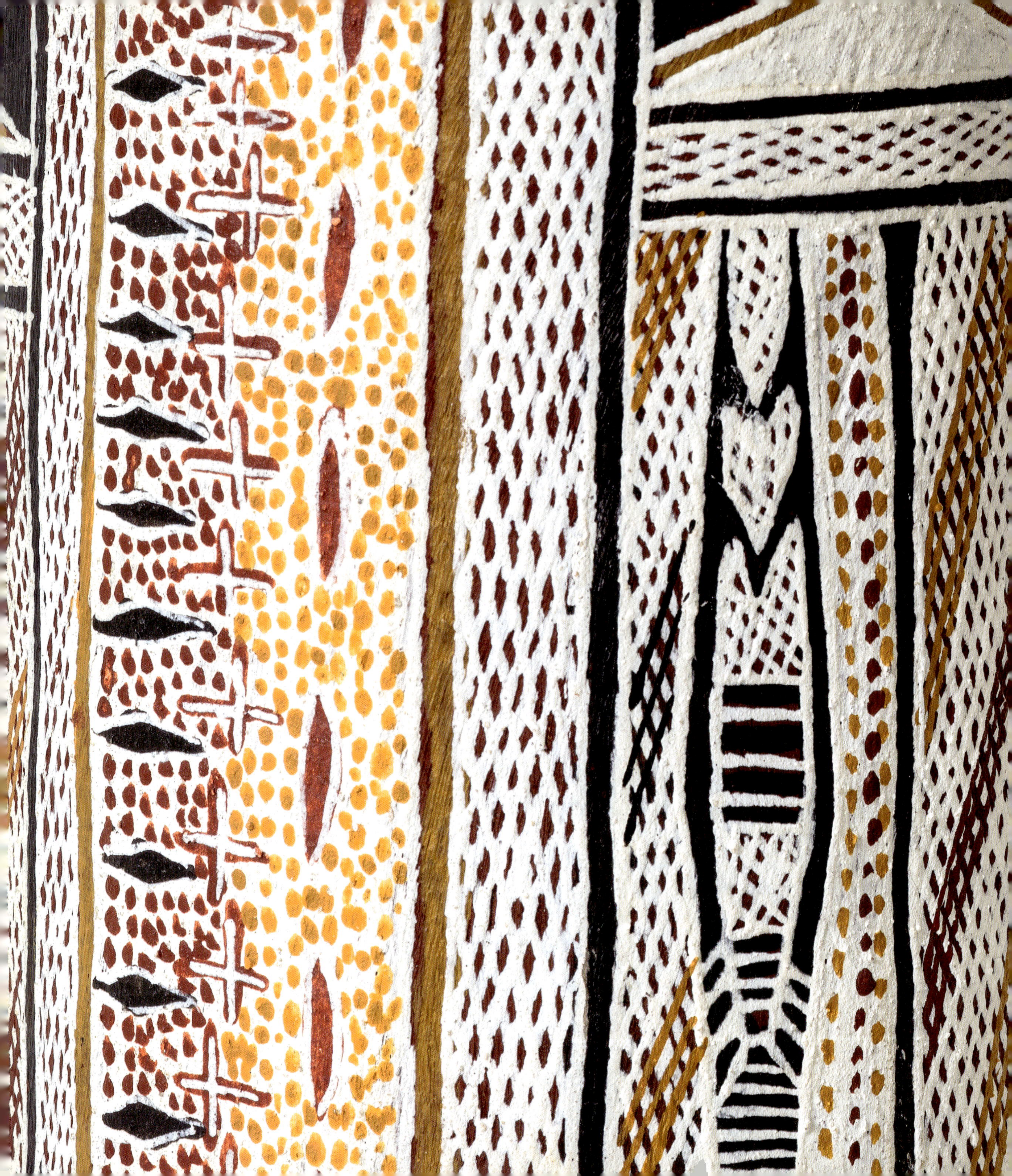

YIRRKALA

Buyaŋgirr Ganambarr
Gunybi Ganambarr
Yalkundi Ganambarr
Malaluba Gumana
Manini Gumana
Djul'djul Gurruwiwi
Bambarrar Marawili
Djambawa Marawili
Noŋgirrŋa Marawili
Nuwandjali Marawilli
Dhurrumuwuy Marika
Baluka Maymuru
Galuma Maymuru
Naminapu Maymuru-White
Barayuwa Munuŋgurr
Beyamarr Munuŋgurr
Marrnyula Munuŋgurr
Rerrkirrwaŋa Munuŋgurr
Yimula Munuŋgurr
Buwathay Munyarryun
Mapunu Ŋurruwuthunm
Djalpat Wanambi
Garawan Wanambi
Guwaykuway Wanambi
Wukun Wanambi
Yalanba Wanambi
Mulkun Wirrpanda
Nawurapu Wunuŋmurra
Gulumbu Yunupiŋu
Nyapanyapa Yunupiŋu

Baluka Maymuru, *Maŋgalili* (detail), 2016 (see p. 123)

Our Destiny in the *Larrakitj*

Wukun Wanambi

In the beginning, the *larrakitj* was sacred. It was used as a coffin. Human bones would be placed inside the hollow log, to commit those remains to their destiny in the *larrakitj*. The *larrakitj* is a ceremonial pole for when someone has passed away. After the body of the dead had been dried in a tree, and the bones were all crunchy, they would be placed inside, and this way, they would go down to the land. *Larrakitj* would be painted with clan designs that represented who the deceased was. These designs represent a whole identity for who he or she was as they were lying in the ground. We would do ceremony for a month or even a year to celebrate that, to respect that.

That was what *larrakitj* were used for in the olden times, and today the elders have given us authority to use them in our art. They said, "OK, now today we are using *larrakitj* as art."

The reason why the old people have given this authority is so that we—the Yolŋu people—can maintain our culture and pass it onto the generations that come after us, to build up their strength and wisdom. But *larrakitj* can't stand by himself: *larrakitj's* identity comes from its family, and this attaches it to our culture and Law. *Balanda* (non-Aboriginal people) need to understand the whole structure—not just the art part—or they will never understand.

Larrakitj need their family because it gives them strength and power. One *larrakitj* on its own is like nothing—it doesn't mean anything—but if you put three or four together in one group it is like a family: they have the strength of the family ties from that area. When we see that *gadayka* (stringybark tree) family, it makes us happy—because there is a family. When you look at the trees, all together, rotating around each other, that is how it is like with me.

When I was a little child, I remember, I sat down on the ground and I listened to my father and grandfather and the old people of the Marrakulu and Rirratjiŋu clans. I listened to them. They were not talking about the *larrakitj*, they were talking about the painting, about how you paint and how you put your symbols down in a different way; how you can protect your patterns, but still pass these designs on to my generation so that we wouldn't lose our identity. All paintings have layers, but we Yolŋu need to break that down, we need to change our paintings so that *we* understand the meaning, but so that *balanda* don't understand. *Balanda* can see the surface side of the designs—like looking at the surface of the water—but underneath is the bigger part that only we know.

First there is the surface of the water. When you paint, you look at the surface and you say, "ok, how do I paint?" For us

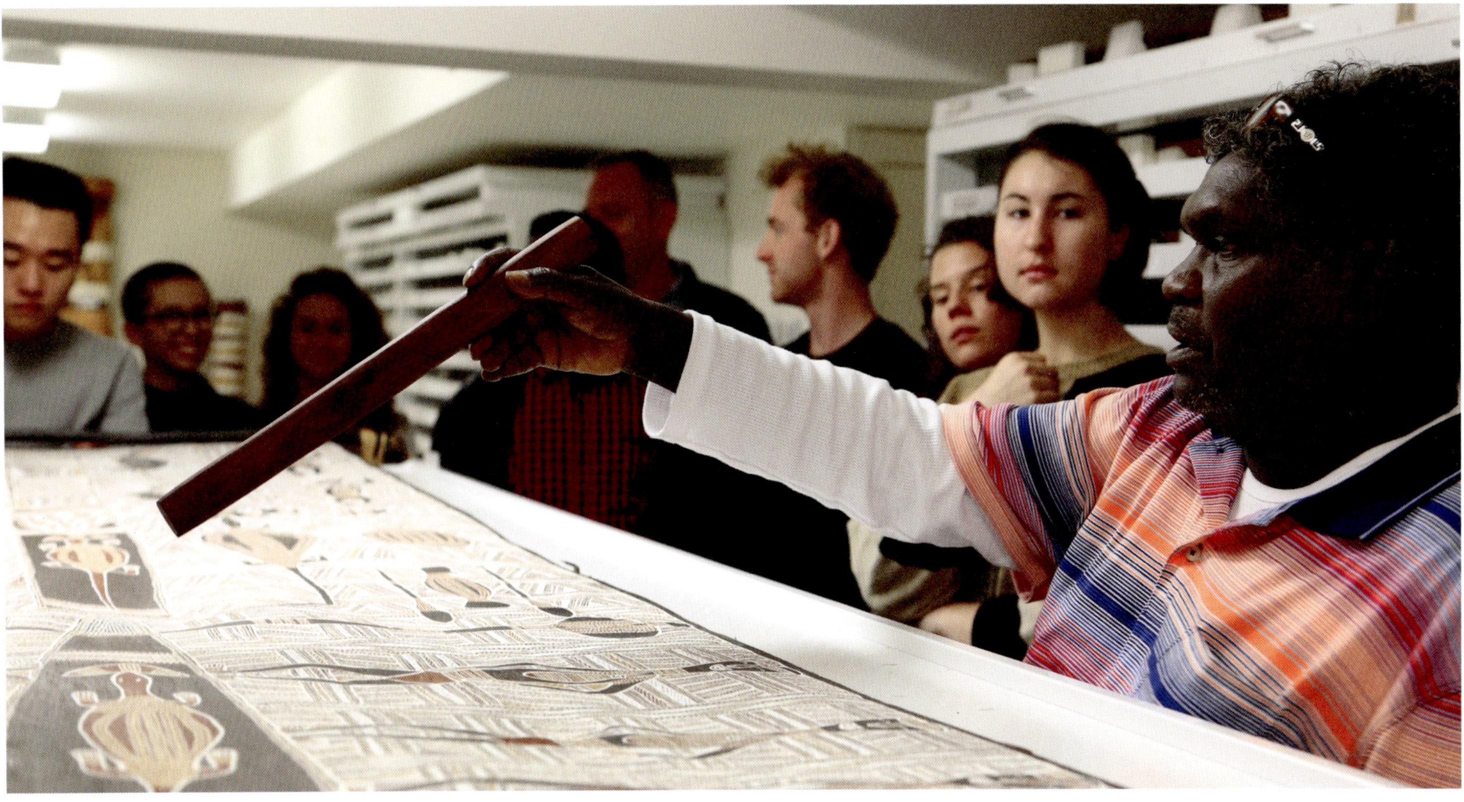

Fig. 1. Wukun Wa<u>n</u>ambi teaching students at the Kluge-Ruhe Aboriginal Art Collection at the University of Virginia

Yolŋu, we know every songline. We know what animals we can paint. The surface is a flat surface that you can play on in art; but then there is a second layer, and a third layer that only the elders can see. When they recognize this, the elders can say, "you are now holding the true identity of this painting"—and it shows that I have pride, that I have a position of authority, that I can do this. I can know this, but I cannot show other people: I can only show them the shadow side until they too understand about the Law. You know how you go to university to get your degree? It is the same steps that we do in our art. When you want to start doing bark painting, you are just a child doing it, and as you grow you are shown by the old men how to develop that bark. As you get older, that gets you a little bit of power, but not the full power or identity. But when you pass that degree—to become a doctor or master of your art—then it shows that you have done that learning.

Every painting is either Dhuwa or Yirritja. It's like *yin* and *yang*. Everything in the world is either Dhuwa or Yirritja—every plant, every place, every clan and every person. We cannot marry someone from the same side—we must always marry the opposite. We are the ceremonial manager or *djuŋgayi* of the other side too—so I am *djuŋgayi* for Yirritja clans. I need to authorize what Maŋgalili—my mother clan—can do. I can make a song schedule for the Maŋgalili and people from Gurrumuru and Gangan can come and talk to me and they do my schedule. It is complementary. It holds everything together. Dhuwa and Yirritja: we have to play our parts separately. All our designs—called *ma<u>d</u>ayin miny'tji*—are separate too—but the *djuŋgayi* understands which is right for people to paint.

Today, I am doing a *<u>l</u>arrakitj*. When my father passed away he gave knowledge to some special people. We call it *djirrikay*: the highest authority, who stands in the middle. They gave me that strength and I started doing my *<u>l</u>arrakitj*. All my paintings comes from Gurka'wuy, where I come from. My vision comes from where my family come from and have passed through. Our great-grandfathers sang the same songs, or *buŋgul*, that we sing today, the same ceremonies that are still run by Marrakulu. But we are taking it forward. It is a time to move forward rather than

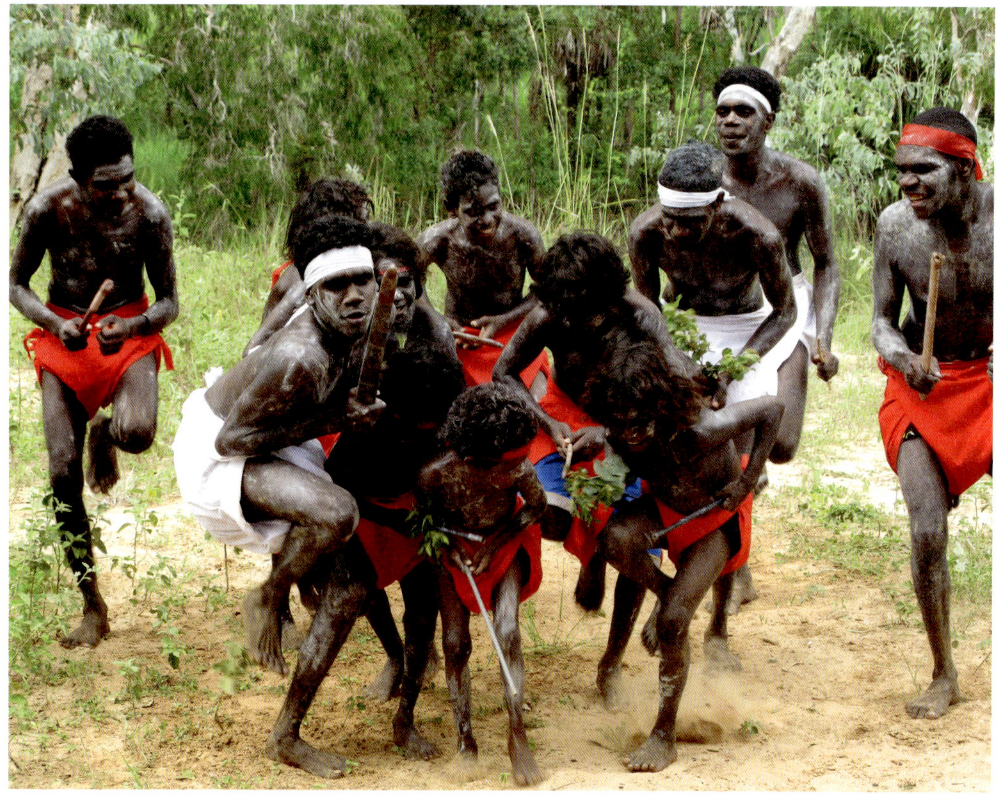

Fig. 2. Boys dancing at Wandawuy, March 2009. Image courtesy of the Mulka Project

go backwards. I want to show *l̲arrakitj* in a different way; for how your mind dives beneath the water, and how the fish move from ocean to ocean, and how the people of Gurka'wuy move like those fish in their ceremony.

The *l̲arrakitj* is made from a Wan̲ambi tree that we call *gaḏay'ka*. I have authority over that tree: the stringybark tree (*Eucalyptus tetradonta*). Whatever is painted on a *l̲arrakitj*, the skin and the flesh belongs to the Wan̲ambi people. And when people chop it every day, it reminds me they are chopping up pieces of me. But the backbone remains, and the symbolism of that is maintained. Our flesh and bone is still there: because that is attached. *Gaḏay'ka* is very, very important. When we chop that *gaḏay'ka*, we sing that *gaḏay'ka*. We sing that stringy-bark: we sing all the bits and pieces. And every little piece represents Marrakulu people—like our flesh and our bones. The outside, every time they cut it, we say "wow, the trees are falling down, we are getting weak. We are not getting stronger." So the tree represents Marrakulu. That *gaḏay'ka* represents Marrakulu.

The flesh, the smooth part of the *l̲arrakitj*, that is like our backbone. When we draw something on the *l̲arrakitj*, we are drawing on the backbone of the Marrakulu. I always say why not use a Yirrjitja tree?—but it doesn't work. So they still use the Dhuwa tree to cut it. *N̲uwayak*, bark for painting on comes from the same tree. The *yiḏaki* (didjeridu) comes from the same tree.

We look around for the right tree to make *l̲arrakitj*. We find a special one—sometimes it is straight, sometime it's a bendy one with bumps. And when we get that *l̲arrakitj* we take it back to the Buku-Larrŋgay Mulka art center and they cut the skin off. Both the outside and inside of the *l̲arrakitj* is sacred to us. My fathers and grandfathers have given us the authority to paint *l̲arrakitj*. Some know the correct way, but some do not know. Because right now, I am the Marrakulu leader, I can approach them and tell the correct way.

When we cut the *gaḏay'ka* down, we sand it until it is really fine, smooth—it is our backbone. When we die, that is what it represents. Every time when we die, it represents that. So what

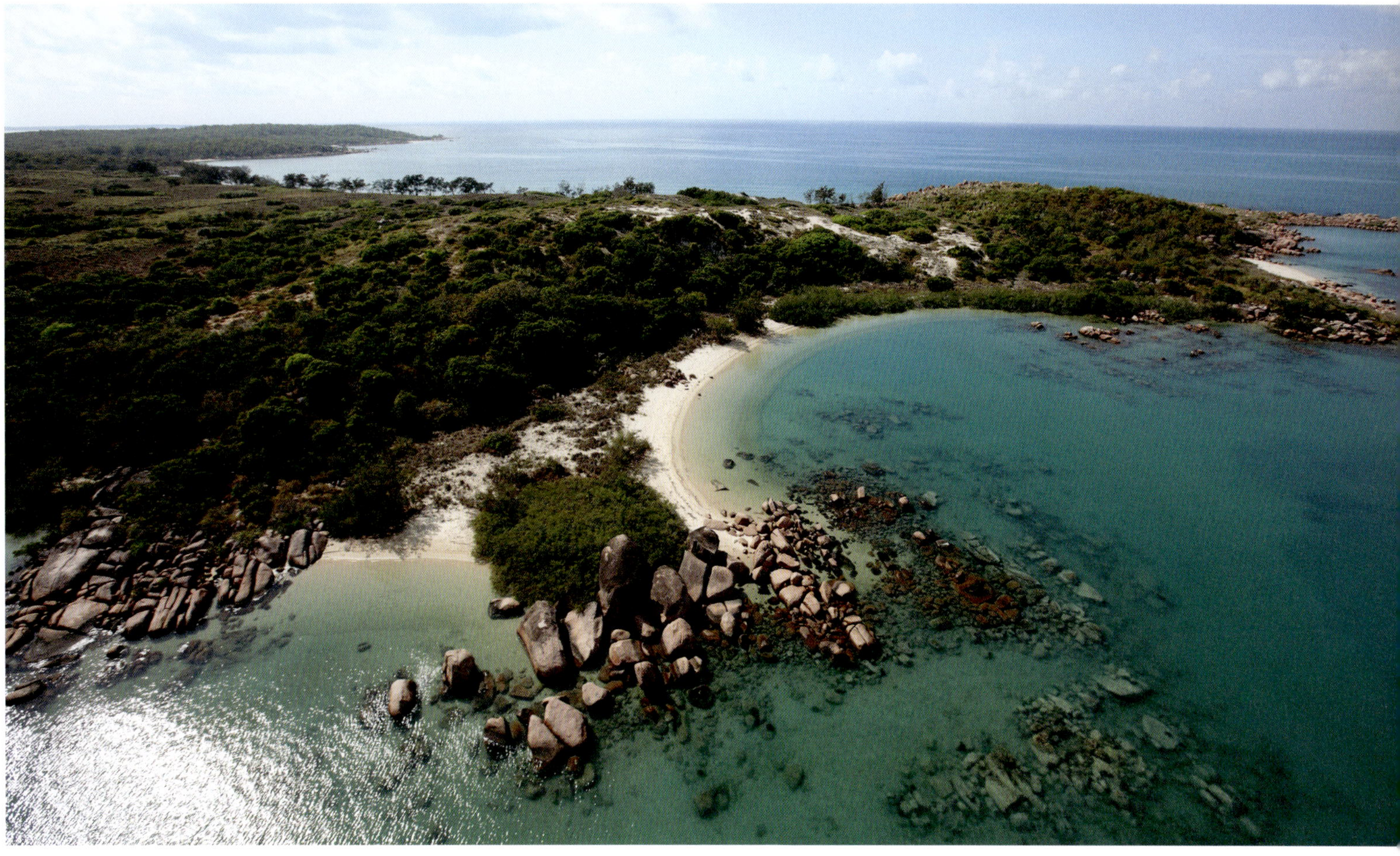

Fig. 3. Gurka'wuy (Trial Bay). Photograph by Peter Eve

I am trying to do is break down Yolŋu theology. There are bigger words, but I am trying to break it down into small terms to put on a piece of paper: the philosophy of the *l̲arrakitj*—as represented for all *l̲arrakitj*—especially for Yolŋu *l̲arrakitj* that travels around the world. They always used *gaḏay'ka*—the Marrakulu tree—it's been there from the beginning. In the old days no ladies could paint on *l̲arrakitj* or see it before it was finished. Today we say ladies can paint. But it still needs to come through the leaders. Because of the art industry, they want to show the rest of the world that they can do it.

The *l̲arrakitj* comes from the ocean. I paint my *l̲arrakitj* with a fish that is called mullet. The mullet travel from river to river, creek to creek, ocean to ocean, looking for their destiny.

In Marrakulu ceremony we dance towards a spear that represents the rock *Bamurruŋu*, surrounded by *wawurritjpal* that we call *marparrarr*, or milk fish, somewhat like a large mullet. It's a bigger name for another fish, and how it swims too, along the same pathway. The more we dance, the more we get strength, showing the culture and the Law of how the fish rotate. Fish are similar to human beings, big travels, how far we see, that's how far we travel, beyond that horizon. Now, today, we are using the same symbol in dancing; and the same symbol, in the same way of how fish rotate, we are dancing to represent how the mullet travel to look for their destiny. It never stays still, it moves. It's like you and me, when we go through the internet, we look for our destinies, to find our great-great-great grandfathers and grandmothers or we go to the museum and we look around for them. It's not easy to explain; when fish find their destiny, that's where he lays down his spirit, like when we die, us like a fish, our spirit goes down, and dives down into our country, into our land. Our land called Trial Bay—Gurka'wuy (Fig. 3). It's about three or four hours' drive from Yirrkala.

I am the cultural director of the Mulka Project and assistant advisor to the Buku-Larrŋgay art center. Mulka is the media center. When I do meetings for Buku-Larrŋgay, I am just an advisor: to advise the Yolŋu and keep them on track on how the system of the art center must run. The art center is important because people want to know what Yolŋu art is like: and they want know how our identity is strong. If we don't show that, our art will mean nothing to the outside world. But showing them that we have our own art, that we have our own art center, and it is strong with culture and Law, is a better way. *Balanda* got law. *Balanda* got art. But *balanda* always keep it in out in the open. We Yolŋu don't keep it out in the open, except in the art gallery and that means stepping out from the *ŋärra* (closed ceremony): out from the parliament into the public to show the world. Even though there is *maḏayin* sacred stuff there, according to the system of the art it has come out from the parliament to the public where the public can see it. But the foundation is now laid down to show the world that we as a small community have still got the culture and the Law, we have land rights, and we are strong.

My grandfathers were all artists, but that wasn't my project when I was a kid: my project was to be a politician. But then I came to be an artist, because my father was passing on, so I had to show that I came from a family of artists to show what I could do. I want to share my identity to the other side of the world so they can understand that it is completely different to what they have. In their world, they use a coffin—but we can present *larrakitj* as a different method. It is important to show our culture to the other side of the world, like they are sharing their identity by showing their fancy coffins. And we are showing, in a modern way, a very old way of doing it.

But art only goes one way to understanding. I want the politicians to listen that education is very important for Yolŋu. We want them politicians to understand that we have the real art. All the politicians should come to Buku-Larrŋgay and see what is happening here. Otherwise they are sitting there talking about art, but they are not supporting the art. Education and health, that is public. Our art is also public. But we need those in charge in Canberra to come out to Yirrkala and talk about it, and find the real story and put it in the media that we have the strongest art. We want the things from the grass-root level to come out into the open space so that Canberra can talk about it. Bring the root out, take the root out and say, "here's the information about Yirrkala for example, and its art is good." And support the outstations, and the local Rirratjiŋu. We've got the power and the strength here because of the land rights. White people say I own the land: but the Yolŋu know it belongs to the clan. Art can show culture, but initiation and ceremony is very important too. The body painted with clan designs is representative of the *maḏayin*. It is all part of the same structure. *Balanda* need to understand the whole structure or they will never find a better way of being.

Yimula Munuŋgurr, *Djapu*, 2016. Earth pigments on wood, 67¼ in. (170.9 cm)

Marrnyula Munuŋgurr, *Djapu Larrakitj*, 2016. Earth pigments on wood, 87⅜ in. (222 cm)

Yimula Munuŋgurr, *Djapu*, 2016. Earth pigments on wood, 50⅜ in. (128 cm)

Yimula Munuŋgurr, *Djapu*, 2016. Earth pigments on wood, 88⅝ in. (225 cm)

Beyamarr Munuŋgurr, *Garrapara*, 2006. Earth pigments on wood, 81⅞ in. (208 cm)

Yimula Munuŋgurr, *Djapu*, 2016. Earth pigments on wood, 65⅛ in. (165.5 cm)

Noŋgirrŋa Marawili, *Baypina*, 2006. Earth pigments on wood, 64½ in. (164 cm)

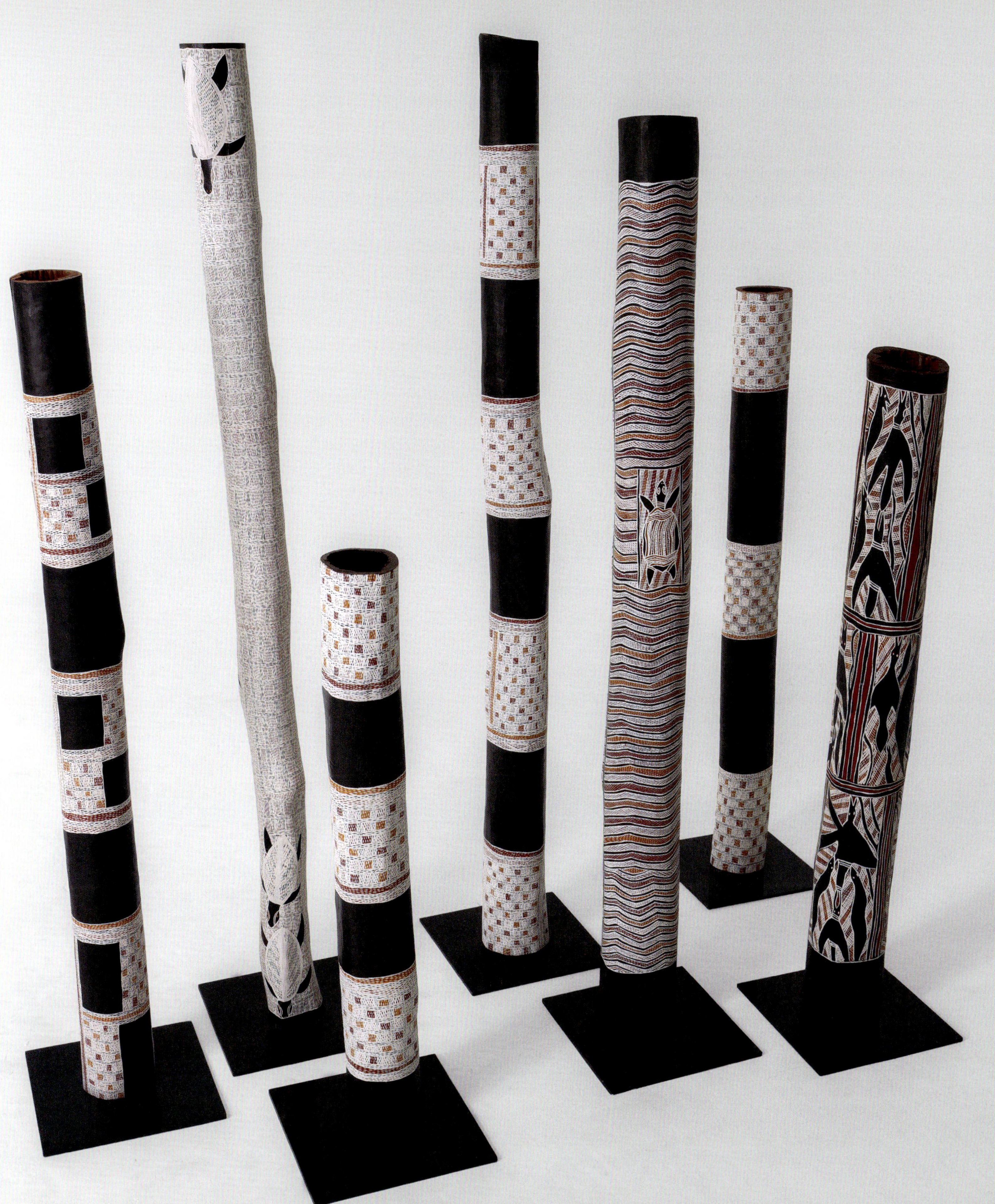

Noŋgirrŋa Marawili, *Baypina*, 2006. Earth pigments on wood, 64½ in. (164 cm).

Djalpat Wan̲ambi, *Marrakulu L̲arrakitj*, 2006. Earth pigments on wood, 55⅛ in. (140 cm)

Djul'djul Gurruwiwi, *Wititj*, 2006. Earth pigments on wood, 68⅛ in. (173 cm)

Buyaŋgirr Ganambarr, *Warrukay*, 2006. Earth pigments on wood, 82¼ in. (209 cm)

Mulkun̲ Wirrpanda, *Yalata*, 2006. Earth pigments on wood, 64⅞ in. (165 cm)

Yalkundi Ganambarr, *Bul'manydji*, 2006. Earth pigments on wood, 75¼ in. (191 cm)

Beyamarr Munuŋgurr, *Garrapara*, 2006. Earth pigments on wood, 81⅞ in. (208 cm)

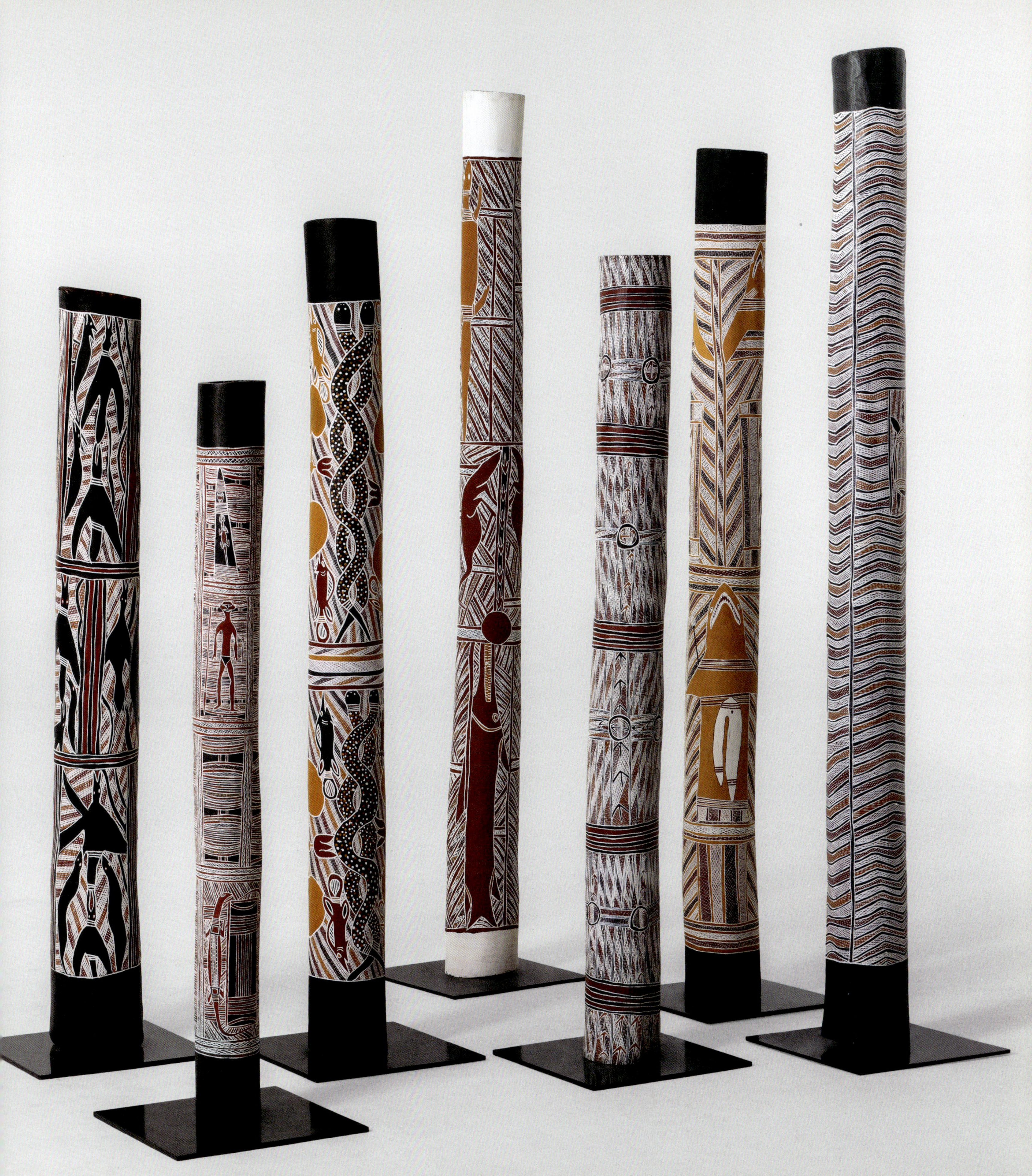

Bambarrar Marawili, *Maḏarrpa Larrakitj*, 2006. Earth pigments on wood, 72⅞ in. (185 cm)

Buwathay Munyarryun, *Waŋgurri Larrakitj*, 2006. Earth pigments on wood, 56¼ in. (143 cm)

Nuwandjali Marawilli, *Garraŋali*, 2006. Earth pigments on wood, 87¾ in. (223 cm)

Mapunu Ŋurruwuthunm, *Yarrinya (Slaughter of Totemic Whale)*, 2006. Earth pigments on wood, 70⅛ in. (178 cm)

Buwathay Munyarryun, *Waŋgurri Larrakitj*, 2006. Earth pigments on wood, 60¼ in. (153 cm)

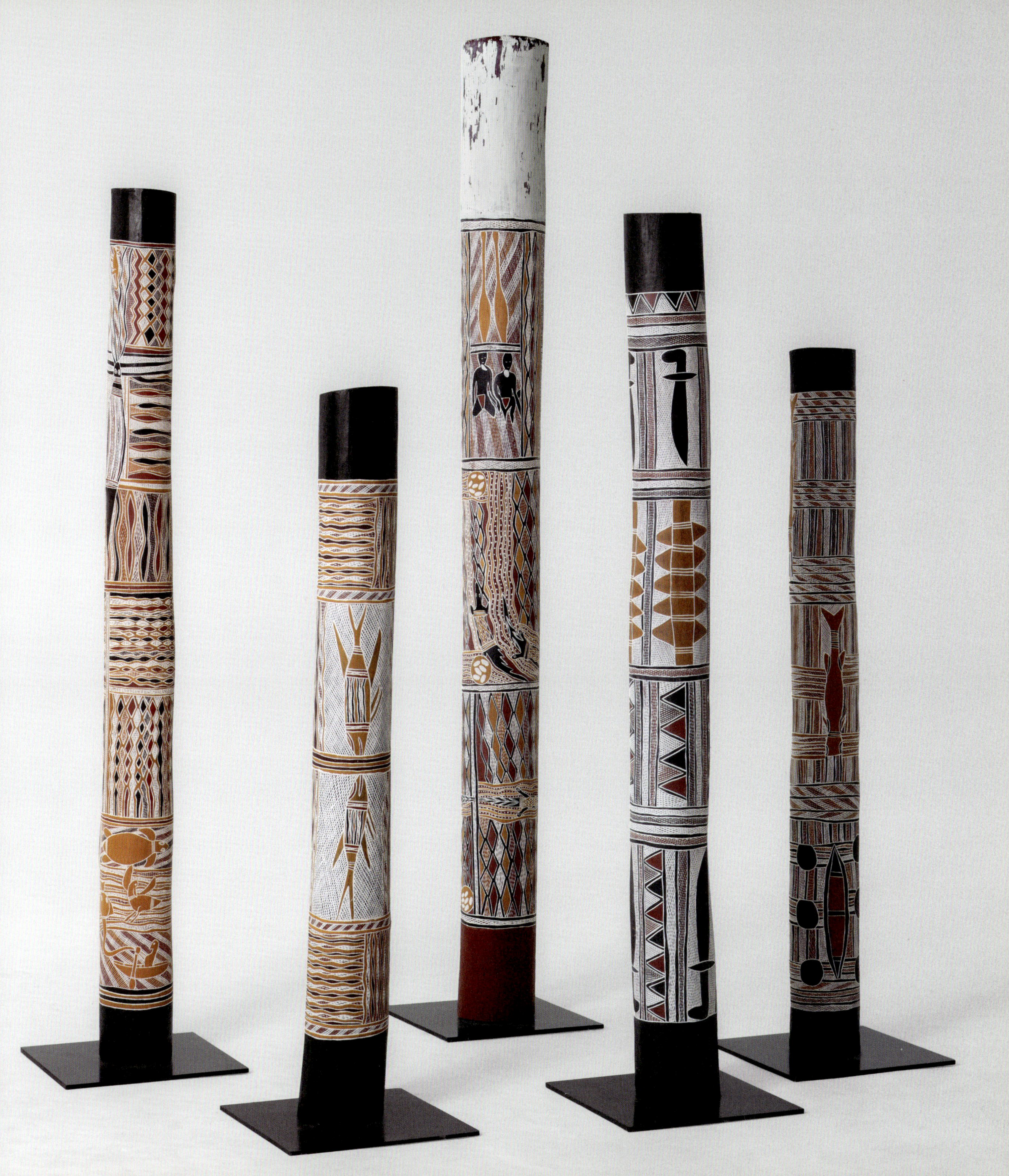

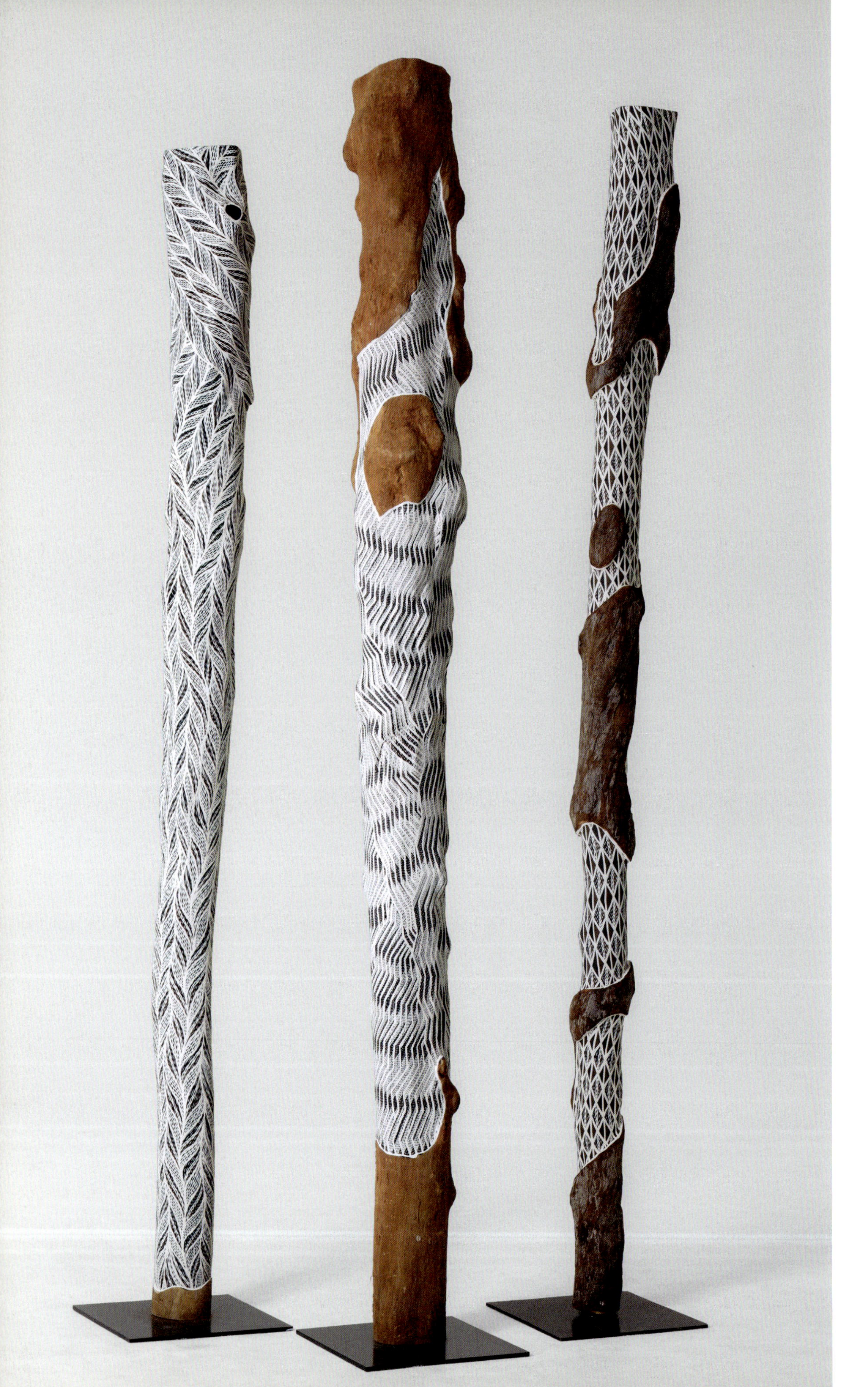

Opposite:

Gunybi Ganambarr, *Milŋurr Ŋaymil*, 2016. Earth pigments on wood, 116⅛ in. (295 cm)

Gunybi Ganambarr, *Garraparra and Gunyuru*, 2016. Earth pigments on wood, 110⁵⁄₁₆ in. (280 cm)

Gunybi Ganambarr, *Buyku*, 2016. Earth pigments on wood, 109⅛ in. (277 cm)

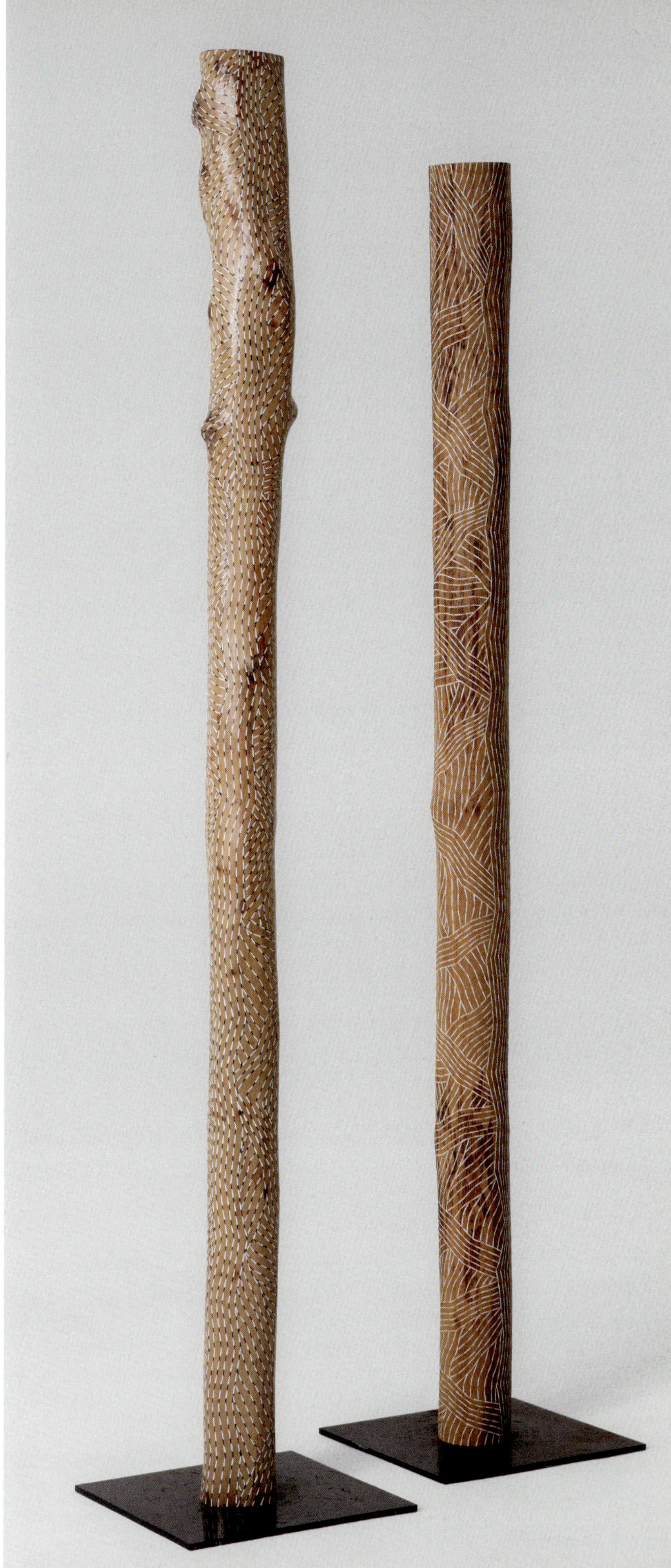

Manini Gumana, *Garraparra*, 2016. Earth pigments on wood, 86⅝ in. (220 cm)

Manini Gumana, *Garraparra*, 2016. Earth pigments on wood, 81½ in. (207 cm)

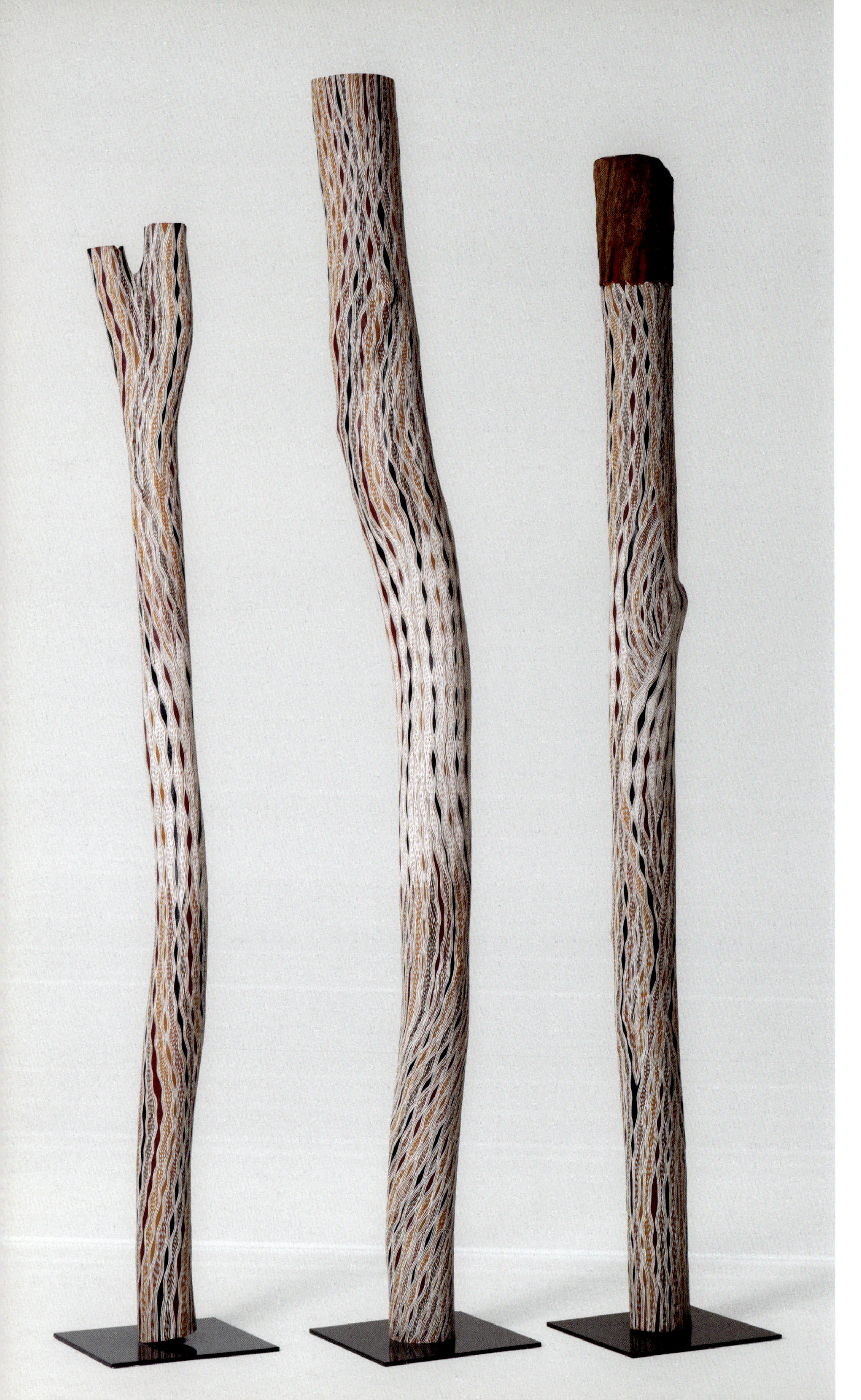

Djambawa Marawili, *Dhakandjali*, 2016. Earth pigments on wood, 98⅜ in. (250 cm)

Djambawa Marawili, *Dhakandjali*, 2016. Earth pigments on wood, 119⅝ in. (304 cm)

Djambawa Marawili, *Dhakandjali*, 2016. Earth pigments on wood, 102⅝ in. (260 cm)

Opposite:
Dhurrumuwuy Marika, *Rulyapa*, 2016. Earth pigments on wood, 75$\frac{3}{16}$ in. (191 cm)

Dhurrumuwuy Marika, *Rulyapa*, 2016. Earth pigments on wood, 90½ in. (230 cm)

Dhurrumuwuy Marika, *Rulyapa*, 2016. Earth pigments on wood, 70 in. (178 cm)

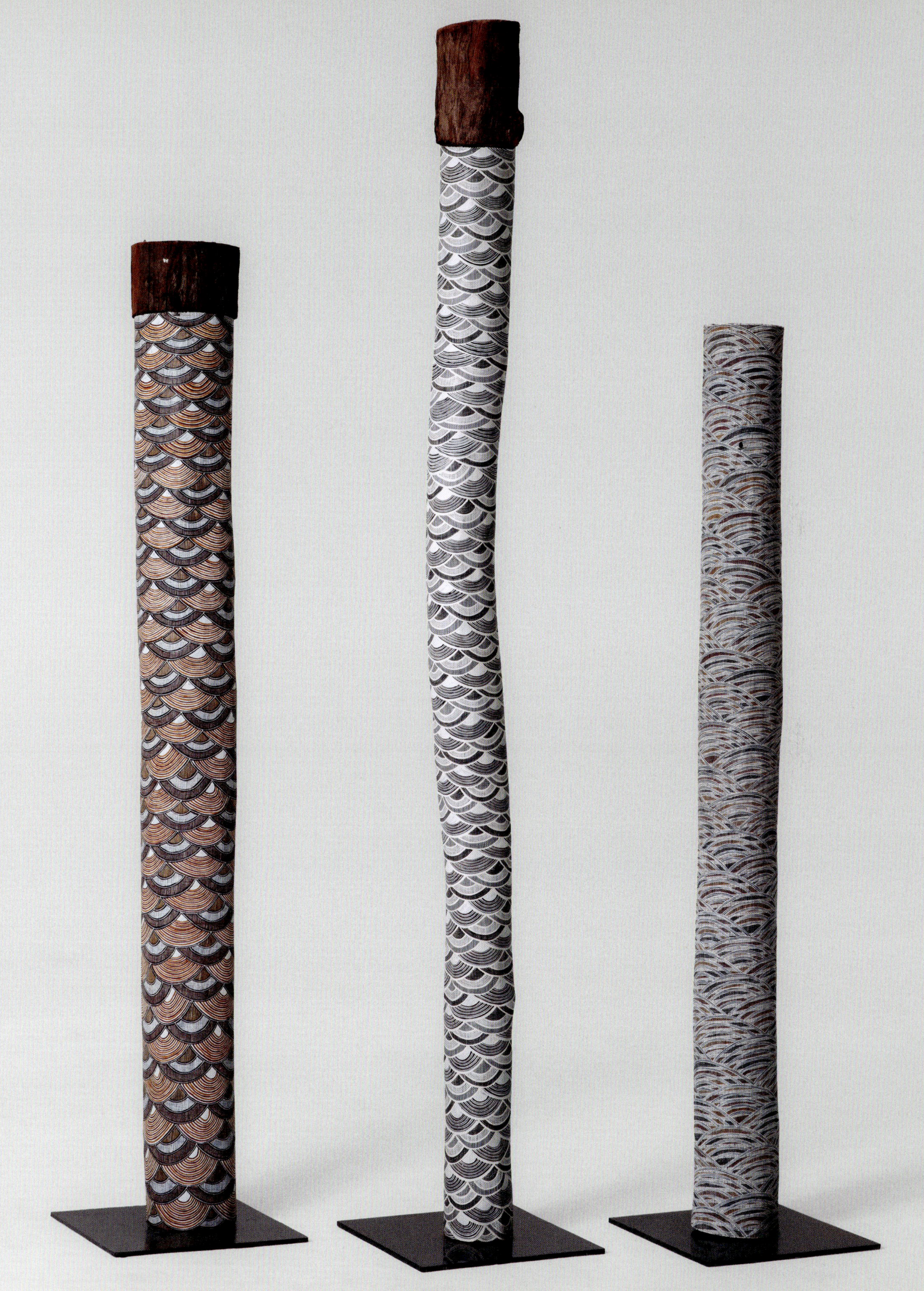

Noŋgirrŋa Marawili, *Yurr'yun*, 2015, Earth pigments on wood, 105 15/16 (269 cm)

Noŋgirrŋa Marawili, *Yurr'yun*, 2015. Earth pigments on wood, 107 in. (272 cm)

Noŋgirrŋa Marawili, *Yurr'yun*, 2015. Earth pigments on wood, 103 1/8 in. (262 cm)

Noŋgirrŋa Marawili, *Yurr'yun*, 2015. Earth pigments on wood, 105 5/16 in. (269 cm)

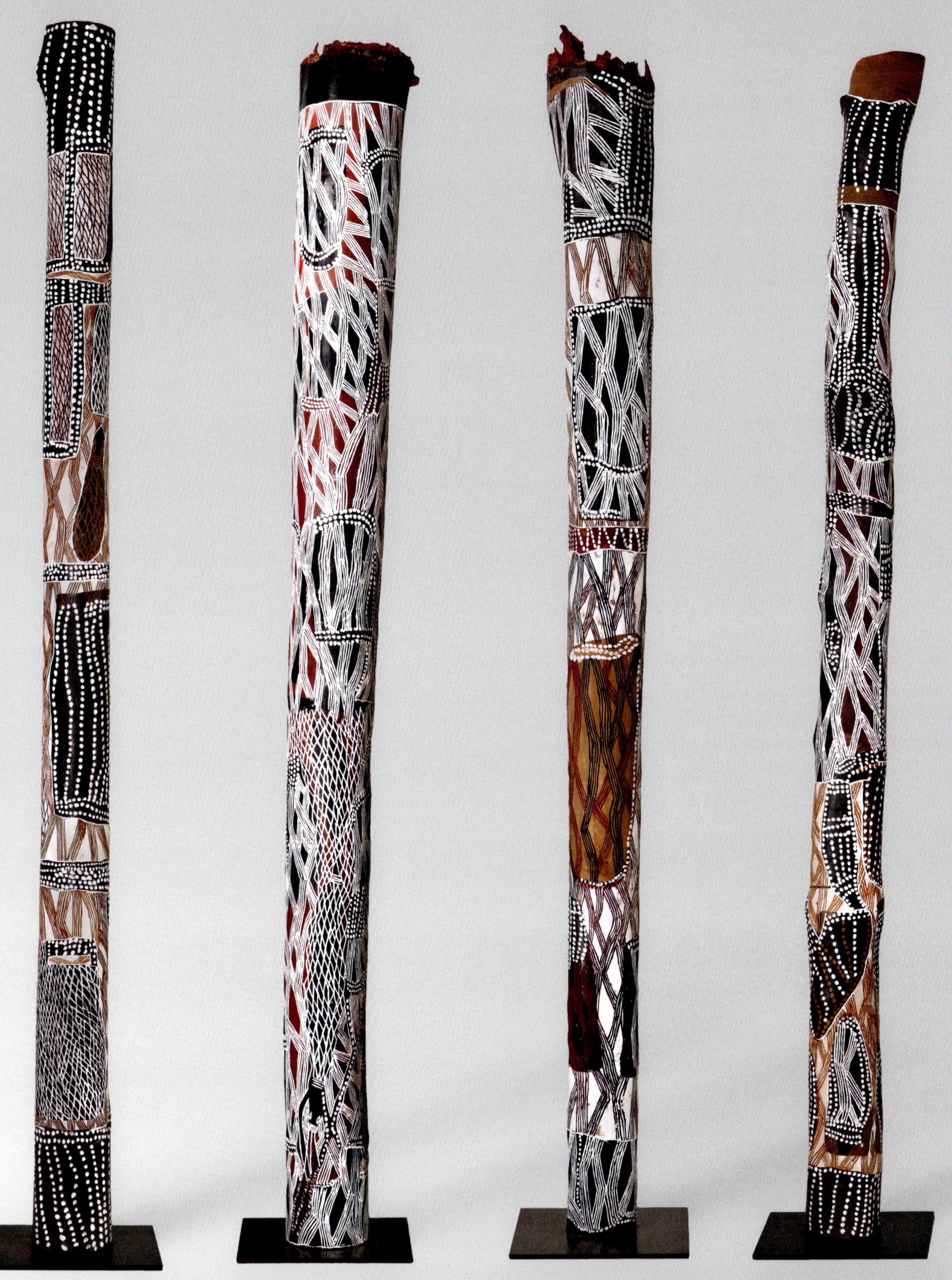

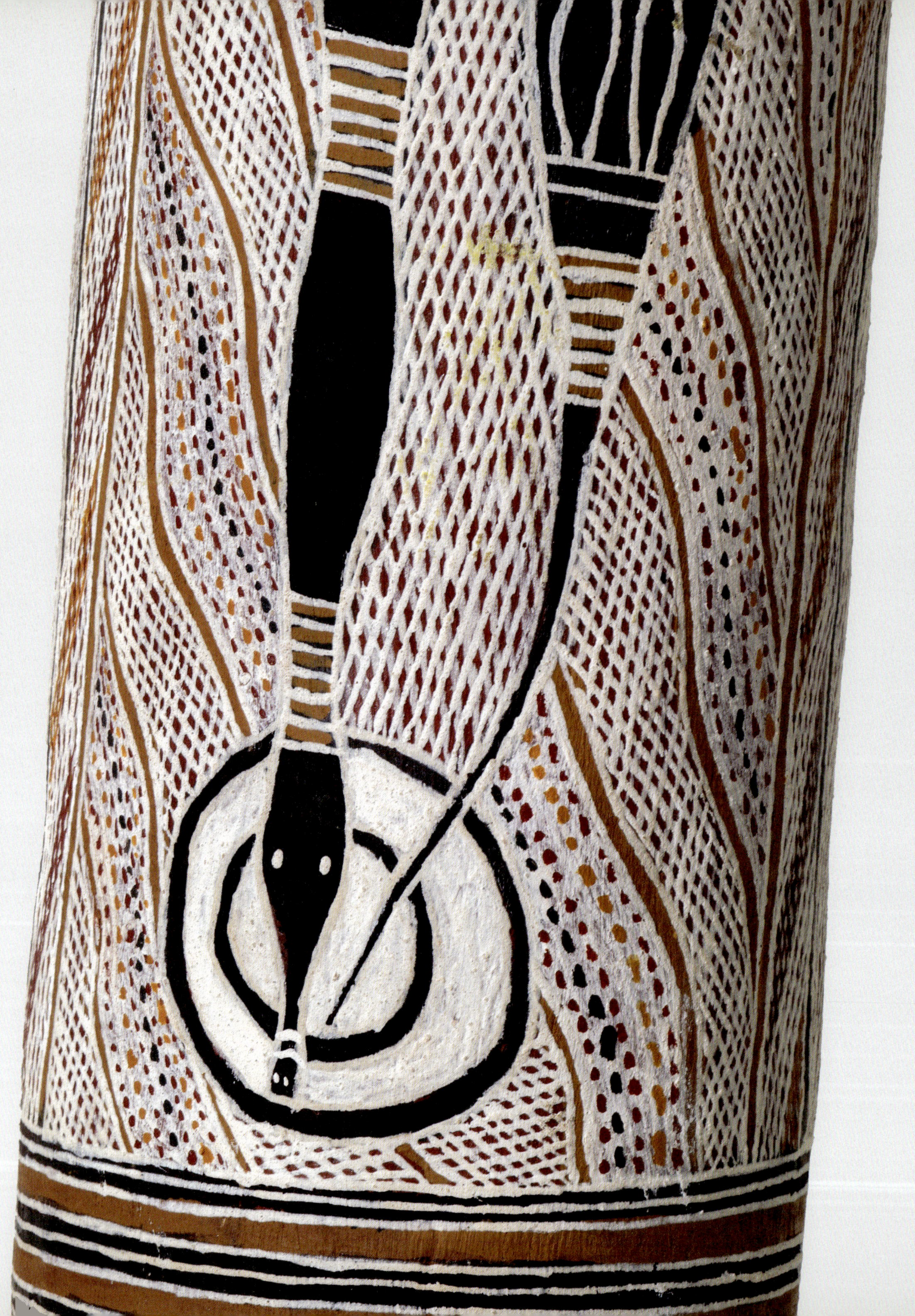

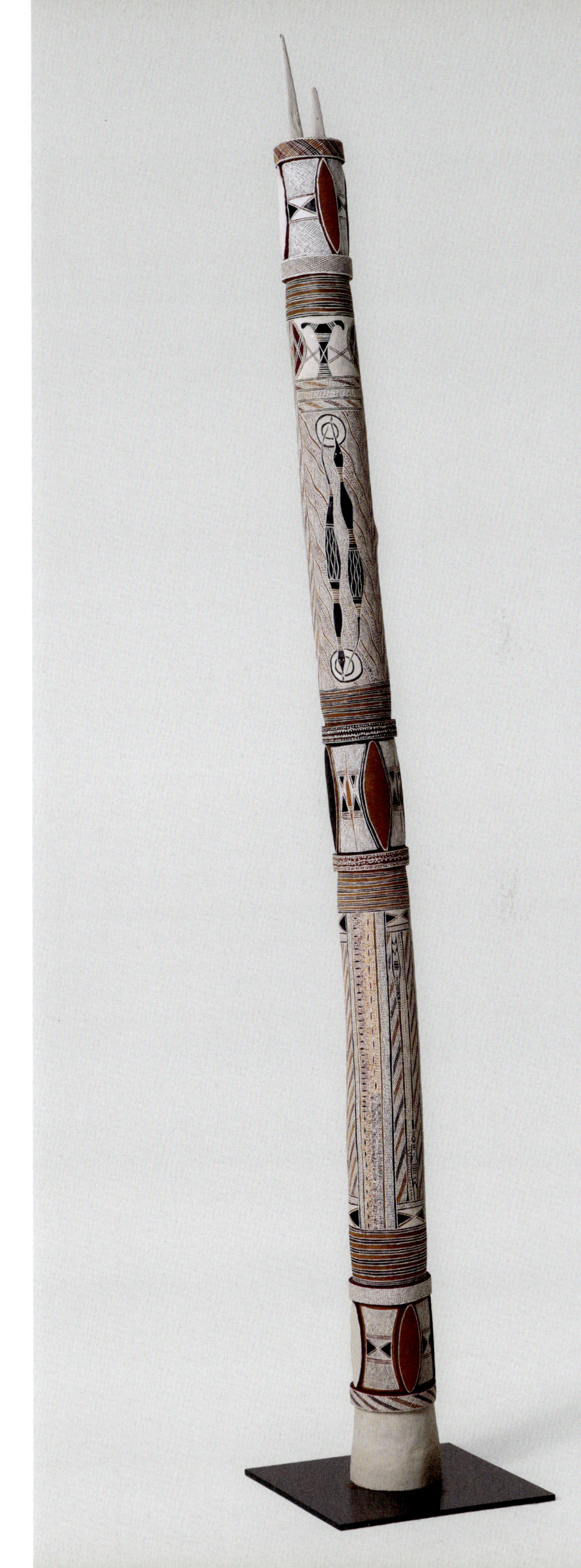

Baluka Maymuru, *Maŋgalili*, 2016. Earth pigments on wood, 96 in. (244 cm)

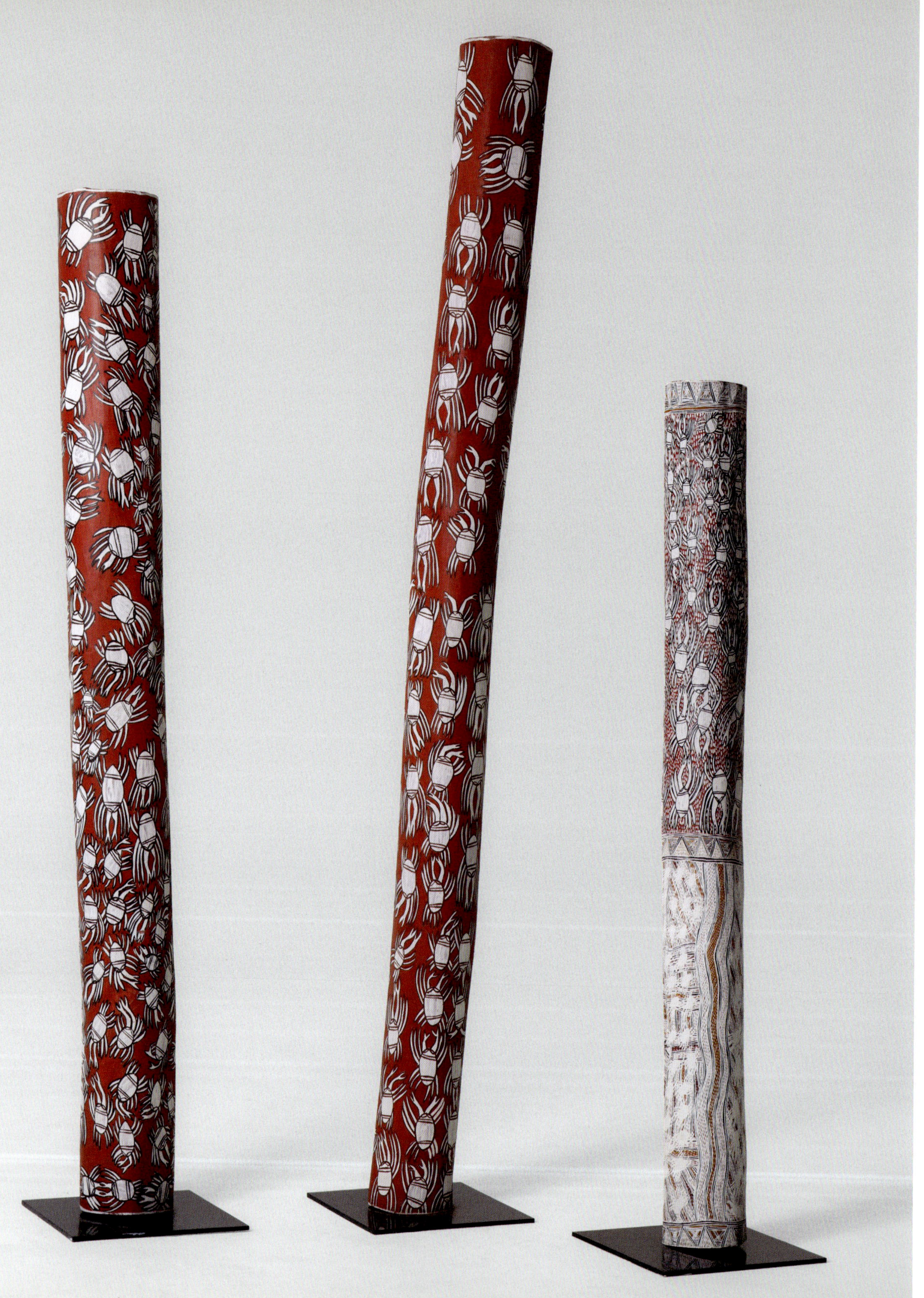

Opposite:

Galuma Maymuru, *Ŋoykal*, 2016. Earth pigments on wood, 86⅝ in. (220 cm)

Galuma Maymuru, *Ŋoykal*, 2016. Earth pigments on wood, 102⅜ in. (260 cm)

Galuma Maymuru, *Ŋoykal*, 2016. Earth pigments on wood, 71 in. (180 cm)

Naminapu Maymuru-White, *Milŋiyawuy (Milky Way)*, 2016. Earth pigments on wood, 63¾ in. (162 cm)

Naminapu Maymuru-White, *Milŋiyawuy (Milky Way)*, 2016. Earth pigments on wood, 90⅛ in. (229 cm)

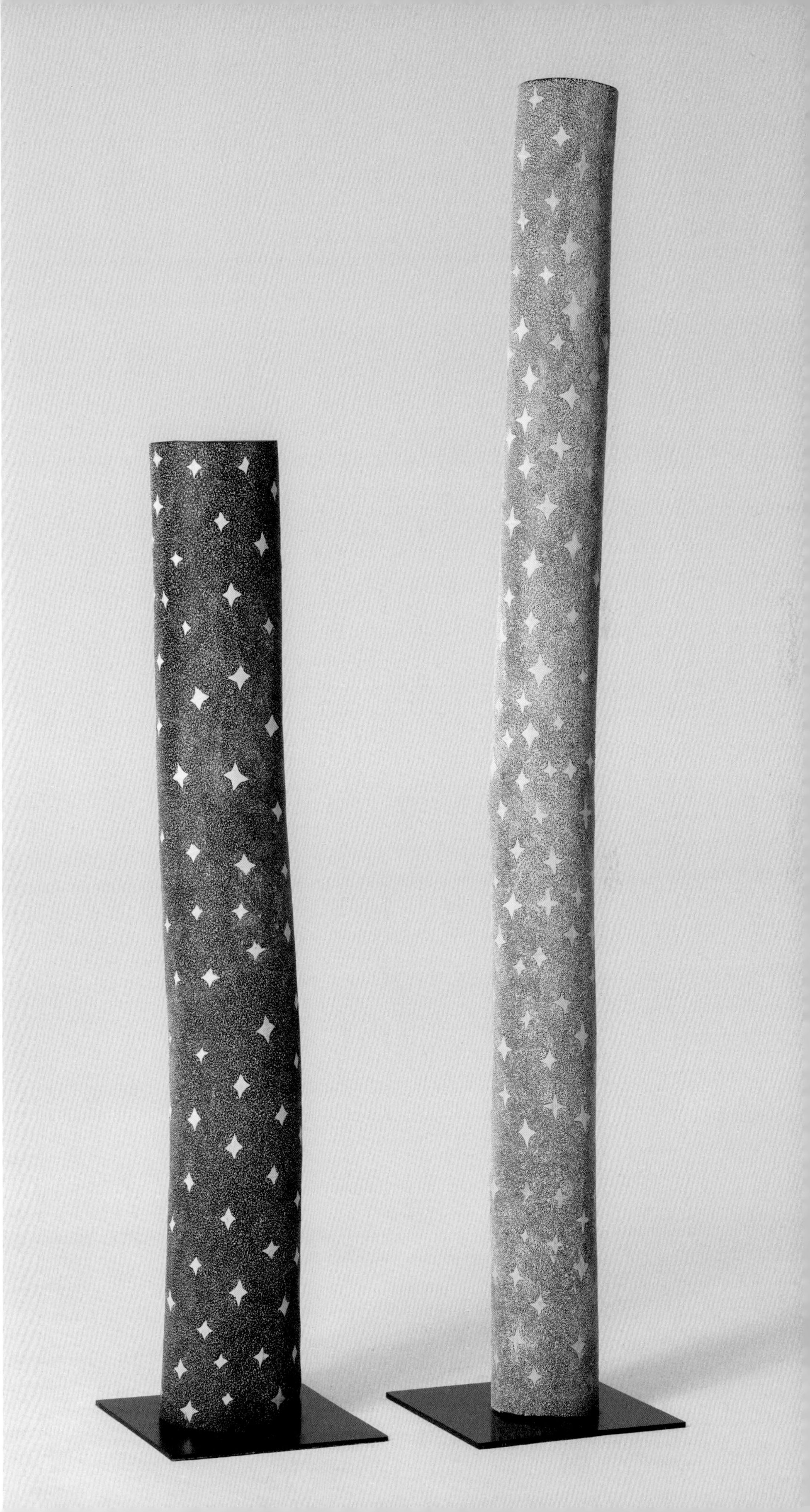

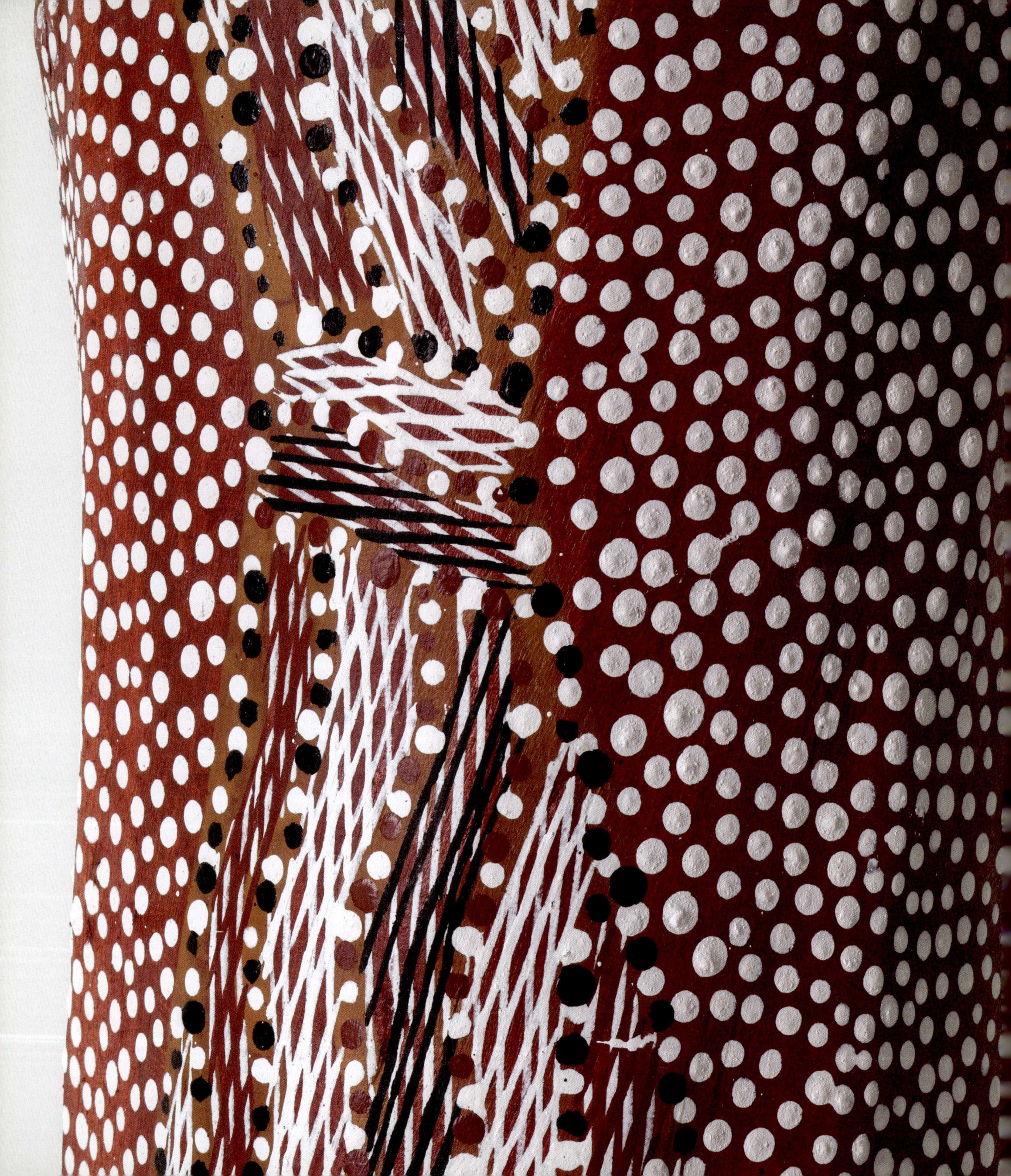

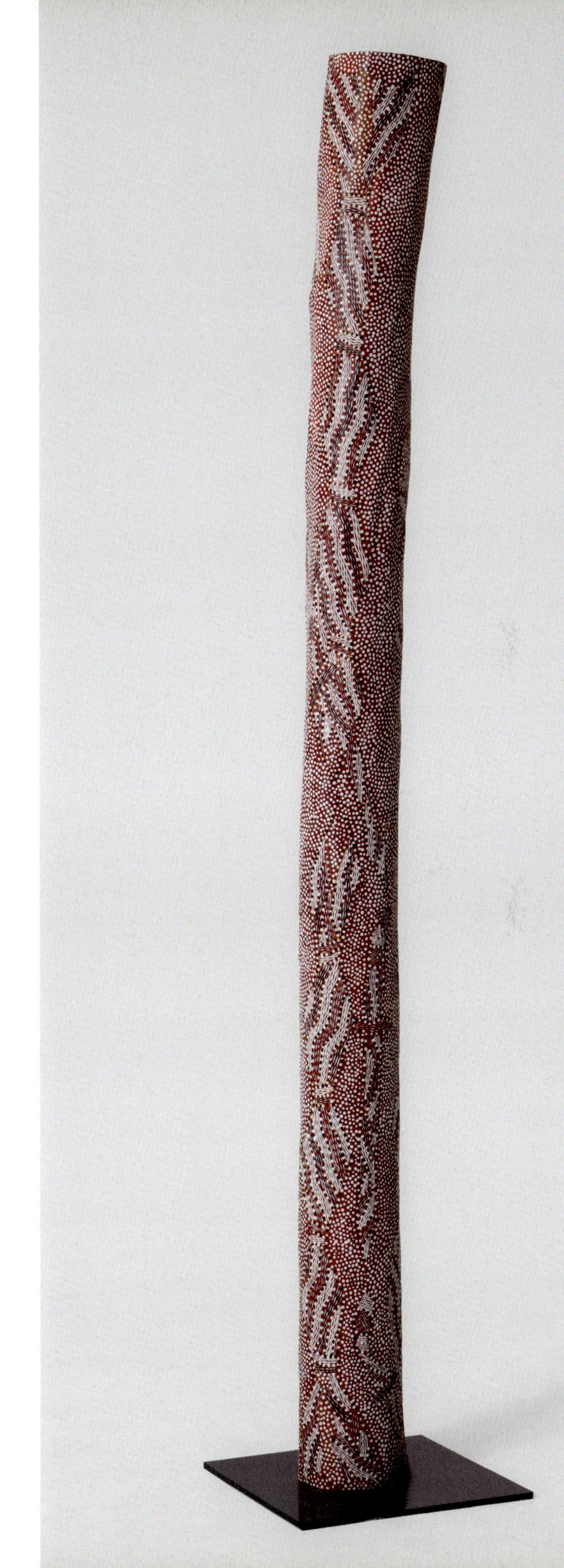

Barayuwa Munuŋgurr, *Yarrinya*, 2016. Earth pigments on wood, 86¼ in. (219 cm)

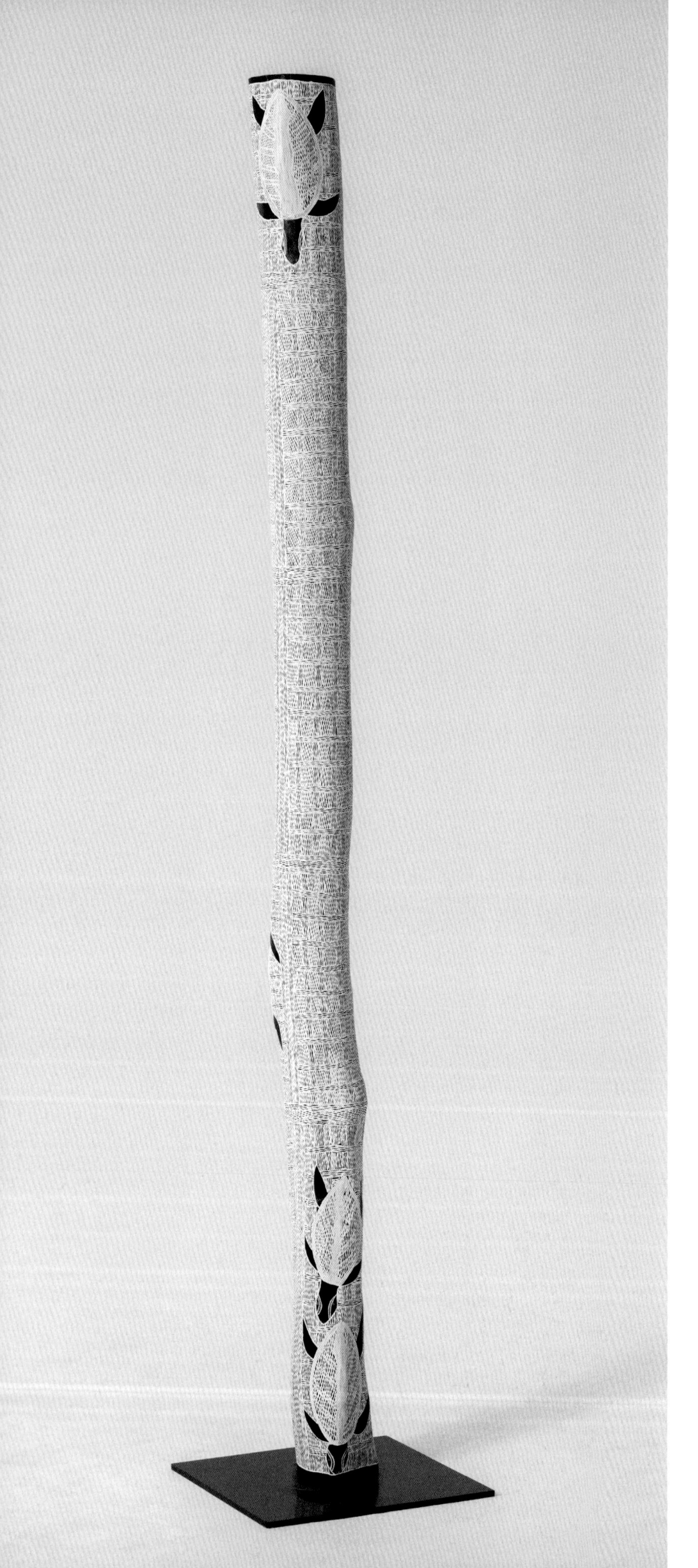

Marrnyula Munuŋgurr, *Djapu Ḻarrakitj*, 2016. Earth pigments on wood, 87⅜ in. (222 cm)

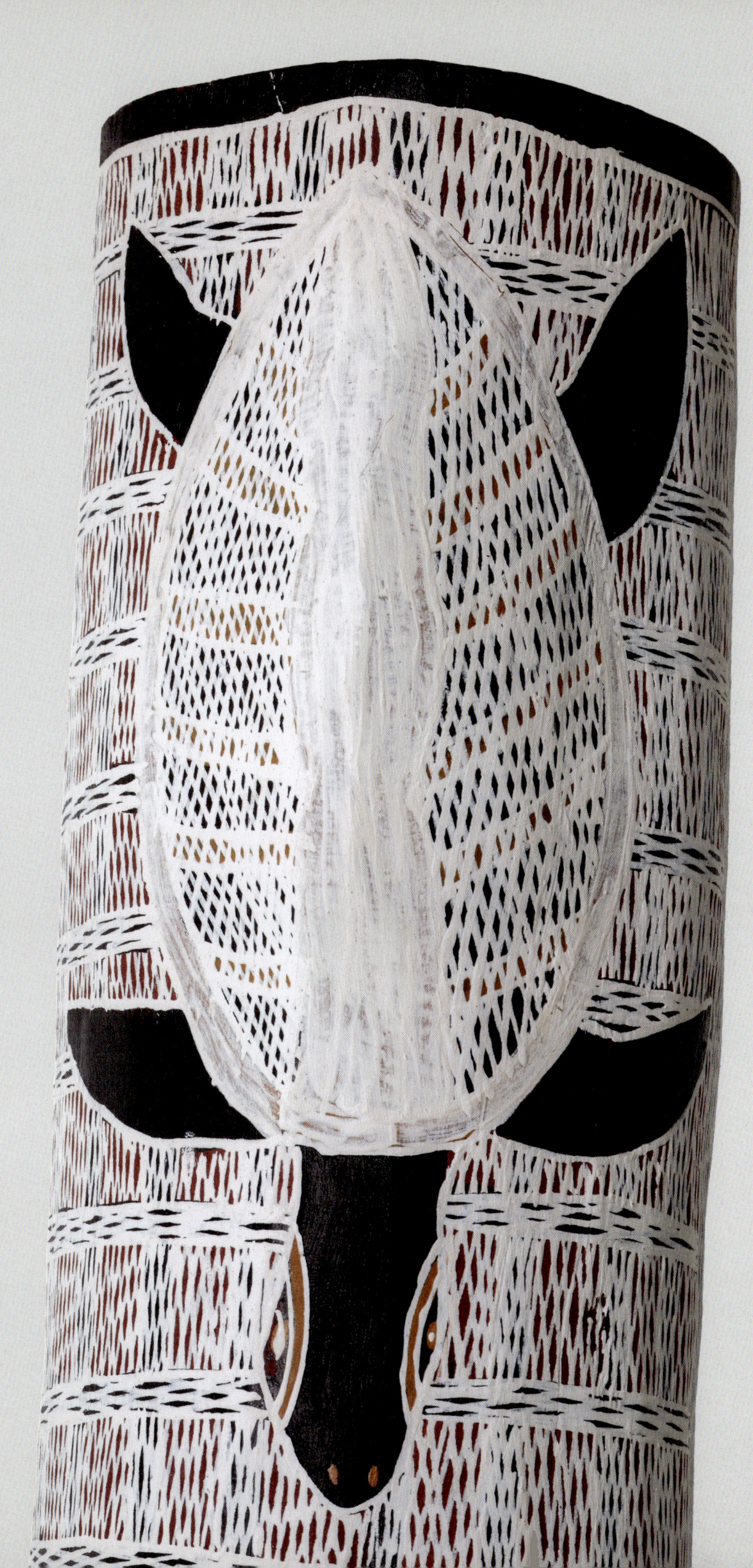

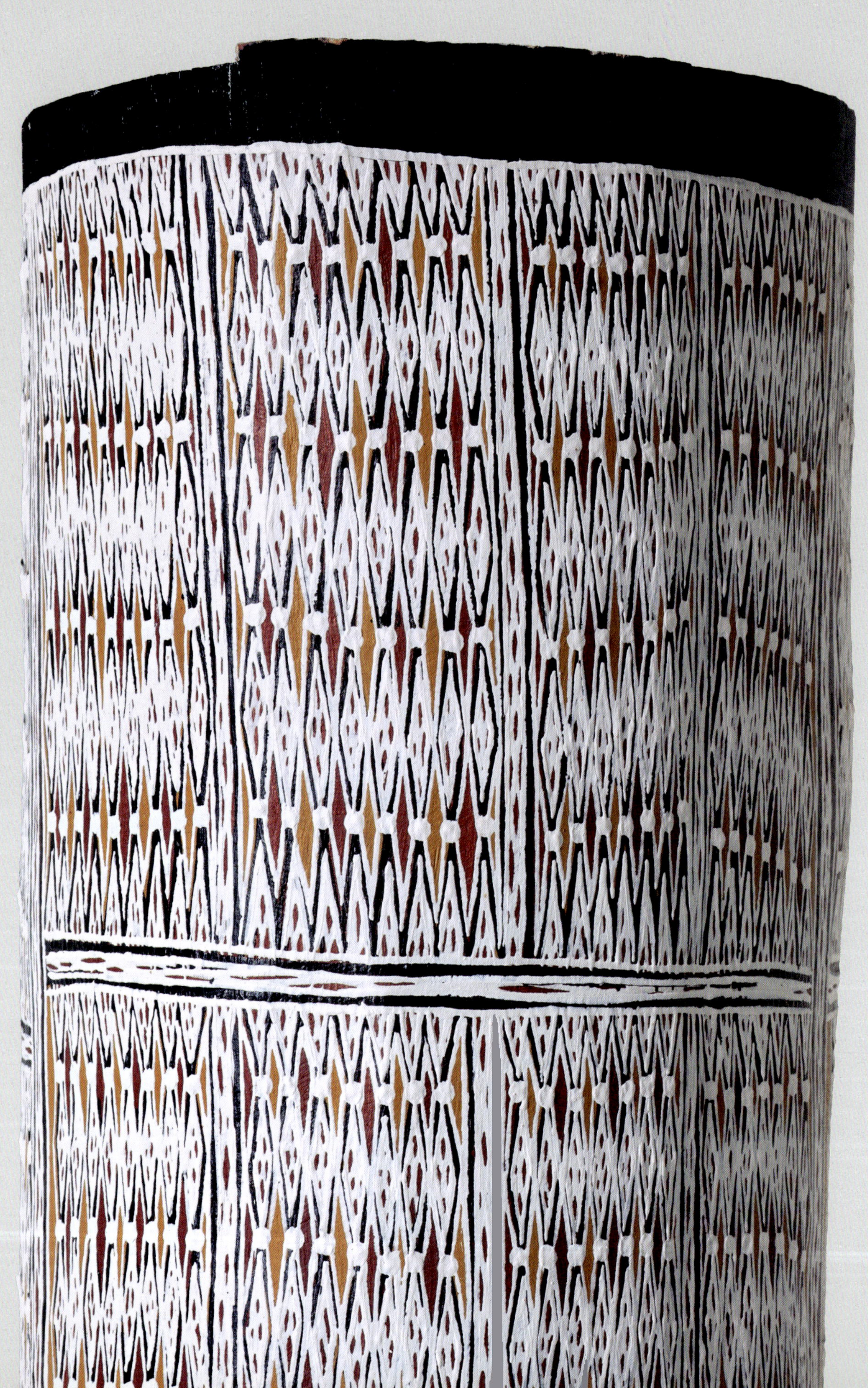

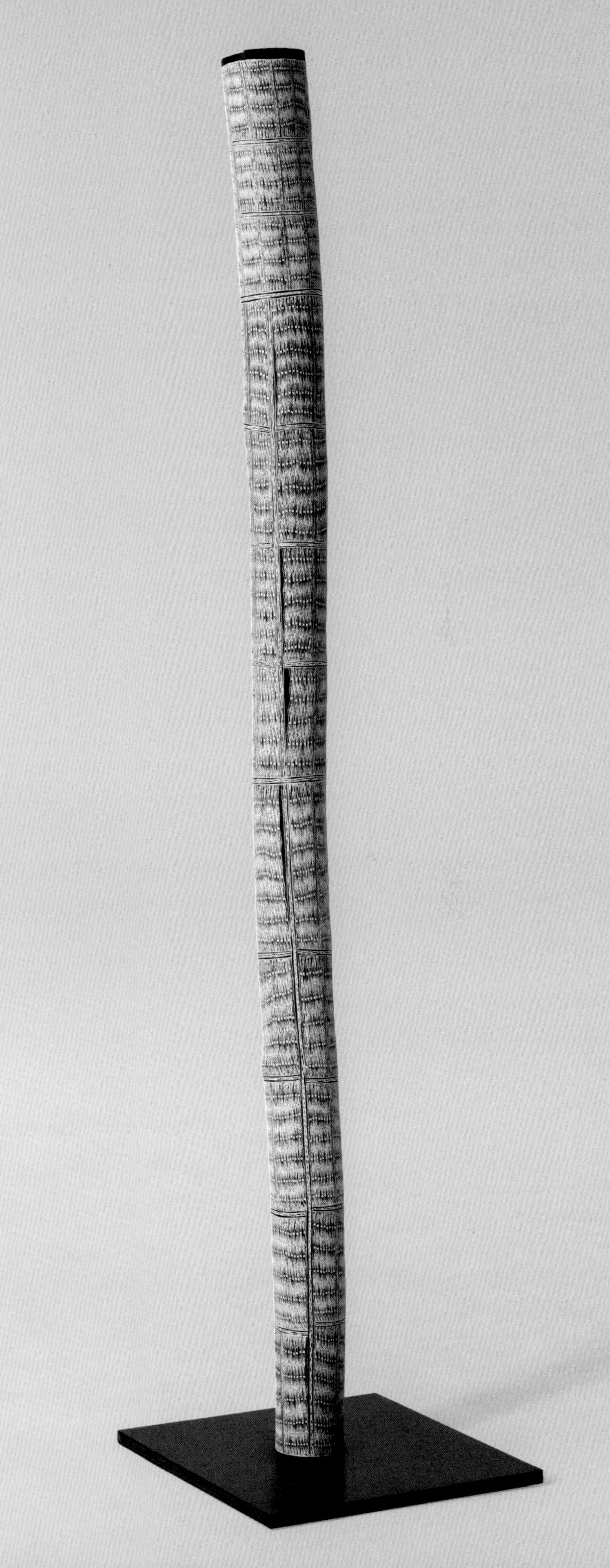

Rerrkirrwaŋa Munuŋgurr, *Gurtha*, 2016. Earth pigments on wood, 72¼ in. (186 cm)

Yimula Munuŋgurr, *Djapu*, 2016. Earth pigments on wood, 67¼ in. (170.9 cm)

Yimula Munuŋgurr, *Djapu*, 2016. Earth pigments on wood, 50⅜ in. (128 cm)

Yimula Munuŋgurr, *Djapu*, 2016. Earth pigments on wood, 88⅝ in. (225 cm)

Yimula Munuŋgurr, *Djapu* 2016. Earth pigments on wood, 65⅛ in. (165.5 cm)

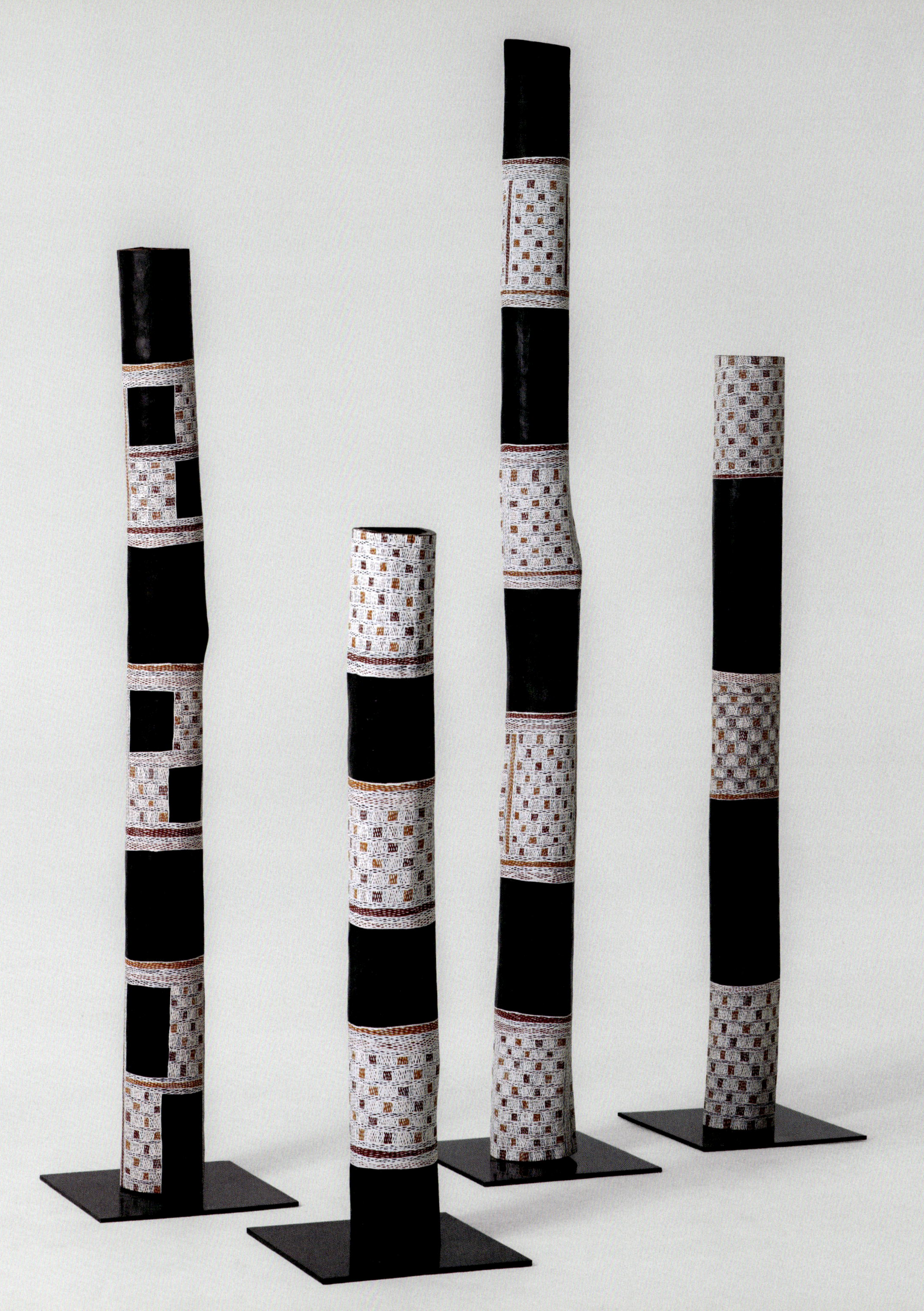

Wukun Waṉambi, *Bamurruŋu*, 2016. Earth pigments on wood. Installation of seven poles. Dimensions variable

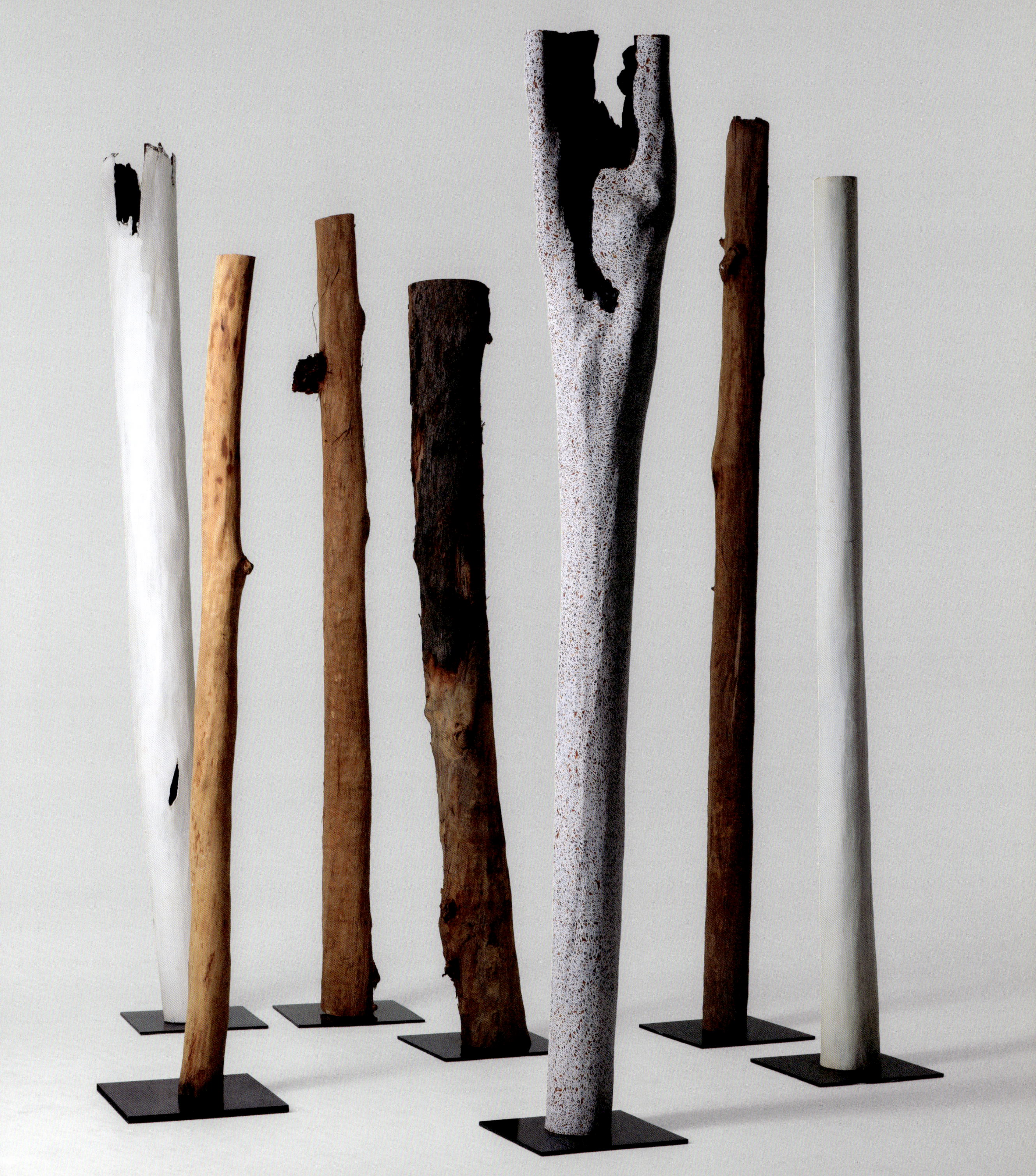

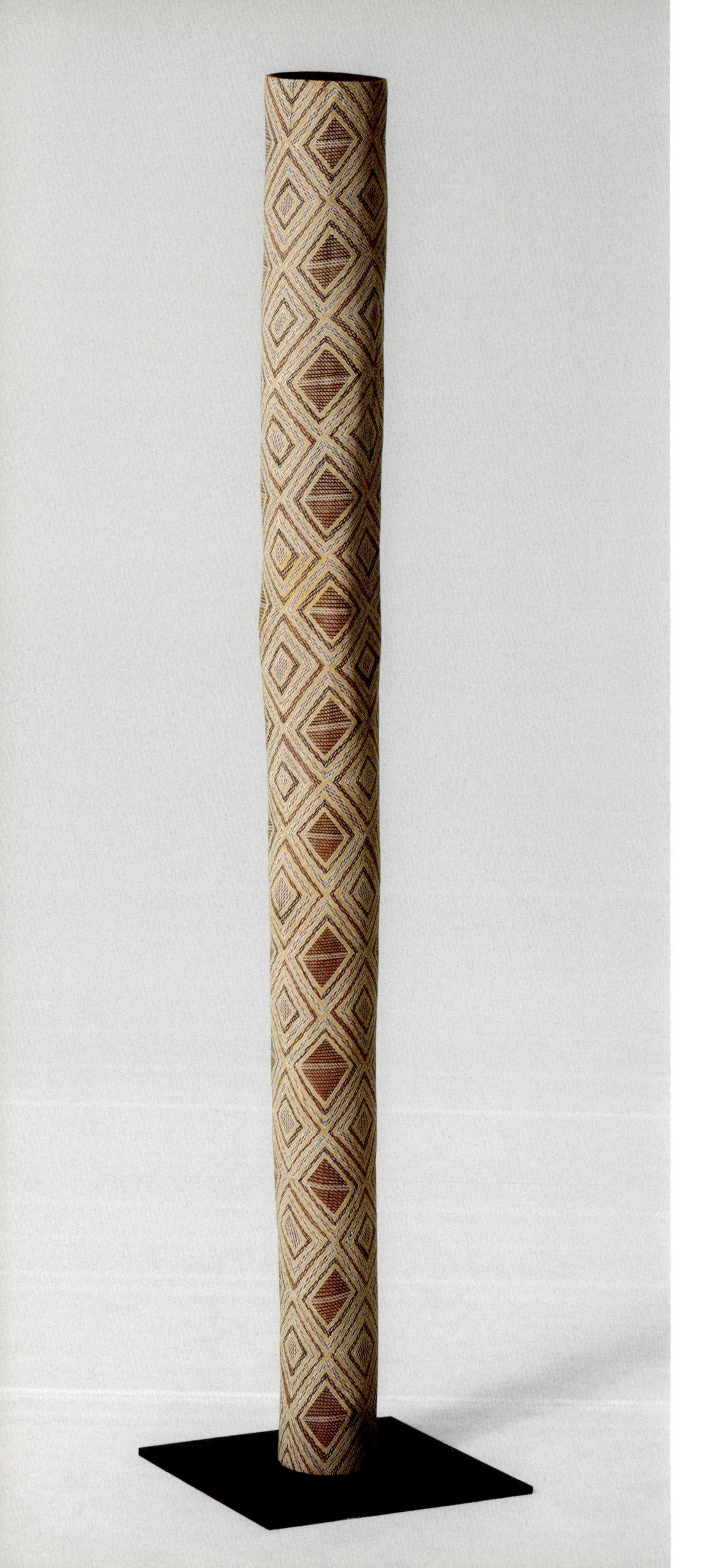

Garawan Wa<u>n</u>ambi, *Marraŋu*, 2011. Earth pigments on wood, 72 in. (184 cm)

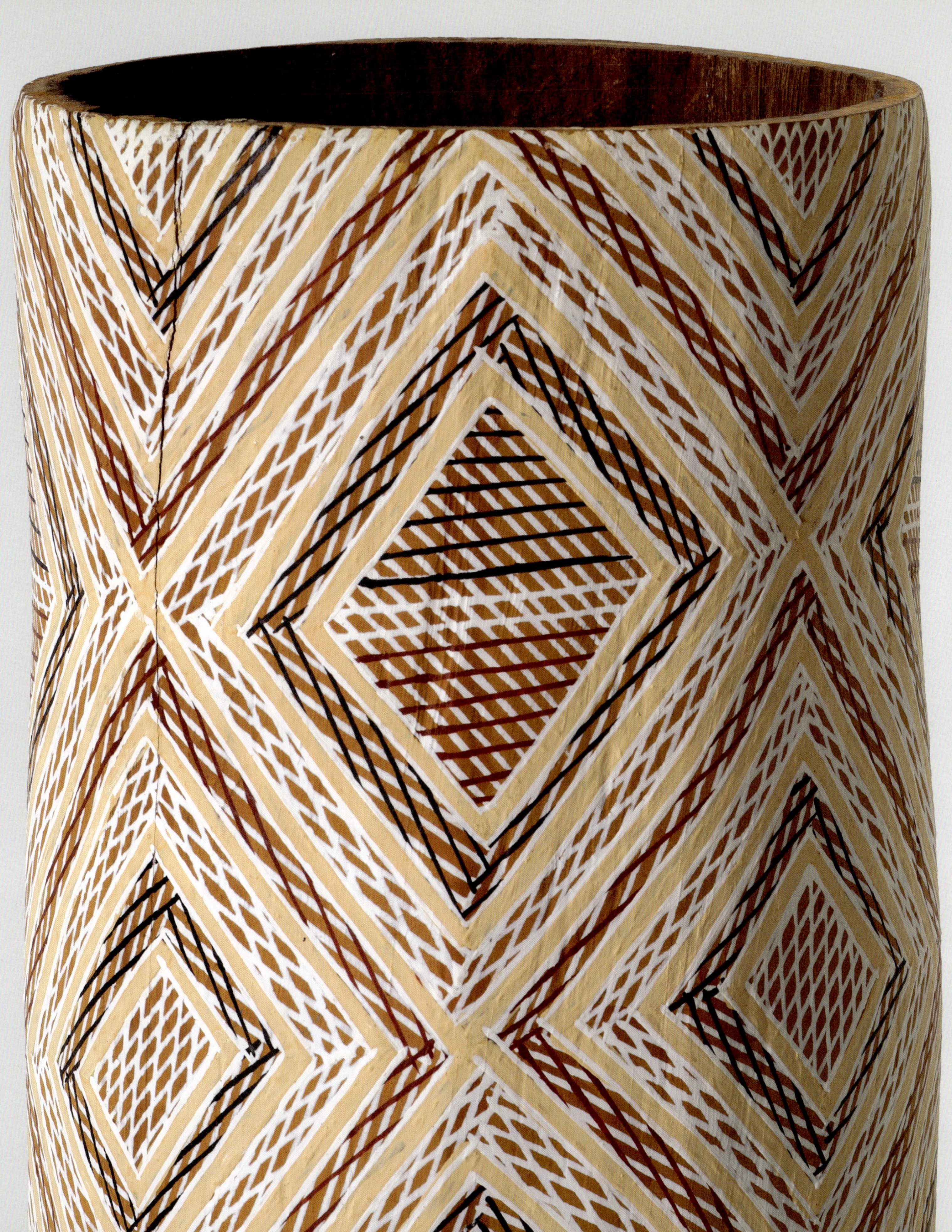

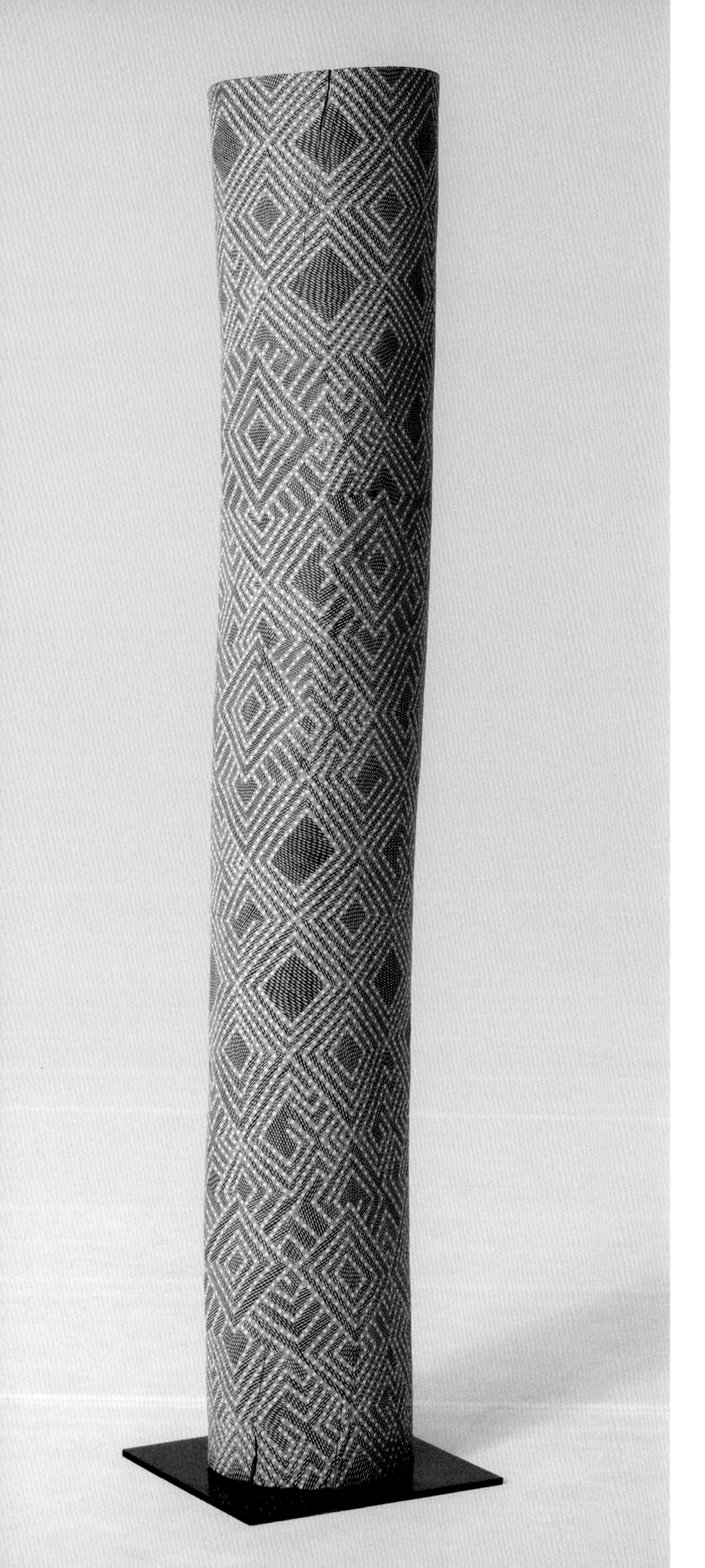

Garawan Wa̱ŋambi, *Marraŋu*, 2016. Earth pigments on wood, 75¼ in. (191 cm)

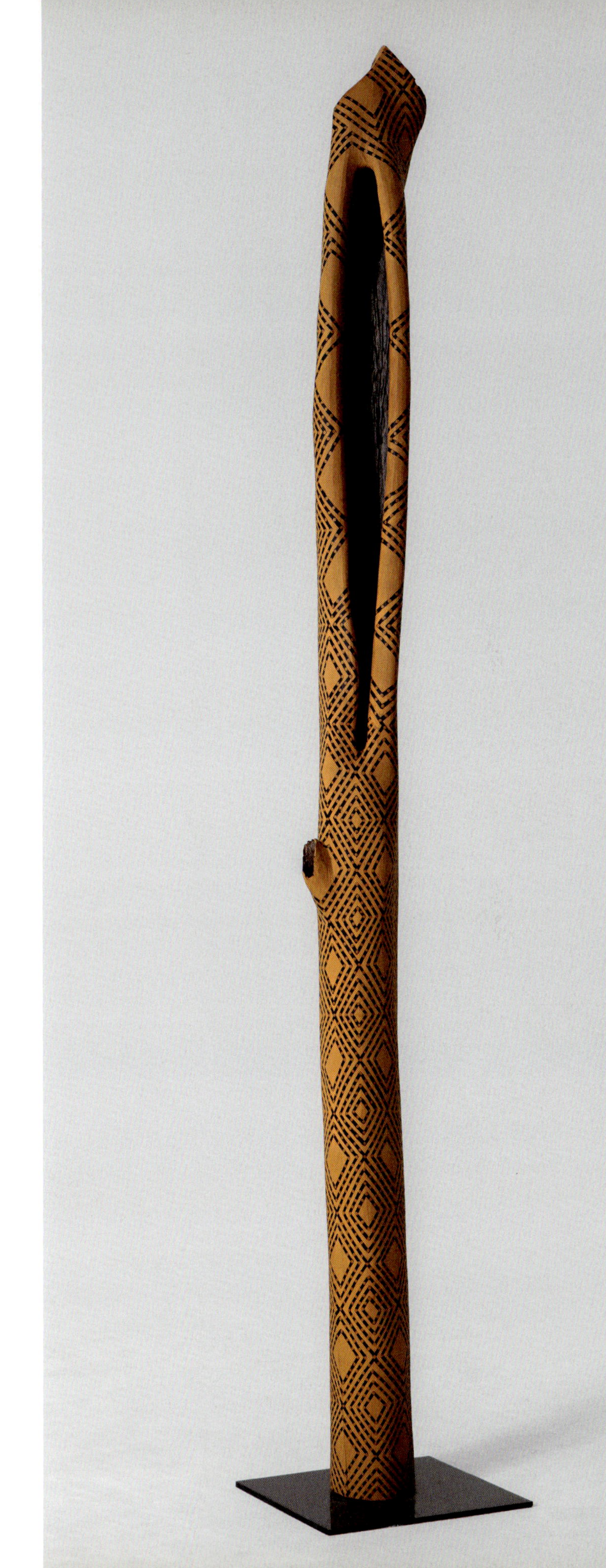

Garawan Waṉambi, *Marraŋu*, 2016. Earth pigments on wood, 100½ in. (255 cm)

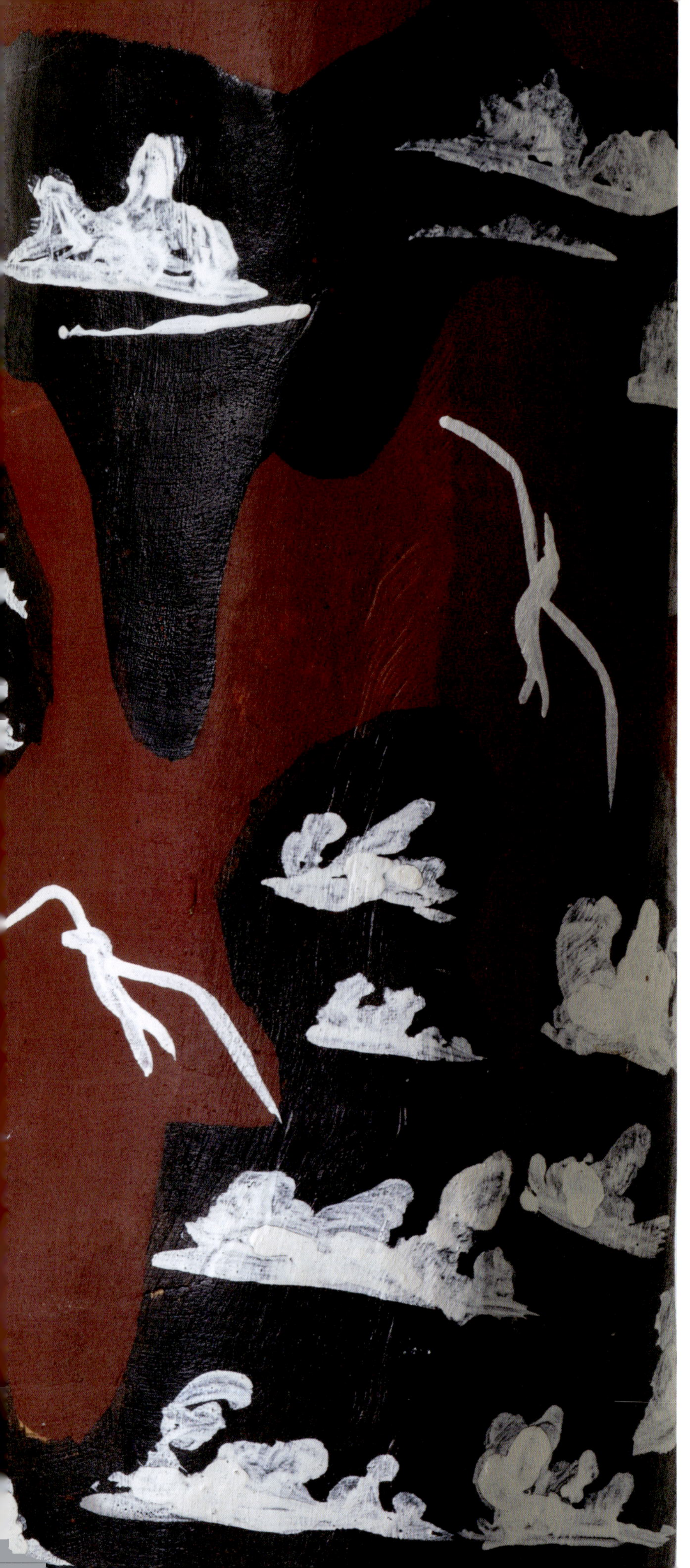

Nawurapu Wunuŋmurra, *Garraparra*, 2016. Earth pigments on wood, 87⅛ in. (221cm)

Nawurapu Wunuŋmurra, *Garraparra*, 2016. Earth pigments on wood, 70 in. (178 cm)

Nawurapu Wunuŋmurra, *Muŋurru* 2016. Earth pigments on wood, 106$^{5}/_{16}$ in. (270 cm)

Nawurapu Wunuŋmurra, *Waŋupini*, 2016. Earth pigments on wood, 87¾ in. (223 cm)

Nawurapu Wunuŋmurra, *Clouds at Garraparra*, 2016. Earth pigments on wood, 83⅞ in. (213 cm)

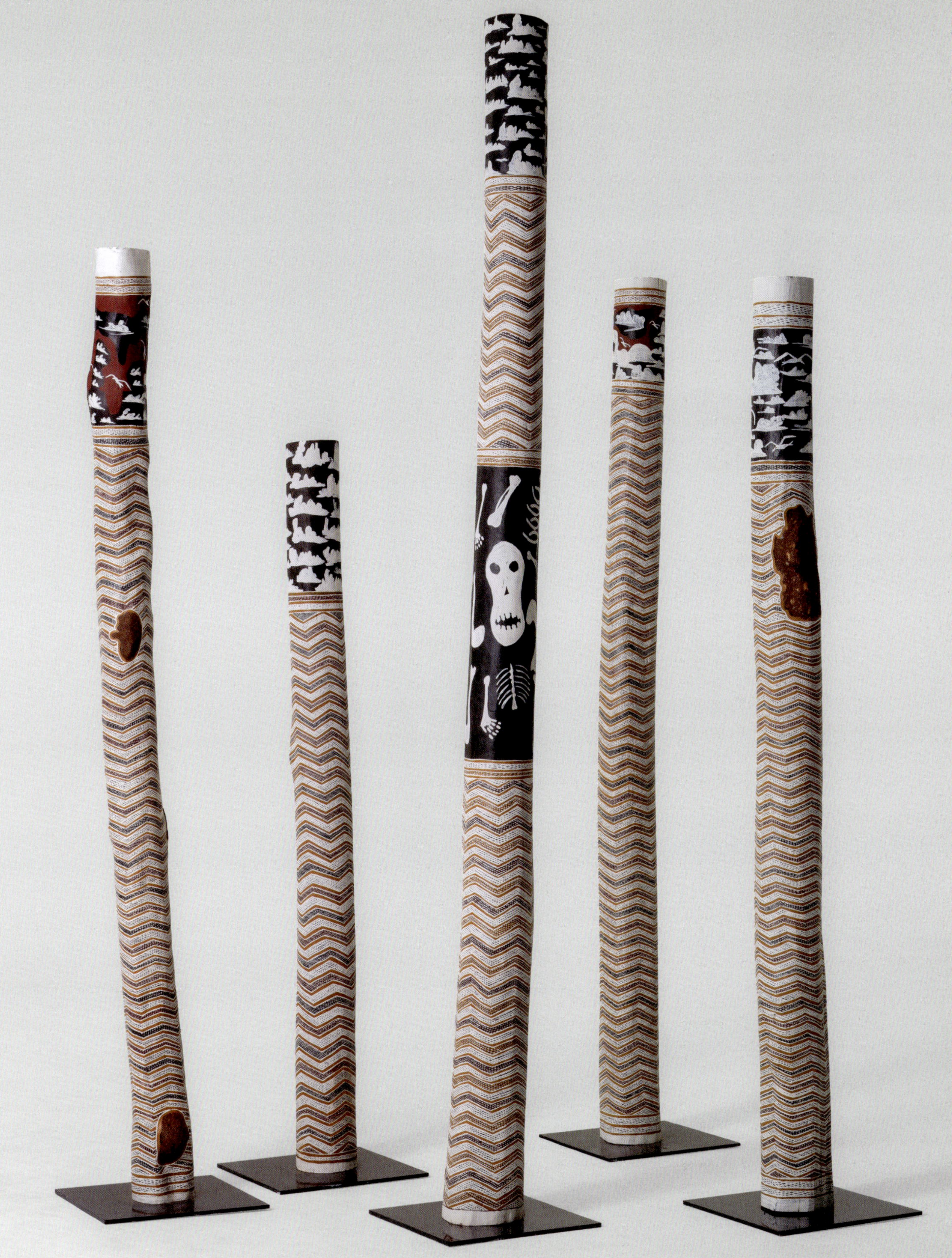

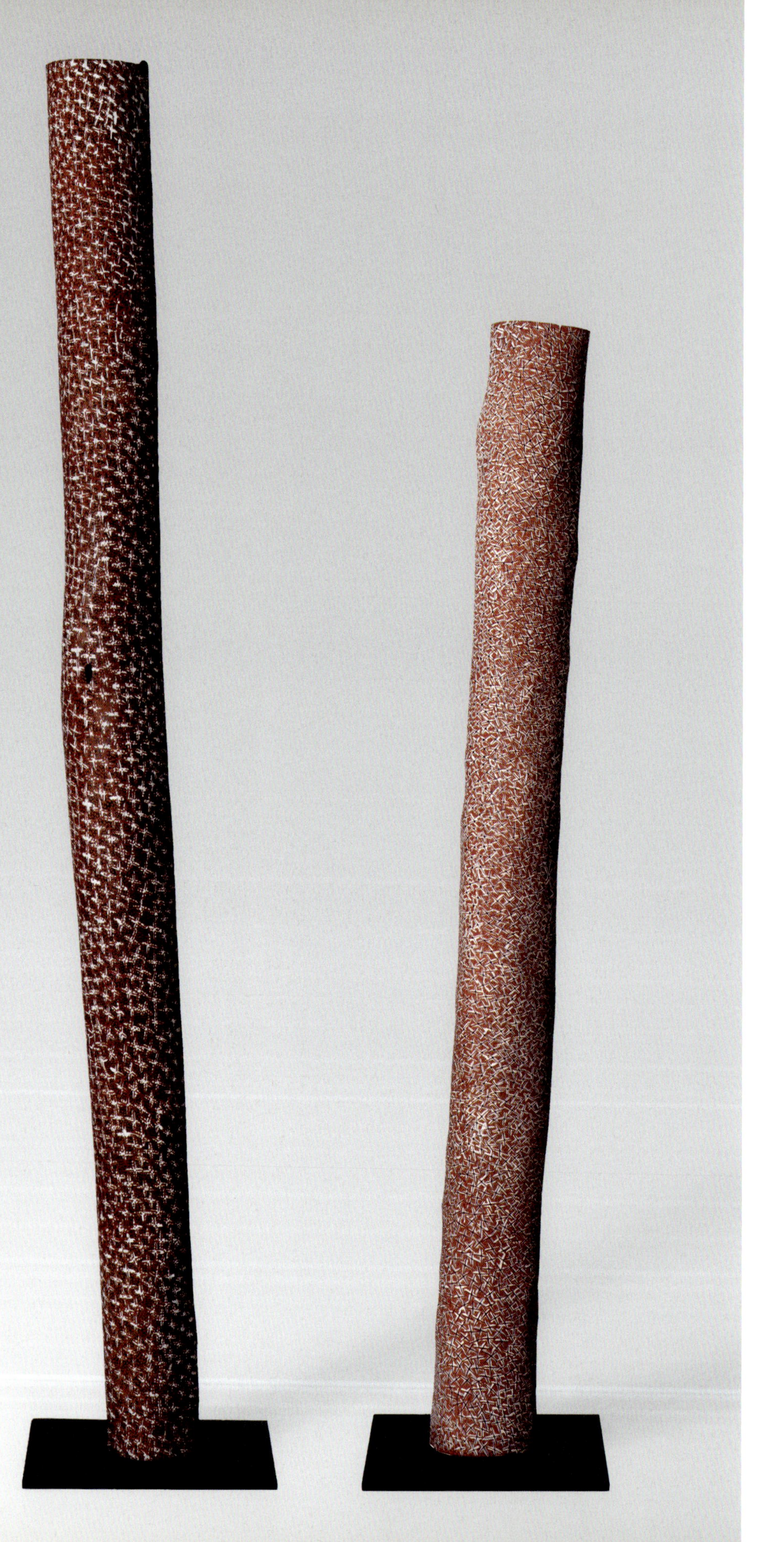

Gulumbu Yunupiŋu, *Ganyu (Stars)*, 2004. Earth pigments on wood, 94½ in. (240 cm).

Gulumbu Yunupiŋu, *Gärak*, 2011. Earth pigments on wood, 71⅝ in. (182 cm)

Opposite:
Nyapanyapa Yunupiŋu, *Untitled*, 2013. Earth pigments on wood, 84¼ in. (214 cm).

Nyapanyapa Yunupiŋu, *Untitled*, 2013. Earth pigments on wood, 83⅞ in. (213 cm).

Nyapanyapa Yunupiŋu, *Untitled*, 2013. Earth pigments on wood, 94⅞ in. (241 cm).

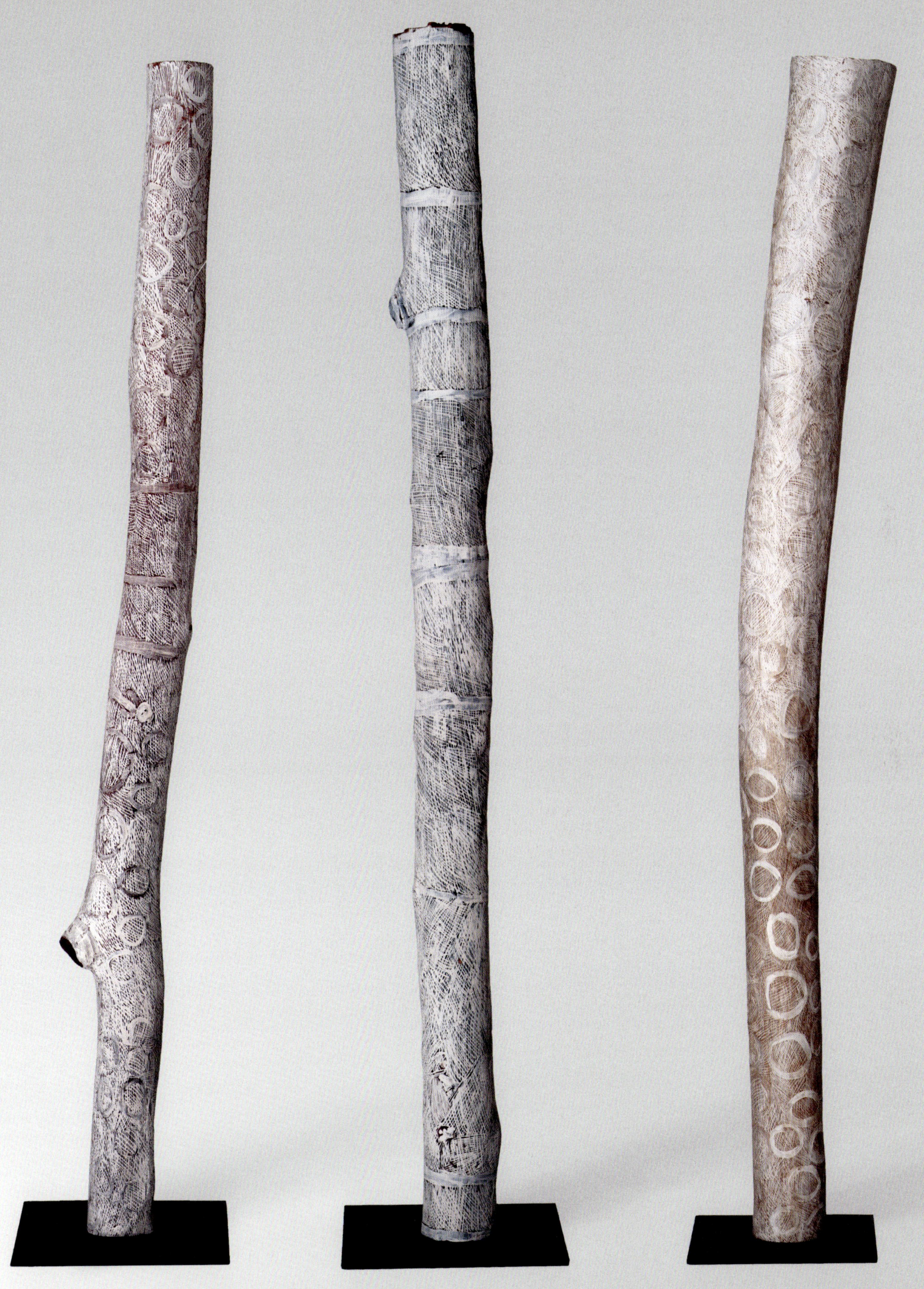

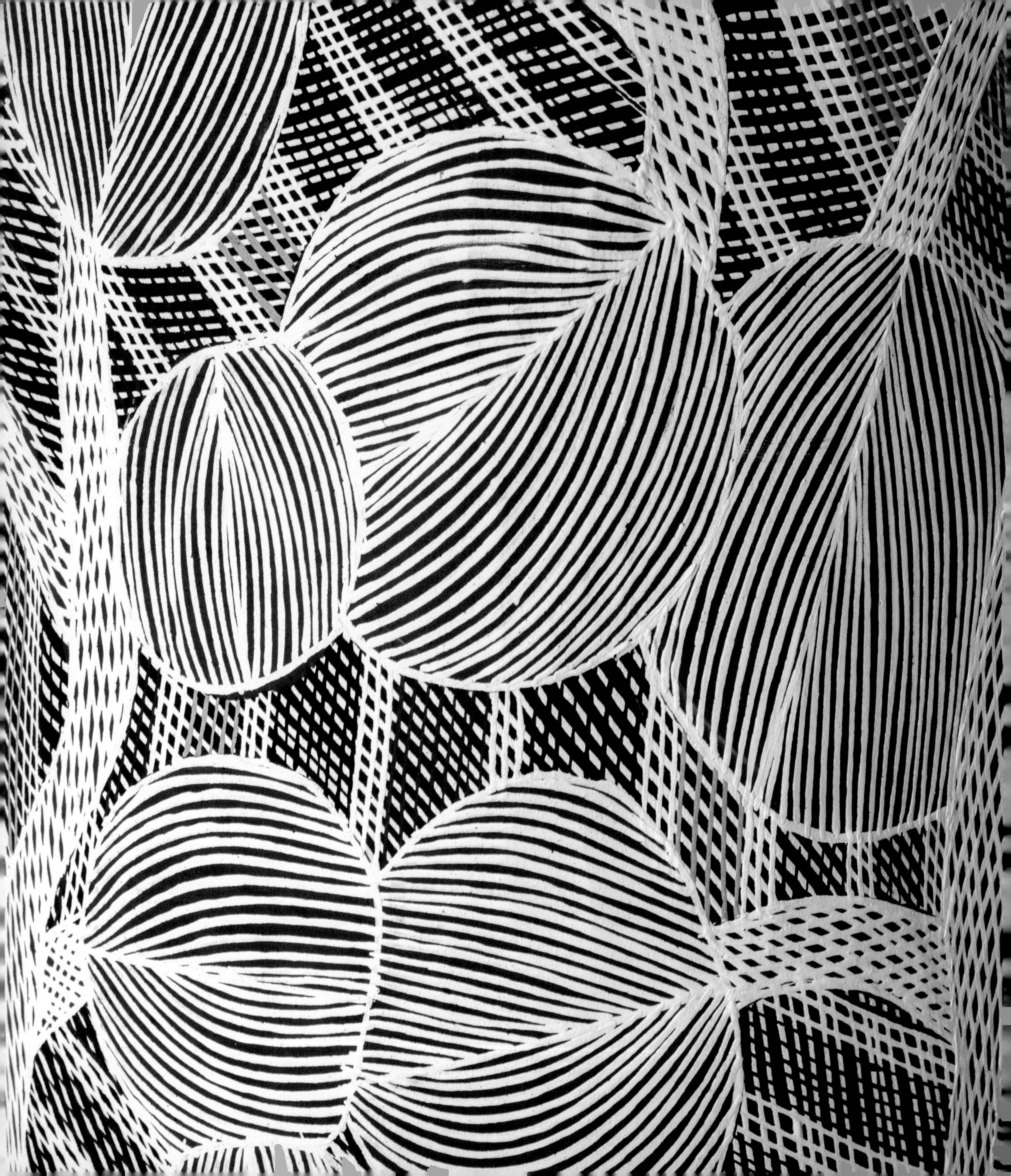

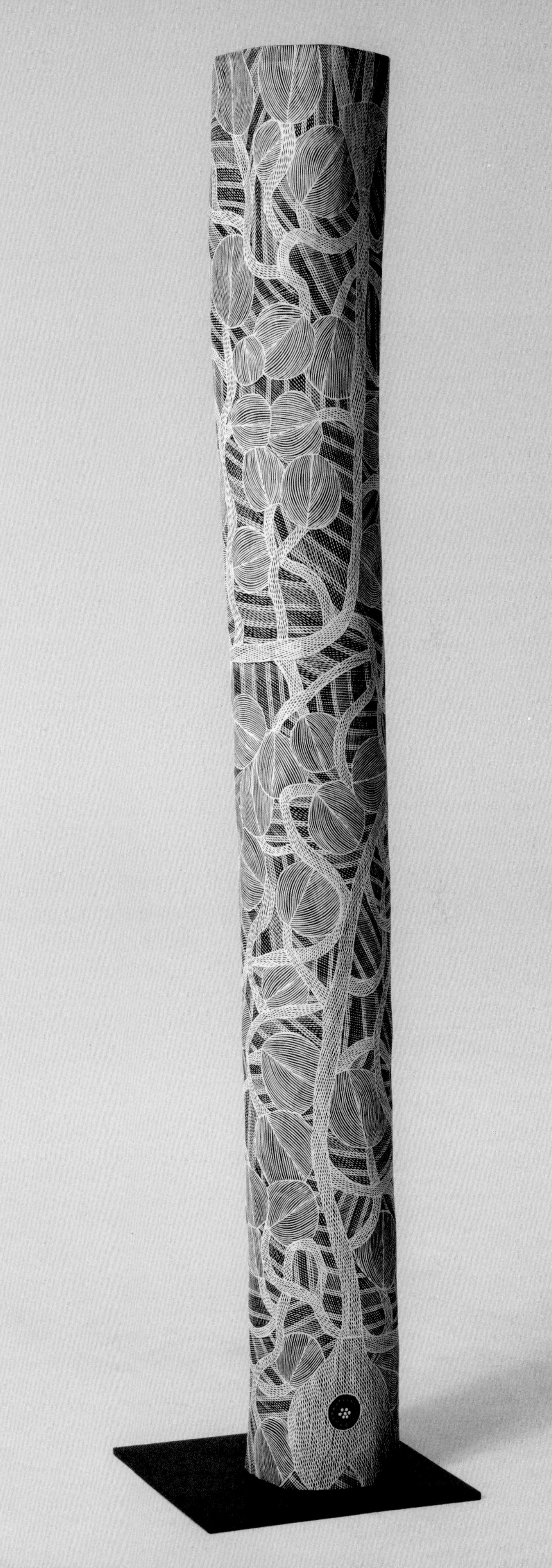

Malaluba Gumana, *Dhatam (Waterlilly)*, 2015. Earth pigments on wood, 75½ in. (191.7 cm)

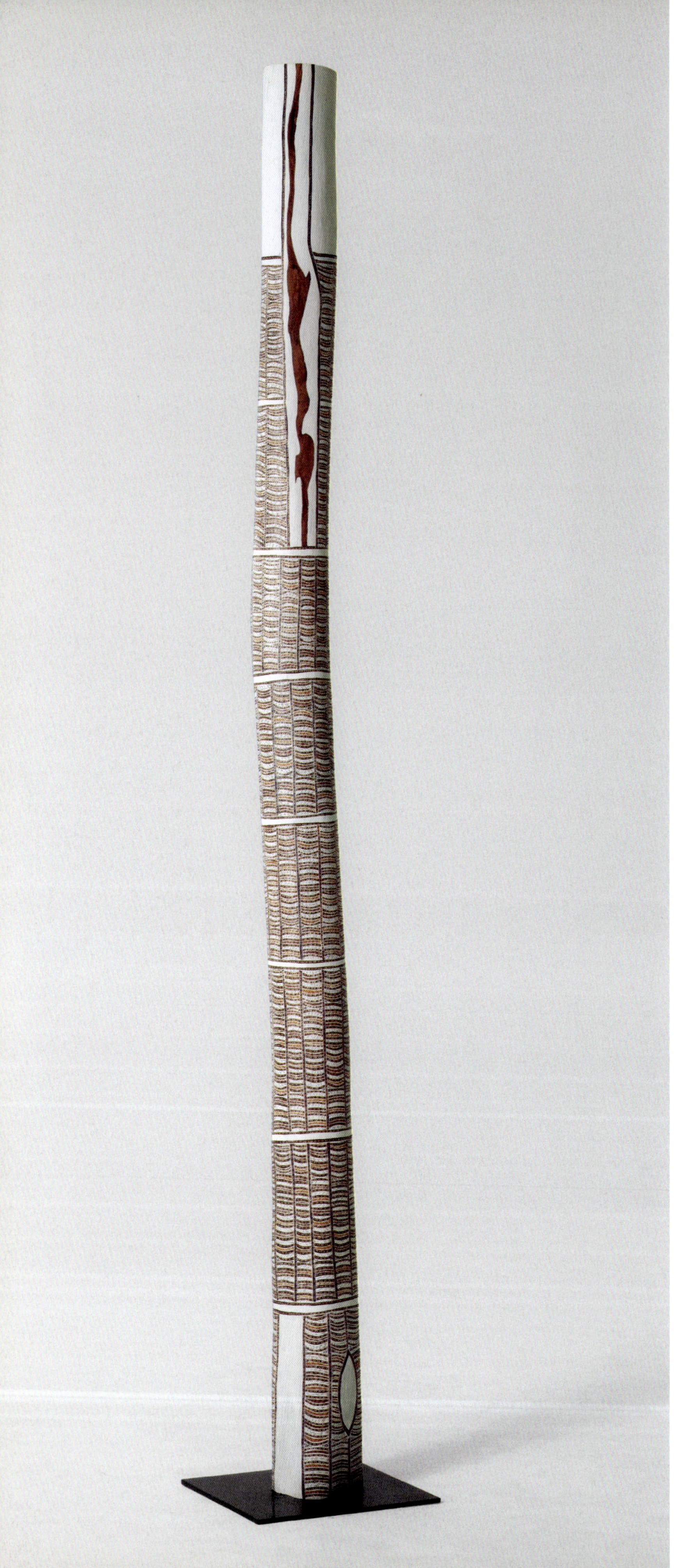

Guwaykuway Waṉambi, *Yanawal*, 2016. Earth pigments on wood, 111⅜ in. (283 cm)

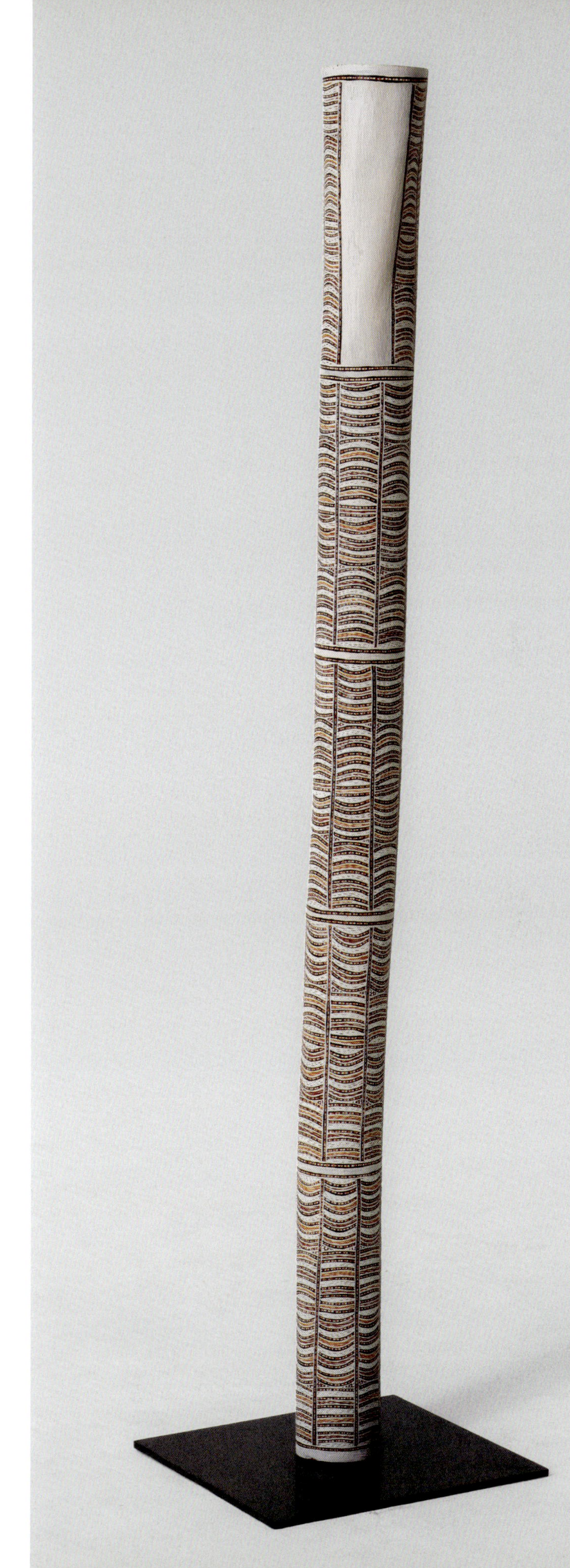

Guwaykuway Wan̲ambi, *Yanawal*, 2016. Earth pigments on wood, 68⅞ in. (175 cm)

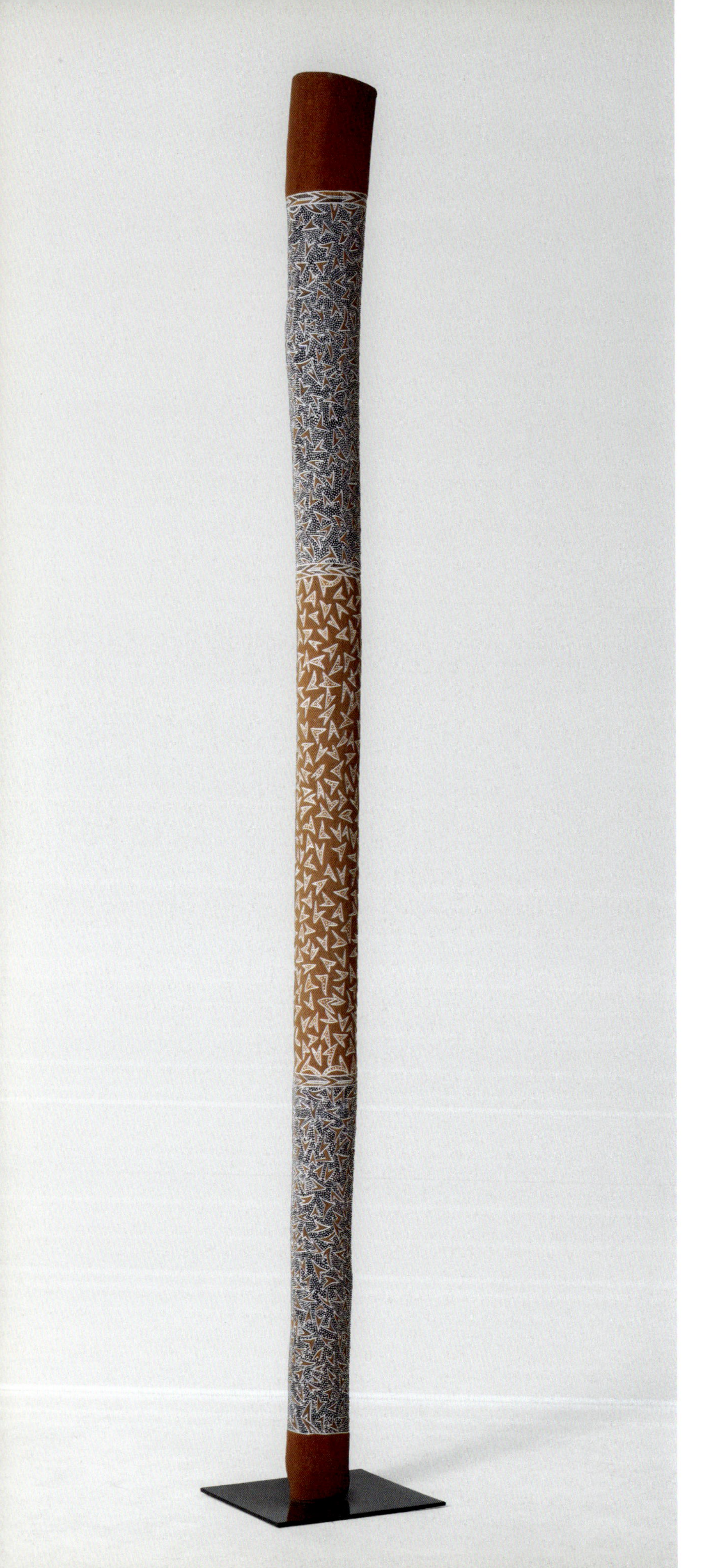

Yalanba Waṉambi, *Trial Bay*, 2016. Earth pigments on wood, 120 in. (305 cm)

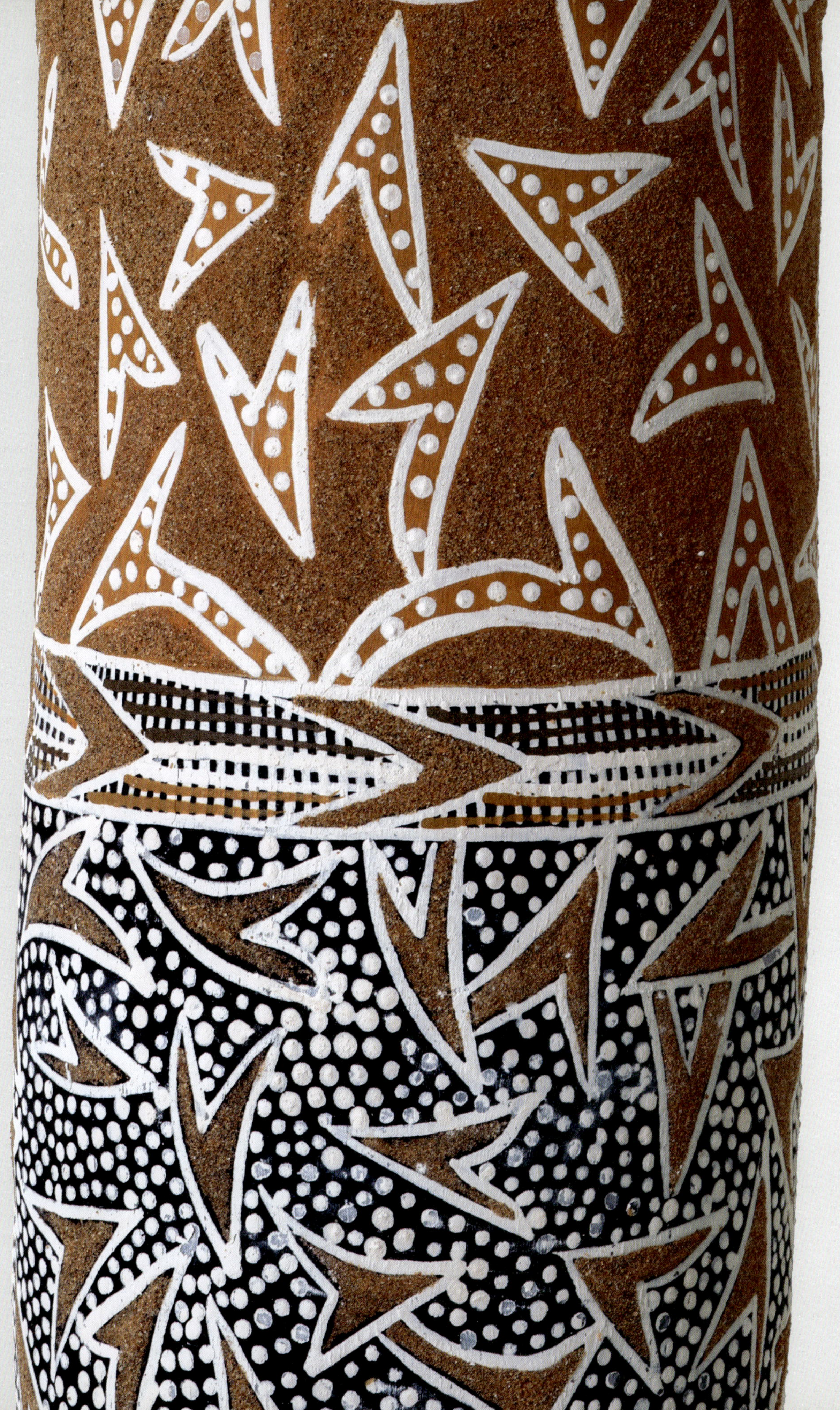

Notes

The Inside World

1. The most notable example of these being the touring exhibition *Larrakitj* curated by Anne Marie Brody from the Kerry Stokes Collection. See Anne Marie Brody, *Larrakitj–Kerry Stokes Collection* (Perth: Australian Capital Equity, 2011).
2. This includes the use of macrons to indicate retroflexed sounds as well as the velar nasal (or "tailed n" [Ŋ:ŋ]) used in northeastern Arnhem Land to denote the *ng* sound.
3. Howard Morphy, *Ancestral Connections: Art and an Aboriginal System of Knowledge* (Chicago: Chicago University Press, 1991), 109–10.
4. In this painting there are four ceremonial *burala* (two black, one white and one yellow). The white *burala* is called Goluk. The black *burala* is called Djaŋalan, and the yellow *burala* is called Ŋarrinya Ŋgarrinya. Although not included in this painting, there is also a red *burala* called Gurrtjuna. I am indebted to Joe Dhamanydji and Chris Durkin from Milingimbi Art and Culture for sharing this reading of Buŋuwuy's painting with me.
5. Morphy, *Ancestral Connections*, 79.
6. Wukun Waṉambi, in *Unsettled: Stories Within*, National Museum of Australia. http://www.nma.gov.au/exhibitions/unsettled/wukun_wanambi, accessed August 15, 2018.
7. This is something that I have taken up at greater length in the essay, "'A Stitch in Time': How Aboriginal Australian Artists are Reweaving Our World," in *Everywhen: The Eternal Present in Indigenous Art from Australia*, ed. Stephen Gilchrist (Cambridge, Mass.: Harvard University Press, 2016), 16–27.
8. Morphy, *Ancestral Connections*, 300.
9. Peter Osborne, *Anywhere or Not at All: Philosophy of Contemporary Art* (London: Verso, 2013), 50. This is particularly evident in the philosophical tendency to look to "pre-modern" and Indigenous modes of thought as a corrective to the dominance of Enlightenment epistemology. See for instance, Bruno Latour, *We Have Never Been Modern*, trans. Catherine Porter (Cambridge, Mass.: Harvard University Press, 1993); Levi Bryant, *The Democracy of Objects* (Ann Arbor: Open Humanities Press, 2011); Jane Bennett, *The Enchantment of Modern Life: Attachments, Crossings and Ethics* (Princeton: Princeton University Press, 2001); and Jane Bennett, *Vibrant Matter: A Political Ecology of Things* (Durham, NC.: Duke University Press, 2010). A similar tendency can be seen in a populist guise in Wade Davis, *The Wayfinders: Why Ancient Wisdom Matters in the Modern World* (Toronto: Anansi Press, 2009).
10. Djon Mundine, in *From the Southern Cross: Australian Biennale 1988: A View of World Art* (Sydney: Sydney Biennale, 1988), 230.
11. Terry Smith, "Public Art between Cultures: The 'Aboriginal Memorial,' Aboriginality, and Nationality in Australia," *Critical Inquiry* 27, no. 4 (2001): 636.
12. Terry Smith, *Contemporary Art: World Currents* (London: Laurence King Publishing, 2011), 212.
13. Nigel Lendon, "Relational Agency: Rethinking *The Aboriginal Memorial*," *EMAJ* 9 (2016), 1–28.
14. Andreas Huyssen, "Present Pasts: Media, Politics, Amnesia," *Public Culture* 12, no. 1 (Winter 2000): 21.
15. Huyssen, "Present Pasts," 22.
16. Osborne, *Anywhere or Not at All*, 17.
17. See for instance, Christine Ross, *The Past Is the Present; It's the Future, Too: The Temporal Turn in Contemporary Art* (New York: Continuum, 2012).
18. Hal Foster, *The Return of the Real: Art and Theory at the End of the Century* (Cambridge, Mass: MIT Press, 1996), 186.
19. Jill Bennett, *Empathic Vision: Affect, Trauma, and Contemporary Art* (Stanford: Standford University Press, 2005), 7.
20. Jennifer Loureide Biddle, "Anthropology as Eulogy: On Loss, Lies and License," in *World Memory: Personal Trajectories in Global Time*, Jill Bennett and Rosanne Kennedy, eds. (New York: Palgrave Macmillan, 2003), 52.
21. The notion of "aesthetic contours" is borrowed from Robyn Ferrell, *Sacred Exchanges: Images in Global Context* (New York: Columbia University Press, 2012).

Larrakitj

1. In the Preface to Anne Marie Brody's edited volume, *Larrakitj–Kerry Stokes Collection* (Perth: Australian Capital Equity, 2011), the Yolŋu artist and ceremonial leader Gawirrin Gumana (1935–2017) wrote "*Larrakitj* is like a new skin for the bones." Brody's book provides the most detailed account of the history and iconography of hollow-log coffins in eastern Arnhem Land, with a primary focus on works from Yirrkala. Nicolas Peterson, "Mortuary customs of North East Arnhem Land: an account compiled from the fieldnotes of Donald Thomson," *Memoirs of the National Museum of Victoria* 37 (1976), 97–108, provides an overview of mortuary rituals as they were at the beginning of intensive European colonization in the 1930s.
2. This history of change is the subject of Frances and Howard Morphy's chapter, "Soon we will be spending all our time in funerals. Yolŋu mortuary rituals in an epoch of constant change," in Signe Howell and Aude Talle: *Returns to the Field—Multitemporal Research and Contemporary Anthropology* (Bloomington: Indiana University Press, 2011), 49–72. While the focus is on changes that have occurred in eastern Arnhem Land similar processes have occurred across Australia.
3. Ian Dunlop's film *Maḏarrpa Funeral at Gurka'wuy* (Sydney: Film Australia, 1979) and the accompanying monograph by Howard Morphy, *Journey to the Crocodile's Nest* (Canberra: Aboriginal Studies Press, 1984), provide a detailed documentary account of a Yolŋu funeral ceremony.
4. Cecil Holmes's film *Djalambu* (1963), made for the Australian Institute of Aboriginal and Torres Strait Islander Studies is a wonderful record of a Yolŋu hollow-coffin ceremony that took place

at Milingimbi and was led by Djäwa of the Gupapuyŋu clan. The performance spiritual setting was Djiliwirri, the sacred place of the wild honey ancestor Birrkuda. The ceremony was a public performance but the film is now of restricted access. Sequences from it are included in the video produced for the Yolŋu rock band Soft Sands recording of "Djiliwirri" by Joe Gumbula and Fred Dhamarrandji (1997). Gumbula was the son of Djäwa and the film and song express the dynamism and spiritual continuity of Yolŋu systems of knowledge and performance.
5. The most detailed account of western Arnhem Land art is Luke Taylor's *Seeing the Inside—Bark painting in Western Arnhem Land* (Oxford: Clarendon Press, 1996). Recent developments in the region's paintings are covered in Taylor's chapter "Categories of 'old' and 'new' in western Arnhem Land bark painting," in Ann McGrath and Mary Anne Jebb, eds, *Long History, Deep Time: Deepening Histories of Place* (Canberra: ANU Press, 2015), 101–17.
6. The history of the recognition of Aboriginal art from Arnhem Land is the subject of Howard Morphy, *Becoming Art—Exploring Cross-cultural Categories* (Oxford: Berg, 2007). See also Ian McLean, *Rattling Spears: A History of Indigenous Australian Art* (London: Reaktion Books, 2016).
7. The most detailed account of *The Aboriginal Memorial* is Susan Jenkins, "'It is power:' interpretation of the *Aboriginal Memorial* in its ethnographic, museological, art historical and political contexts" (unpublished M.Phil. thesis, Australian National University, 2003). The National Gallery of Australia's website provides an excellent overview: https://nga.gov.au/AboriginalMemorial/home.cfm

A Longer Contemporary

1. Howard Morphy, *Ancestral Connections: Art and an Aboriginal System of Knowledge* (Chicago and London: University of Chicago Press, 1991), 4.
2. Henry Skerritt made the excellent point of this link between the natural and human-made in these works. Henry Skerritt, e-mail message to the author, January 2017.
3. Henry F. Skerritt, "No Boundaries: Aboriginal Australian Contemporary Abstract Painting," in *No Boundaries: Aboriginal Australian Contemporary Abstract Painting*, ed. Henry F. Skerritt (Reno and Munich: Nevada Museum of Art and Prestel, 2015), 12.
4. Morphy, *Ancestral Connections,* 4.

Sharing Culture to Maintain a Future

1. Wukun Wan̲ambi, in *Unsettled: Stories Within*, National Museum of Australia. http://www.nma.gov.au/exhitions/unsettled/wukun_wanambi, accessed August 15, 2018.
2. The neologisim "everywhen" was coined by W. E. H. Stanner in his 1953 essay "The Dreaming." Stanner noted, "One cannot 'fix' The Dreaming in time: it was, and is, everywhen." In 2016, Yamatji curator Stephen Gilchrist used it as the title of the exhibition *Everywhen: The Eternal Present in Indigenous Art from Australia* at Harvard Art Museums. See W. E. H. Stanner, *The Dreaming and Other Essays*, (Melbourne: Black Inc. Agenda, 2009), 57–72; and Stephen Gilchrist, ed. *Everywhen: The Eternal Present in Indigenous Art from Australia* (Cambridge, Mass.: Harvard University Press, 2016).
3. Tony Birch, "Our Red Sands Dug and Sifted: Sovereignty and the Act of Being," in *Sovereignty*, ed. Paola Bella and Max Delany (Melbourne: Australian Centre for Contemporary Art, 2016), 17.
4. Djon Mundine, "Saltwater," in *Saltwater: Yirrkala Bark Paintings of Sea Country* (Buku-Larrŋgay Mulka Centre and Jennifer Isaacs Publishing, 1999), 20.
5. Mundine, "Saltwater."
6. Lindy Lee interview with Djon Mundine, OAM, *Artlink* 35, no.2 (June 2015), 34.
7. Paola Bella, "Sovereignty: Inalienable and Intimate," in *Sovereignty*, ed. Bella and Delany, 11.
8. Mundine, "Saltwater," 22.
9. Will Stubbs, "Reflections on the Yirrkala Church Panels," *L̲arrakitj—The Kerry Stokes Collection,* ed. Anne Marie Brody (Perth: Australian Capital Equity, 2011), 45.

***Nawarddeken Lorrkkon dja* Injalak Arts**

1. Unless otherwise noted, all quotes are taken from interviews with the author, February–March 2018.
2. Gabriel Maralngurra, interviewed by Lauren van Nest, March 26, 2018.
3. See Dan Kennedy, "Kabimbebme: It Really Pops!" *Artlink* 36, no. 2 (June 2016): 60–62.
4. Gabriel Maralngurra, quoted in Henry Skerritt, "Is Art History Any Use to Aboriginal Artists? Gabriel Maralngurra's *Contact Paintings,*" in *Double Desire: Transculturation and Indigenous Contemporary Art,*" ed. Ian McLean (Newcastle upon Tyne: Cambridge Scholars Press, 2014), 239.

Memories of a *Lorrkkon* Ceremony at Maningrida

1. Spelled *lárrkkan* in the Ndjébbana language of Maningrida.

Garrawurra D̲upun

1. William Lloyd Warner, *A Black Civilization: A Social Study of an Australian Tribe* (revised edition) (New York: Harper and Brothers, 1969), 431.
2. Warner, *A Black Civilization*, 431.
3. Apolline Kohen, "Maningrida," in *Beyond Sacred: Recent Painting from Australia's Remote Aboriginal Communities. The Collection of Colin and Elizabeth Laverty* (Prahan, Victoria: Hardie Grant Books, 2008), 270.
4. Andrew Blake, "Wukun Wan̲ambi from Yirrkala," in *Beyond Sacred*, 300.
5. A. Borsboom, "Dreaming Clusters Among Marangu Clans," in *Australian Aboriginal Concepts* (Canberra: Australian Institute of Aboriginal Studies, 1974), 115.

6. Howard Morphy, "Larrakitji—Death and the Celebration of Life," in *Larrakitj. Kerry Stokes Collection*, ed. Anne Marie Brody (Perth: Australian Capital Equity, 2011), 27.
7. N. Garrawurra, interview with the author, Darwin, NT: 2017.
8. Morphy, "Larrakitji—Death and the Celebration of Life," 30.
9. Louise Hamby, *Containers of Power: Women with Clever Hands* (Melbourne: Utber & Patullo Publishing, 2010), 13.
10. Ian Keen, "Metaphor and the Metalanguage: 'Groups' in Northeast Arnhem Land," *American Ethnologist*, 22, no. 3 (1995): 73.
11. Ian Keen, *One Ceremony, One Song: An Economy of Religious Knowledge among the Yolngu of North-East Arnhem Land* (Canberra: The Australian National University, 1978), 73.
12. Wally Caruana, "Liya-gawumirr and Manyar-rngu people and Balmbi people," in *Le Mémorial: un chef-d'oeuvre d'art aborigène / The Memorial: a Masterpiece of Aboriginal Art* (Lausanne and Canberra: Musée Olympique and the National Gallery of Australia, 1999), 104; B. Westley and S. Westley, "Mickey Durrng—Artist of East Arnhem Land," *Aboriginal Art Online*. Accessed. http://www.aboriginalartonline.com/resources/articles2.php.
13. Westley and Westley, "Mickey Durrng."
14. Amy Corfield, *Amy Corfield diary kept on South Goulburn Island Mission, August 1916–15 August 191, with transcription by Deborah Stummer, 2008*, transcription Deborah Stummer (Goulburn Island: 1916, 1919).
15. C. S. G. H. Wilkins, *Undiscovered Australia* (New York and London: G. P. Putnam's Sons, 1929), 157, Fig. 13-16-80 and 13-16-123.
16. Wilkins, *Undiscovered Australia*.
17. Warner, *A Black Civilization*, 504.
18. Oc1925,1113.35 and 36.
19. 1985.0072.0090.
20. Lindy Allen and Louise Hamby, "A History of the Art from Milingimbi," in *Art from Milingimbi: Taking Memories Back*, ed. Cara Pinchbeck (Sydney: Art Gallery of New South Wales, 2017).
21. Louise Hamby and Dr. Gumbula, "Development of Collecting at the Milingimbi Mission," in *Strings of Connectedness: Essays in Honour of Ian Keen*, ed. P. G. Toner (Canberra: ANU Press, 2015).
22. Susan Jenkins, "Remembrance and Renewal: An Overview of Aboriginal Burial Practices and Their Contemporary Significance," in Susan Jenkins, "Remembrance and Renewal: An Overview of Aboriginal Burial Practices and their Contemporary Significance," in *Le Mémorial: un chef-d'oeuvre d'art aborigène / The Memorial: a Masterpiece of Aboriginal Art*, 32–44. *The Memorial. A Masterpiece of Aboriginal Art* (Lausanne: Musée Olympique, 1999), 32–44.
23. Henry Skerritt, "Choosing Who Will Keep the Stories Strong," *Artlink* 23, no. 3 (2009), 74–76.
24. Joyce Naliyabu, interview with the author, Milingimbi, NT, 2017.
25. N. Garrawurra, interview with the author, Darwin, NT, 2017.
26. Skerritt, "Choosing Who Will Keep the Stories Strong," 74–76.
27. Skerritt, "Choosing Who Will Keep the Stories Strong," p. 76.
28. Chris Durkin, interview with the author, Milingimbi, NT, 2017.
29. Westley and Westley, "Mickey Durrng."
30. Westley and Westley, "Mickey Durrng."

Selected Bibliography

Allen, Lindy. *Ancestral Power and the Aesthetic.* Melbourne: Ian Potter Museum of Art, 2009.

Altman, Jon, and Luke Taylor. "Too Many Dreamings: Diversity and Change in Bark Paintings from West Arnhem Land." In *Indigenous Art at the Australian National University*, edited by Claudette Chubb and Nancy Sever, 63–101. Melbourne: Macmillan, 2009.

Australia Council Aboriginal Arts Board. *Oenpelli Bark Painting.* Sydney: Ure Smith, 1979.

Balla, Paola, and Max Delany, eds., *Sovereignty.* Melbourne: Australian Centre for Contemporary Art, 2016.

Barber, Marcus. "Coastal Conflicts and Reciprocal Relations: Encounters between Yolngu People and Commercial Fishermen in Blue Mud Bay, North-East Arnhem Land." *Australian Journal of Anthropology* 21, no. 3 (2010): 298–314.

Batty, Philip, Lindy Allen, and John Morton, eds. *The Photographs of Baldwin Spencer*. Carlton: Miegunyah Press, Melbourne University Publishing, 2005.

Bennett, Jane. *The Enchantment of Modern Life: Attachments, Crossings and Ethics*. Princeton: Princeton University Press, 2001.

——. *Vibrant Matter: A Political Ecology of Things*. Durham, NC.: Duke University Press, 2010.

Bennett, Jill. *Empathic Vision: Affect, Trauma, and Contemporary Art.* Stanford: Stanford University Press, 2005.

Berndt, Ronald. *Kunapipi*. Melbourne: Cheshire, 1951.

——. "A Living Aboriginal Art: The Changing Inside and Outside Contexts." In *Aboriginal Arts and Crafts and the Market*, edited by Peter Loveday and Peter Cooke, 29–36. Canberra: North Australia Research Unit, Australian National University, 1983.

Berndt, Ronald, and Catherine Berndt. *Arnhem Land, Its History and Its People*. Melbourne: Cheshire, 1954.

——. *Man, Land and Myth in North Australia: The Gunwinggu People*. East Lansing: Michigan State University, 1970.

Biddle, Jennifer Loureide. "Anthropology as Eulogy: On Loss, Lies and License." In *World Memory: Personal Trajectories in Global Time,* edited by Jill Bennett and Roseanne Kennedy, 43–58. New York: Palgrave McMillan, 2003.

Borsboom, Ad. "Dreaming Clusters Among Marrangu Clans." In *Australian Aboriginal Concepts,* edited by L.R. Hiatt, 106–21. Canberra: Australian Institute of Aboriginal Studies, 1978.

Brody, Anne Marie, ed. *L̲arrakitj—Kerry Stokes Collection.* Perth: Australian Capital Equity, 2011.

Bryant, Levi. *The Democracy of Objects*. Ann Arbor: Open Humanities Press, 2011.

Buku-Larrŋgay Mulka Centre. *Saltwater: Yirrkala Bark Paintings of Sea Country*. Yirrkala: Buku-Larrŋgay Mulka and Jennifer Isaacs Publishing, 1999.

Bullock, Natasha, and Genevieve O'Callaghan. *John Mawurndjul: I am the Old and the New.* Sydney and Adelaide: Museum of Contemporary Art Australia and the Art Gallery of South Australia, 2018.

Chaloupka, George. *Journey in Time*. Chatswood: REED, 1993.

Chaseling, Wilbur. *Yulengor: Nomads of Arnhem Land*. London: Epworth Press, 1957.

Cole, Keith. *A History of Oenpelli*. Darwin: Nungalinya Publications, 1975.

Davis, Wade. *The Wayfinders: Why Ancient Wisdom Matters in the Modern World*. Toronto: Anansi Press, 2009.

Deger, Jennifer. "Seeing the Invisible: Yolngu Video as Revelatory Ritual." *Visual Anthropology* 20 (2007): 103–21.

Dunlop, Ian. *Mad̲arrpa Funeral at Gurka'wuy.* Sydney: Film Australia, 1979.

Dyer, Christine Adrian, ed., *Kunwinjku Art from Injalak, 1991–1992: The John W. Kluge Commission.* North Adelaide, South Australia: Museum Art International, 1994.

Elkin, Adolphus Peter, Catherine Berndt, and Ronald Berndt. *Art in Arnhem Land*. Chicago: University of Chicago Press, 1950.

Ferrell, Robyn. *Sacred Exchanges: Images in Global Context.* New York: Columbia University Press, 2012.

Foster, Hal. *The Return of the Real: Art and Theory at the End of the Century.* Cambridge, Mass.: MIT Press, 1996.

Hamby, Louise, ed. *Twined Together: Kunmadj Njalehnjaleken.* Gunbalanya: Injalak Arts and Crafts, 2005.

——. *Containers of Power: Women with Clever Hands.* Melbourne: Utber and Patullo Publishing, 2010.

Hamby, Louise and Dr. Gumbula. "Development of Collecting at the Milingimbi Mission." In *Strings of Connectedness: Essays in Honour of Ian Keen,* edited by P. G. Toner, 187–214. Canberra: ANU Press, 2015.

Huyssen, Andreas. "Present Pasts: Media, Politics, Amnesia." *Public Culture* 12, no. 1 (Winter 2000): 21–38.

Jenkins, Susan. "'It is Power': Interpretation of the Aboriginal Memorial in its Ethnographic, Museological, Art Historical and Political Contexts." MPhil thesis, Australian National University, 2003.

Kaufman, Christian, ed. *Rarrk—John Mawurndjul: Journey through Time in Northern Australia*, Basel: Museum Tinguely, 2005.

Keen, Ian. "One Ceremony, One Song: An Economy of Religious Knowledge Among the Yolngu of North-East Arnhem Land." Ph.D. thesis, Australian National University, 1978.

——. *Knowledge and Secrecy in an Aboriginal Religion*. Oxford: Oxford University Press, 1994.

——. "Metaphor and Metalanguage: 'Groups' in Northeast Arnhem Land." *American Ethnologist* 22, no. 3 (1995): 502–27,

——. "Ancestors, Magic and Exchange in Yolngu doctrines: extensions of the person in time and space." *Journal of the Royal Anthropological Institute* 12 (2006), 515–53.

Lane, Robert Lazarus. "Wukun Wanambi's *Nhina, Nhäma, Ga Ngäma* (Sit, Look, and Listen)." In *Indigenous Archives: The Making and Unmaking of Aboriginal Art*, edited by Darren Jorgensen and Ian McLean, 227–49. Crawley: UWA Publishing, 2017.

Latour, Bruno. *We Have Never Been Modern.* Translated by Catherine Porter. Cambridge, Mass.: Harvard University Press, 1993.

Lendon, Nigel. "Visual Evidence: Space, Place and Innovation in Bark Paintings of Central Arnhem Land." *Australian Journal of Art* 12, no. 1, 1994, 55–74.

———. "Relational Agency: Rethinking *The Aboriginal Memorial." EMAJ* 9 (2016): 1–28.

Marawili, Djambawa. "On Homelands and Caring for Indigenous Knowledge." *ANKAAA Arts Backbone* 14, no. 2 (December 2014–January 2015): 2–3.

———. "The Land and the Sea Can't Talk, We have to talk for them." *Artlink* 36, no. 2 (June 2016): 26–31.

May, Sally K. "Learning Art, Learning Culture: Art, Education, and the Formation of New Artistic Identities in Arnhem Land, Australia." In *Archaeologies of Art: Time Place, Identity*, edited by Ines Domingo Sanz, Danae Fiore and Sally K. May, 171–94. Walnut Creek, California: Left Coast Press, 2008.

McLean, Ian. "Crossing Country: Tribal Modernism and Kuninjku Bark Painting." *Third Text* 20, no. 5 (September) 2006: 599–616.

———. *Rattling Spears: A History of Indigenous Australian Art.* London: Reaktion Books, 2016.

Morphy, Frances, and Howard Morphy. "Tasting the Waters: Discriminating Identities in the Waters of Blue Mud Bay." *Journal of Material Culture* 11 (2006): 67–85.

———. "Soon we will be spending all our time at funerals": Yolngu Mortuary Rituals in an Epoch of Constant Change." In *Returns to the Field: Multitemporal Research and Contemporary Anthropology*, edited by Signe Howell and Aud Talle. Bloomington: Indiana University Press, 2011: 49–72.

Morphy, Howard. *Journey to the Crocodile's Nest.* Canberra: Aboriginal Studies Press, 1984.

———. "From Dull to Brilliant: The Aesthetics of Spiritual Power Among the Yolngu." *Man* 24, no. 1 (March 1989): 21–40.

———. *Ancestral Connections: Art and an Aboriginal System of Knowledge.* Chicago: Chicago University Press, 1991.

———. "Landscape and the Reproduction of the Ancestral Past." In *The Anthropology of Landscape*, edited by Erich Hirsch and Michael O'Hanlon. Oxford: Clarendon Press, 1995: 184–207.

———. *Aboriginal Art.* London: Phaidon, 1998.

———. *Becoming Art: Exploring Cross-cultural Categories.* Oxford: Berg, 2007.

Mundine, Djon. *They are Meditating: Bark Paintings from the MCA's Arnott's Collection.* Sydney: Museum of Contemporary Art, 2008.

Mundine, Djon, and Bernice Murphy, eds. *The Native Born: Objects and Representations from Ramingining, Arnhem Land*. Sydney: Museum of Contemporary Art, 1996.

Musée Olympique. *Le Mémorial: un chef-d'oeuvre d'art aborigène / The Memorial: a Masterpiece of Aboriginal Art.* Lausanne and Canberra: Musée Olympique and the National Gallery of Australia, 1999.

National Museum of Australia. *Old Masters: Australia's Great Bark Artists.* Canberra: National Museum of Australia, 2013.

———. *Unsettled: Stories Within.* http://www.nma.gov.au/exhibitions/unsettled/wukun_wanambi.

Osborne, Peter. *Anywhere or Not at All: Philosophy of Contemporary Art*. London: Verso, 2013.

Perkins, Hetti, ed. *Crossing Cultures: The Alchemy of Western Arnhem Land Art.* Sydney: Art Gallery of New South Wales, 2004.

———, ed. *Earth and Sky: John Mawurndjul and Gulumbu Yunupingu*, Healesville, Victoria: TarraWarra Museum of Art, 2015.

Peterson, Nicolas. "Mortuary customs of north-east Arnhem Land: An account compiled from Donald Thomson's fieldnotes," *Memoirs of the National Museum of Victoria* 37 (1976): 97–108.

Pinchbeck, Cara, ed. *Art from Milingimbi: Taking Memories Back.* Sydney: Art Gallery of New South Wales, 2017.

———, ed. *Noŋgirrŋa Marawili: Living Landscapes.* Sydney: Art Gallery of New South Wales, 2018.

———, ed. *Yirrkala Drawings*. Sydney and Munich: Art Gallery of New South Wales and Prestel Publishing, 2014.

Russ, Vanessa. *Milingimbi: A Living Culture.* Perth: University of Western Australia, Berndt Museum of Anthropology, 2017.

Ryan, Judith. *Spirit in Land: Bark Paintings from Arnhem Land*. Melbourne: National Gallery of Victoria, 1990.

Skerritt, Henry. "Choosing Who Will Keep the Stories Strong." *Artlink* 29, no. 3 (September 2009): 74–76.

———. "Is Art History Any Use to Aboriginal Artists? Gabriel Maralngurra's *Contact Paintings*." In *Double Desire: Transculturation and Indigenous Contemporary Art,* edited by Ian McLean, 223–41. Newcastle: Cambridge Scholars Publishing, 2014.

———, ed. *No Boundaries: Contemporary Aboriginal Australian Abstract Painting.* Reno and Munich: Nevada Museum of Art and Prestel Publishing, 2015.

———. "Seeing Through Spencer: Gabriel Maralngurra's Paintings of Baldwin Spencer." *Pacific Arts: The Journal of the Pacific Arts Association,* 14, no. 1–2 (2015): 106–19.

———. "A Stitch in Time: How Aboriginal Australian Artists are Reweaving Our World." In *Everywhen: The Eternal Present in Indigenous Art from Australia*, edited by Stephen Gilchrist. Cambridge, Mass.: Harvard Art Museums, 2016: 16–27.

———. ed. *Marking the Infinite: Contemporary Women Artists from Aboriginal Australia.* Reno and Munich: Nevada Museum of Art and Prestel Publishing, 2016.

Smith, Terry. *Contemporary Art: World Currents.* London: Laurence King Publishing, 2011.

———. "Public Art Between Cultures: The 'Aboriginal Memorial,' Aboriginality, and Nationality in Australia." *Critical Inquiry* 27, no. 4 (2001): 629–61.

Smith Boles, Margaret, and Howard Morphy. *Art from the Land: Dialogues with the Kluge-Ruhe Collection of Australian Aboriginal Art.* Charlottesville: University of Virginia, Kluge-Ruhe Aboriginal Art Collection, 1999.

Spilia, Elina. "A World in a Turtle Egg." *Meanjin* 65, no. 1 (2006): 154–63.

———. "Shark People: Djapu Painting and the Miny'tji Buku Larrnggay Collection." *Art Bulletin of Victoria* 47 (2007): 6–15.

———. "Gulumbu Yunupingu: Into the Light." *Art and Australia* 47, no. 1 (Spring 2010): 118–23.

Sprague, Quentin. "White Lines: The Recent Work of Nyapanyapa Yunupingu." *Discipline* 3 (Winter 2013): 59–68.

Stanner, W. E. H. *The Dreaming and Other Essays*. Melbourne: Black Inc. Agenda, 2009.

Stubbs, Will. "A Short History of Yolngu Activist Art." *Artlink* 36, no. 2 (2016): 18–25.

Studd, Annie, ed. *Balnhdurr—A Lasting Impression*. Yirrkala: Buku-Larrŋgay Mulka Centre, 2015.

Sydney Biennale. *From the Southern Cross: Australian Biennale 1988.* Sydney: Sydney Biennale, 1988.

Taylor, Luke. "Categories of 'Old' and 'New' in Western Arnhem Land Bark Painting." In *Long History, Deep Time: Deepening Histories of Place,* edited by Ann McGrath and Mary Anne Jebb, Canberra: ANU Press, 2015, 101–17.

———. *Seeing the Inside: Bark Paintings in Western Arnhem Land.* Oxford: Clarendon Press, 1996. Canberra: ANU Press, 2015.

Thomson, Donald. *Economic Structure and the Ceremonial Exchange Cycle in Arnhem Land*. Melbourne: Macmillan, 1949.

———. *Donald Thomson in Arnhem Land*. Melbourne: Gordon & Gotch, 1983.

Volkenandt, Claus and Christian Kaufmann, eds. *Between Indigenous Australia and Europe: John Mawurndjul*. Berlin: Dietrich Reimer Verlag GmbH, 2009.

Wa<u>n</u>ambi, Wukun and Ishmael Marika. "The Mulka Project," *Artlink* 36:2 (June 2016): 82–84.

Wa<u>n</u>ambi, Wukun with Henry Skerritt. "The Mulka Project: The Whole Picture." *Art Monthly Australia* 282 (August 2015): 30–31.

Warner, William Lloyd. *A Black Civilization: A Social Study of an Aboriginal Tribe.* Revised edition. New York: Harper and Brothers, 1963.

Webb, T. T. *From Spears to Spades*. Melbourne: The Book Depot, 1938.

Wells, Ann E. *Milingimbi: Ten Years in the Crocodile Islands of Arnhem Land.* Sydney: Angus and Robertson, 1963.

Westley, Brenda, and Steve Westley. "Mickey Durrng: Artist of East Arnhem Land." *Aboriginal Art Online*, http://www.aboriginalartonline.com/resources/articles2.php.

Wilkins, C. S. G. H. *Undiscovered Australia.* London: G. P. Putnam's Sons, 1929.

Williams, Nancy. *The Yolngu and Their Land*. Stanford: Standford University Press, 1986.

Wolseley, John, and Will Stubbs, eds. *Mi<u>d</u>awarr: Harvest.* Canberra: National Museum of Australia, 2017.

Wright, Felicity. *Contemporary Paintings from Western Arnhem Land*. Adelaide: Flinders Art Museum, Flinders University, 2002.

Author Biographies

Murray Garde is a consultant anthropologist and linguist who works with the Bininj people of western Arnhem Land and Kakadu National Park. Garde has lived on remote outstation communities and in larger towns of the region since the 1980s. He currently manages a community language maintenance project supporting the Bininj Kunwok languages of the region and is interested in advocacy for these languages in both the Indigenous and non-Indigenous communities. Garde is keenly involved in the documentation of art through the artists' own languages, and in particular Indigenous ecological knowledge which continues to be applied by Bininj involved in the many land-management groups of the region. He currently spends much of his time producing digital resources that assist in the intergenerational transfer of this knowledge.

Louise Hamby is the Chief Investigator on the ARC Linkage Grant, *50 Years of Collecting at the Milingimbi Mission* and is a Visiting Research Fellow in the School of Archaeology and Anthropology at the Australian National University. Indigenous fiber arts, the material culture of Arnhem Land, Indigenous collection-based research and digital repatriation and re-documentation of museum collections and archival material are her research topics. She has been an honorary associate of Museum Victoria since 2003. Through her research she has developed a number of collaborative curatorial projects working with Indigenous Australians supported by VISIONS grants: *Art on a String* (2001), *Twined Together: Kunmadj Njalehnjaleken* (2005), and *Women With Clever Hands: Gapuwiyak Miyalkurrwurr Gong Djambatjmala* (2010). The book, *Art on a String: Aboriginal Threaded Objects from the Western Desert and Arnhem Land*, co-authored with Diana Young, is the seminal guide to Aboriginal necklace making.

Howard Morphy is distinguished professor of anthropology in the Research School of Humanities and the Arts at the Australian National University. He is an anthropologist of art and visual anthropology with a major theoretical focus on the nature of cross-cultural categories. His most recent book is *Becoming Art: Exploring Cross-Cultural Categories* (2007). With Frances Morphy, he has worked closely with Yolŋu people for more than forty years. His involvement in e-research and in the development of museum exhibitions reflects his determination to make humanities research as accessible as possible to wider publics and to close the gap between the research process and research outcomes. He is currently working with colleagues at the British Museum and the National Museum of Australia on the concept of the relational museum, linking distributed collections to source communities.

Kimberley Moulton is a Yorta Yorta curator and writer; she is Senior Curator of South Eastern Aboriginal Collections at Museums Victoria. She is an alumna of the National Gallery of Australia Westfarmers Indigenous Leadership Program (2010); the British Council ACCELERATE program (2013); and in 2013 was a National Gallery of Australia International Curatorial Fellow. Moulton's practice looks at the intersection of First Peoples' self-representation and access in museums and galleries. Moulton has curated numerous exhibitions, including *Djambawa Marawili AM: Where the Water Moves, Where It Rests* (Kluge-Ruhe Aboriginal Art Collection, 2015); *RECENTRE-sisters* (City of Melbourne Gallery, 2017); and *Next Matriarch* (Ace Open, TARNANTHI Indigenous Arts Festival Adelaide, 2017).

Diana Nawi is an independent curator based in Los Angeles. She will serve as the co-Artistic Director (alongside Naima J. Keith) of Prospect.5, New Orleans, in 2020. Most recently, she organized *Adler Guerrier: Conditions and Forms for blck Longevity* (2018) at the California African American Museum, Los Angeles. Nawi previously served as Associate Curator at Pérez Art Museum Miami (PAMM) for five years, where she curated exhibitions and published catalogues including *John Dunkley: Neither Day nor Night* (2017), *Nari Ward: Sun Splashed* (2015), *Iman Issa: Heritage Studies* (2015), and *Adler Guerrier: Formulating a Plot* (2014). She also organized newly commissioned projects including *Haroon Mirza: A C I D G E S T* (2017), *Matthew Ronay: When Two Are in One* (2016), *Shana Lutker: Again Against, A Foot, A Back, A Wall* (2015), *Nicole Cherubini: 500* (2014), *Yael Bartana: Inferno* (2013), *Bouchra Khalili: Speeches – Chapter 3: Living Labour* (2013), and *LOS JAICHACKERS: Night Shade/Solanaceae* (Julio César Morales and Eamon Ore-Giron; 2013). Prior to joining PAMM, Nawi worked as an assistant curator on the Abu Dhabi Project of the Solomon R. Guggenheim Foundation and served as a fellow at the Museum of Contemporary Art Chicago and the Massachusetts Museum of Contemporary Art.

Henry Skerritt is the Mellon Curator of the Indigenous Arts of Australia at the Kluge-Ruhe Aboriginal Art Collection of the University of Virginia. He is editor of the books *No Boundaries: Aboriginal Australian Contemporary Abstract Painting* (2015) and *Marking the Infinite: Contemporary Women Artists from Aboriginal Australia* (2016); he was the consulting curator on the identically named touring exhibitions that originated at the Nevada Museum of Art. Skerritt has curated numerous exhibitions, including *Experimental Gentlemen* (2011) at the Ian Potter Museum of Art at the University of Melbourne and *Yimadoowarra: the Art of Loongkoonan* (2016) at the Australian Embassy in Washington, DC, and the Kluge-Ruhe Museum at the University of Virginia. He holds a PhD in art history from the University of Pittsburgh.

Wukun Wa<u>n</u>ambi is a leader of the Marrakulu clan, an acclaimed artist, and the cultural director of The Mulka Project, the Indigenous media unit located at Yirrkala in northeastern Arnhem Land. His works are included in most significant Australian collections, including the National Gallery of Australia, as well as in the British Museum and the Musée de Lyon. His practice ranges from traditional mediums such as bark painting, through to print making and video installation. He is a two-time winner at the National Aboriginal and Torres Strait Islander Art Awards. Wa<u>n</u>ambi is currently one of the lead Yolŋu curators for the exhibition project *Ma<u>d</u>ayin: Eight Decades of Aboriginal Bark Painting from Yirrkala* which will tour the United States in 2021–2.

David Wickens grew up in the Blue Mountains in New South Wales. He has travelled extensively throughout northern and central Australia in an old Land Rover he built in his former career as a mechanic. Settling in the Northern Territory in 2011, Wickens has been involved in many aspects of the Australian arts industry, both as an arts worker and a practicing artist. His time living in remote communities and working closely with Indigenous artists has given Wickens a unique and broad insight into the cultural practices and artistic styles present within northern Australia. From 2014 to 2017 he was assistant manager at Injalak Arts, Kunbarrllanjnja, and in 2018 Wickens relocated to Yirrkala Arnhem Land to work at the Buku-Larrŋgay Mulka art center.

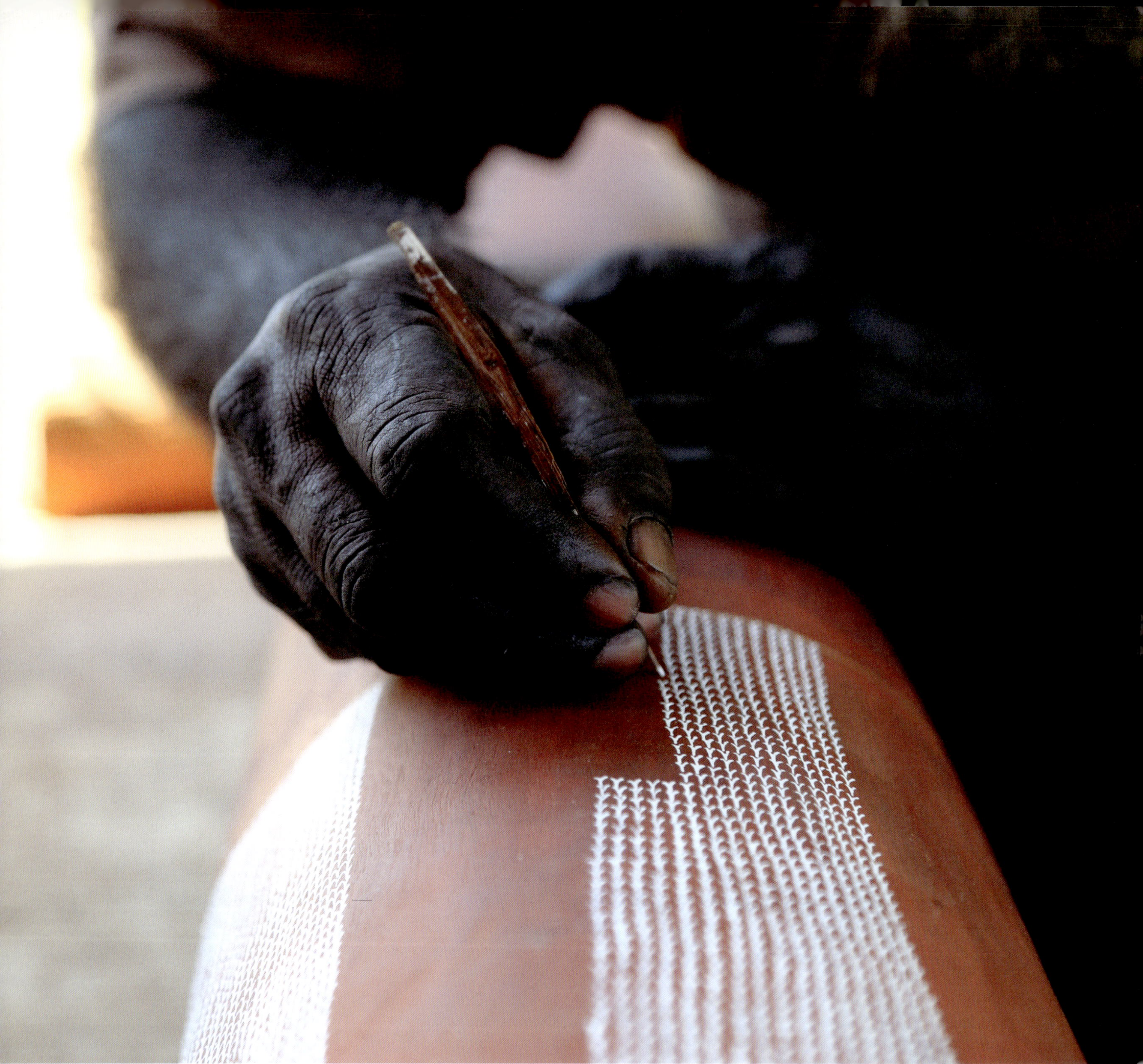

Owen Yalandja. Photograph by Kate O'Hara.

Acknowledgments

Dennis Scholl

With this, the third exhibition of our collection of Aboriginal Australian contemporary art, totaling sixteen venues in six years, our grand Aboriginal Australian art project comes to a close. It has joyfully resulted in Debra and me placing over two hundred works of this amazing art into museums across the United States.

There are so many to thank in an expansive project such as this one. To start, we want to express our appreciation to the Nevada Museum of Art, especially David Walker, JoAnne Northrup, and William Fox for their complete commitment from beginning to end. Without that level of enthusiasm this would have been a far smaller undertaking.

To have so many venues requires a leap of faith by each museum and much thanks go out to the Charles H. Wright Museum of African American History in Detroit, the Fralin Museum of Art at the University of Virginia, and the Patricia and Phillip Frost Art Museum at Florida International University for signing up for this exhibition.

The remote places these art objects have come from contain some of the finest people I have met in the art world. Their aliegiance to the art and artists of their region is unwavering. Our immense gratitude goes to Will Stubbs, Edwina Circuitt, Joseph Brady, Kade McDonald, Andrew Blake, Michelle Culpitt, Kate O'Hara, Dave Wickens, Felicity Wright, Chris Durkin, and Rosita Holmes. We also want to thank the many artists who responded to our request to create these beautiful objects, in many cases restarting the practice of memorial pole art-making in their communities. Commissioning so many works requires trust and faith on both sides. I think the results speak for themselves. I hope the world will embrace this work and continue to support it, so that these artists will be able to continue to practice their craft.

Editorial support for this catalogue was provided by the Kluge-Ruhe Aboriginal Art Collection of the University of Virginia, and we are indebted to their staff: Margo Smith AM, Nicole Wade, Lauren Maupin, and Laura Bendick. We also want to thank our thoughtful essayists, Murray Garde, Louise Hamby, Howard Morphy, Kimberley Moulton, Diana Nawi, Wukun Wan̲ambi, and Dave Wickens for helping to explain the history and mystery of memorial poles in Arnhem Land. Our collection managers Anita Sharma and Emanuel Ribas have gracefully wrangled this work all over the globe, ably assisted by the team of Loriel Beltran, Leandro Vasquez and Domingo Castillo. We are so appreciative of the care they continue to show the works in our collection.

Much of the direction we have followed has come out of many conversations by people who are passionate about this work. They include Fred Myers, Howard Morphy, John and Barbara Wilkerson, Maia Nuku, Robert Kaplan and Margaret Levi, D'Lan Davidson, Greer Adams, Julie Harvey, the late Will Owen and Harvey Wagner, Simon Mordant, Hetti Perkins, Andrea and Peter Hylands, Nicholas Baume, and Djumbawa Marawili AM.

A special thanks to the Australian Embassy in Washington, DC: Ambassador Joe Hockey and his wife Melissa Babbidge, along with Rebecca Allen, Laura Nix, and Fiona Koschade who have supported these exhibitions every step of the way.

When it comes to design aesthetics we have always put ourselves in the hands of Miko McGinty and once again she has delivered beyond our wildest expectations. Much appreciation to Miko, Rita Jules, Claire Bidwell, and Sally Salvesen for their unerring guidance.

The completion of this odyssey is bittersweet, especially because it means I will not be speaking to my friend Henry Skerritt on a daily basis anymore. He has taught me so much about this "inside world" and for that I thank him. We have had such an adventure together, and the commitment he has shown to these three exhibitions and the building of this collection has been extraordinary. For that we are eternally grateful.

My wife Debra and I are approaching our fortieth year together, and she has been the single most important person in my life. She is always there with encouragement and support. None of this would have happened without her love, patience, and spirit of adventure.

Photo Credits

All artwork plates and detail photographs were taken by Sid Hoetzell, Miami.
All artworks from Kunbarrllanjnja © the artists, courtesy of Injalak Arts, Kunbarrllanjnja.
All artworks from Maningrida © the artists and their estates, courtesy of Maningrida Arts and Culture, Maningrida.
All artworks from Milingimbi © the artists, courtesy of Milingimbi Art and Culture, Milingimbi.
All artworks from Yirrkala © the artists and their estates, courtesy of Buku-Larrŋgay Mulka Art Centre, Yirrkala.

p. 12 © The artist's estate, courtesy of Milingimbi Art and Culture. Image courtesy of Kluge-Ruhe Aboriginal Art Collection of the University of Virginia, Charlottesville.
pp. 14–15 © Henry Skerritt.
p. 17 © Janet Fieldhouse. Image courtesy of Kluge-Ruhe Aboriginal Art Collection of the University of Virginia, Charlottesville.
pp. 20–21 © Henry Skerritt.
pp. 22–3 © Creative Cowboy Films.
p. 28 © Nari Ward. Image courtesy of Lehmann Maupin, New York, Hong Kong, and Seoul. Photograph by StudioLHOOQ.
p. 29 © Jeffrey Gibson. Image courtesy of Roberts Projects, Los Angeles. Photograph by Peter Mauney.
p. 30 © Brian Jungen. Image courtesy of the Art Gallery of Ontario.
p. 34 © Henry Skerritt.
p. 36 © The estates of the artists, courtesy of Buku-Larrŋgay Mulka Art Centre, Yirrkala. Image courtesy of Australian Parliament House, Canberra.
p. 37 © National Gallery of Australia, Canberra.
pp. 45–6 © Injalak Arts, Kunbarrllanjnja.
pp. 47–9 © David Wickens and Injalak Arts, Kunbarrllanjnja.
p. 62 © Maningrida Arts and Culture, Maningrida.
p. 63 © Henry Skerritt.
p. 65 © Kate O'Hara, courtesy of Maningrida Arts and Culture, Maningrida.
p. 67 © Copyright the estate of Axel Poignant, courtesy of the National Library of Australia, Canberra.
p. 91 © The Ohio State University, Byrd Polar and Climate Research Center Archival Program, Sir George Hubert Wilkins Papers.
p. 92 © National Museum of Australia. Photograph by George Serras.
p. 92 © Australian Institute of Aboriginal and Torres Strait Islander Studies, Canberra.
p. 93 © Ben Ward, courtesy Milingimbi Art and Culture, Milingimbi.
p. 93 © Rosita Holmes, courtesy Milingimbi Art and Culture, Milingimbi.
p. 94 © Zanette Kahler, courtesy Milingimbi Art and Culture, Milingimbi.
p. 95 © Rosita Holmes, courtesy Milingimbi Art and Culture, Milingimbi.
p. 107 © Kluge-Ruhe Aboriginal Art Collection of the University of Virginia, Charlottesville.
p. 108 © The Mulka Project, Yirrkala.
p. 109 © Peter Eve.
p. 159 Kate O'Hara, courtesy of Maningrida Arts and Culture, Maningrida.

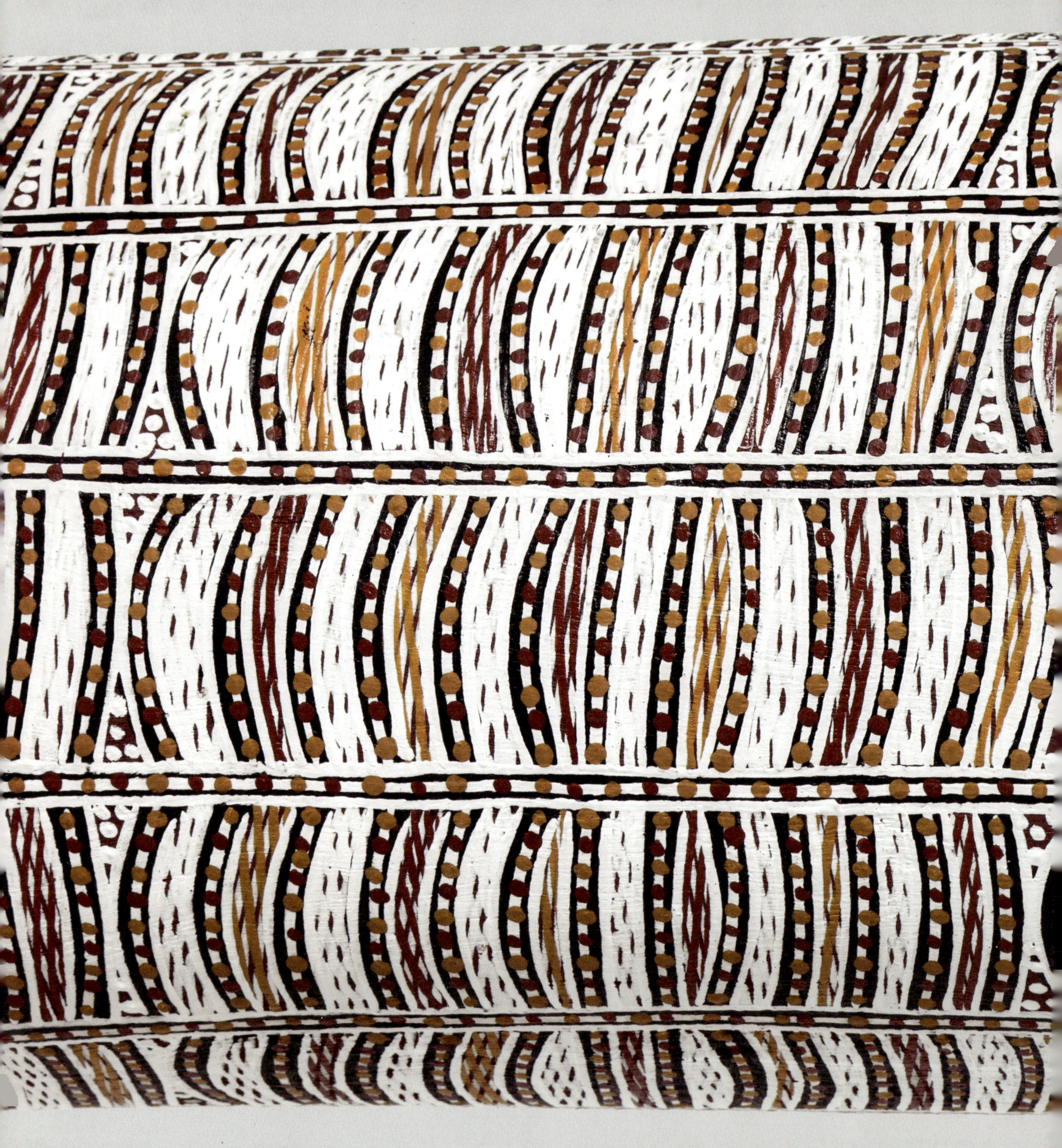